CHRIS DEVON

C# Web Development With ASP.NET
core 3

Copyright © 2024 by Chris Devon

All rights reserved. No part of this publication may be reproduced, stored or transmitted in any form or by any means, electronic, mechanical, photocopying, recording, scanning, or otherwise without written permission from the publisher. It is illegal to copy this book, post it to a website, or distribute it by any other means without permission.

First edition

*This book was professionally typeset on Reedsy.
Find out more at reedsy.com*

Contents

Introduction to ASP.NET Core 3 and Modern C# Web Development	1
Getting Started - Building Your First ASP.NET Core 3 Project	33
Deep Dive into Razor Pages and MVC Architectur	73
Chapter 4: Entity Framework Core - Mastering Data Access and...	111
Advanced Authentication and Authorization Techniques	149
Building RESTful APIs and Integrating Web APIs	189
Integrating Front-End Frameworks (React, Angular, and Vue)	223
Middleware and Dependency Injection in ASP.NET Core	268
Security Essentials for Modern Web Applications	299
Performance Optimization Techniques in ASP.NET Core	332
Testing and Debugging Your ASP.NET Core Application	361
Deployment and Continuous Integration/Continuous Delivery...	398
Building a Full-Scale Real-World Projec	428
ASP.NET Core 3 Beyond the Basics	472
Looking Forward - Preparing for Future ASP.NET Core Versions	509

Introduction to ASP.NET Core 3 and Modern C# Web Development

Overview of ASP.NET Core 3 and Key Differences from Previous Versions

ASP.NET Core 3 is a significant advancement in the .NET ecosystem, designed to offer a robust, high-performance, cross-platform framework for building modern web applications. With its modular design, lightweight architecture, and enhanced performance capabilities, ASP.NET Core 3 provides developers with an agile, scalable foundation that allows for rapid development without sacrificing flexibility or power. This chapter will dive into what ASP.NET Core 3 brings to the table and highlight its key differences from previous versions, particularly ASP.NET Core 2.2 and earlier.

The Evolution of ASP.NET Core

ASP.NET Core was introduced as a reimagining of the .NET Framework, optimized to meet the needs of modern web applications. With its release, Microsoft aimed to create a more versatile framework that would adapt to the increasingly complex demands of cloud-based applications, APIs, and microservices. Unlike the traditional ASP.NET framework tied to Windows, ASP.NET Core is cross-platform, supporting Windows, macOS, and Linux out of the box.

ASP.NET Core 3 represents the latest iteration in this evolution, focusing on three main pillars:

1. **Improved performance and resource efficiency** for building high-scale applications.
2. **Enhanced developer productivity** through streamlined tooling and clearer API design.
3. **Seamless support for modern architectures**, including microservices and containerized deployments.

These pillars underscore the changes introduced in ASP.NET Core 3, which we'll explore in depth to understand why these enhancements are game-changers for modern web development.

Key Features of ASP.NET Core 3

1. .NET Core 3 as the Foundation

ASP.NET Core 3 exclusively targets .NET Core 3, moving away from compatibility with .NET Framework. This transition allows the framework to fully leverage .NET Core 3's optimizations, especially for performance and resource utilization. Additionally, .NET Core 3 introduces several enhancements, such as improved garbage collection, JIT compilation, and support for new C# 8 features, all of which directly benefit ASP.NET Core 3 applications.

2. Blazor and WebAssembly Support

One of the standout additions to ASP.NET Core 3 is Blazor, a framework for building interactive client-side web applications with C# instead of JavaScript. Blazor comes in two forms: Blazor Server, which runs server-side with SignalR to synchronize changes in the browser, and Blazor WebAssembly, which enables running .NET code directly in the browser through WebAssembly. Blazor's inclusion provides a compelling alternative to JavaScript-based frameworks like Angular, React, and Vue, offering a full-stack development experience within the .NET ecosystem.

3. Endpoint Routing for Greater Flexibility

ASP.NET Core 3 introduces endpoint routing, a more efficient, flexible approach to request routing. Previously, routing was tightly coupled to MVC controllers or Razor Pages. Endpoint routing decouples routing from the MVC pipeline, allowing developers to define routes in a more centralized manner. This change benefits not only MVC but also API development and Blazor components, allowing a unified approach to request handling.

4. Generic Host Builder and Worker Services

ASP.NET Core 3 consolidates its hosting infrastructure with the **Generic Host** and introduces the concept of Worker Services. The Generic Host now supports both web and non-web applications, making it easier to standardize application initialization, configuration, and dependency injection across different types of applications. Worker Services enable developers to build background services that can run alongside ASP.NET Core applications, simplifying the development of microservices and background processing systems.

5. Razor Components for Enhanced UI Separation

Razor Components are another major addition in ASP.NET Core 3. Originally introduced as part of Blazor, Razor Components allow developers to create reusable UI components using Razor syntax. Razor Components are server-side rendered, improving server-based UI interactivity and reducing latency issues associated with client-side frameworks. This approach complements Blazor by offering a familiar syntax for creating dynamic, reusable web interfaces.

6. gRPC Support for High-Performance Communication

ASP.NET Core 3 adds built-in support for gRPC (Google Remote Procedure Call), enabling high-performance, low-latency communication in microservices and distributed systems. Unlike REST APIs, which rely on HTTP/1.1 and are often more bandwidth-heavy, gRPC uses HTTP/2, which offers several advantages, including smaller message sizes, multiplexing, and bi-directional streaming. This makes gRPC a natural choice for applications where efficiency and speed are paramount, such as in financial, gaming, and real-time analytics applications.

7. Health Checks and Improved Diagnostics

ASP.NET Core 3 includes health checks, a built-in way to monitor the health of applications. This feature allows developers to define endpoints that check the status of various components (such as database connections, cache services, and external APIs) and is essential for ensuring high availability and reliability in production environments. Coupled with improved diagnostics and logging capabilities, these features simplify monitoring and troubleshooting for cloud-native applications.

Key Differences Between ASP.NET Core 3 and Previous Versions

With the shift to ASP.NET Core 3, Microsoft has made several architectural changes and feature enhancements that set it apart from ASP.NET Core 2.2 and earlier. Here are some of the most impactful differences:

1. .NET Core Exclusivity

In previous ASP.NET Core versions, developers could choose to target either .NET Core or the .NET Framework. However, ASP.NET Core 3 exclusively targets .NET Core 3, fully embracing cross-platform compatibility and cloud readiness. This means no compatibility with the full .NET Framework, marking a shift towards a fully modular, lightweight runtime.

2. New JSON Serialization Library: System.Text.Json

ASP.NET Core 3 replaces the Newtonsoft.Json library with the newly introduced System.Text.Json library as the default JSON serializer. This change results in significant performance improvements in JSON handling, as System.Text.Json is more optimized for .NET Core applications. However, it is less mature than Newtonsoft.Json, which may still be required in applications with complex serialization requirements.

3. Removal of Obsolete Packages and APIs

ASP.NET Core 3 has removed several packages and APIs considered outdated or unnecessary. For example, support for Web Forms, WCF

INTRODUCTION TO ASP.NET CORE 3 AND MODERN C# WEB DEVELOPMENT

(Windows Communication Foundation), and Windows-specific authentication (e.g., Windows Authentication and Active Directory) has been removed, as these features are generally incompatible with cross-platform requirements and cloud-native architectures.

4. Dependency Injection Improvements

Dependency Injection (DI) is a core feature of ASP.NET Core, and ASP.NET Core 3 introduces new improvements to the DI container. This version makes it easier to inject services into hosted services and background tasks. Additionally, the new ServiceProviderOptions allow greater control over dependency resolution, providing advanced configurations for scenarios where DI lifetimes or instantiation patterns need to be explicitly managed.

5. Improved SignalR with JSON and MessagePack Support

SignalR, the library for real-time web functionality, sees enhancements in ASP.NET Core 3. This version introduces native support for MessagePack, a binary serialization format that reduces bandwidth usage compared to JSON. Additionally, SignalR now supports System.Text.Json for JSON serialization, further improving performance for real-time applications.

6. Simplified Startup Configuration

ASP.NET Core 3 includes a simplified approach to configuring services and middleware in the Startup.cs file. This change encourages cleaner, more maintainable code, with less boilerplate needed to configure typical application dependencies. In particular, the IWebHostBuilder class is now deprecated, and all configurations are done through the HostBuilder, making it easier to standardize application setup across projects.

7. C# 8 Features in ASP.NET Core 3

With ASP.NET Core 3's dependency on .NET Core 3, developers can now fully utilize C# 8 features, such as asynchronous streams, nullable reference types, and pattern matching enhancements. These language features offer more expressive syntax and make it easier to handle concurrency, data validation, and complex conditional logic, all of which are common in web development.

8. Enhanced Docker and Kubernetes Integration

Docker and Kubernetes have become foundational technologies in modern software deployment, and ASP.NET Core 3 offers deeper integration with these containerization tools. Docker support is built into the Visual Studio tooling, and developers can easily containerize their ASP.NET Core applications with minimal configuration. Additionally, ASP.NET Core 3 applications are optimized for orchestration in Kubernetes, including built-in health checks and diagnostics that align with Kubernetes' health monitoring features.

ASP.NET Core 3 represents a milestone in the evolution of the ASP.NET ecosystem, delivering new features and performance improvements that empower developers to build modern, high-performance web applications more efficiently than ever before. By adopting .NET Core 3 as its exclusive runtime, ASP.NET Core 3 offers a more streamlined, consistent experience for developers and ensures that applications are built on a cross-platform foundation. With features like Blazor, gRPC, and Razor Components, ASP.NET Core 3 is equipped to meet the demands of both traditional server-rendered web applications and highly interactive, client-side experiences.

The key differences between ASP.NET Core 3 and its predecessors—such as the shift to System.Text.Json, removal of deprecated packages, and enhanced dependency injection—underscore Microsoft's commitment to building a modern framework that is optimized for performance, scalability, and cloud-native architecture. As we proceed through this book, we'll delve into each of these features in greater detail, exploring how ASP.NET Core 3 enables developers to create powerful, maintainable, and efficient web applications tailored for the future of .NET development.

Benefits of Using ASP.NET Core 3 for Modern Web Development

ASP.NET Core 3 offers a range of benefits that address the diverse needs of modern web development, from high performance to scalability and cross-platform compatibility. With its modular framework, comprehensive developer tooling, and support for modern programming paradigms, ASP.NET Core 3 enables developers to build applications that are responsive, resilient, and ready for deployment across various platforms and environments. In this section, we'll cover the primary benefits that ASP.NET Core 3 brings to the table, making it an attractive choice for creating both enterprise-grade and cloud-native applications.

1. Cross-Platform Flexibility and Deployment Options

One of the most significant advantages of ASP.NET Core 3 is its cross-platform nature. Unlike the traditional ASP.NET Framework, which is limited to Windows, ASP.NET Core 3 runs on Windows, macOS, and Linux. This allows developers to choose their preferred operating system, development environment, and deployment strategy, providing unmatched flexibility and expanding potential use cases.

- **Platform-Agnostic Development**: ASP.NET Core 3 applications can be built and run on any operating system supported by .NET Core, offering development teams the freedom to work within the environments that best suit their needs.
- **Containerized Deployments**: ASP.NET Core 3 integrates seamlessly with Docker and Kubernetes, allowing applications to be containerized and orchestrated in modern cloud environments. Containers ensure consistent deployment across different environments, facilitate scalability, and streamline CI/CD workflows.
- **Cloud-Ready by Design**: Designed with cloud environments in mind, ASP.NET Core 3 is optimized for deployment on Azure, AWS, Google Cloud, and other platforms, enabling applications to easily scale based on demand.

2. Performance Optimization and Resource Efficiency

ASP.NET Core 3 is engineered to be lightweight and high-performing, a crucial benefit for web applications where response time and resource utilization are key factors.

- **Improved Throughput**: ASP.NET Core 3 introduces several optimizations that improve throughput, such as an efficient HTTP request pipeline, endpoint routing, and the adoption of System.Text.Json for faster JSON serialization.
- **Reduced Memory Footprint**: With its modular design, ASP.NET Core 3 allows developers to include only the components they need, reducing memory usage and improving load times. This modularity makes it especially suitable for microservices, where efficient resource usage is essential.
- **Kestrel Web Server**: ASP.NET Core 3 relies on Kestrel, a high-performance, cross-platform web server optimized for speed and minimal resource consumption. Kestrel outperforms traditional web servers and handles a large volume of concurrent requests with low overhead, making it ideal for high-traffic applications.
- **Asynchronous Processing**: Asynchronous programming with async/await is fully supported in ASP.NET Core 3, enabling non-blocking operations that improve scalability and reduce resource contention, especially for I/O-bound tasks like database queries and network requests.

3. Enhanced Security Features

Security is a critical consideration in web development, and ASP.NET Core 3 includes a range of features to safeguard applications against common threats.

- **Identity and Authentication Support**: ASP.NET Core Identity, which comes built into ASP.NET Core 3, offers a powerful authentication and authorization system that integrates easily with

OAuth, OpenID Connect, and third-party providers like Google and Facebook. This allows applications to secure user data and provide seamless login experiences across platforms.
- **Improved Protection Against Common Vulnerabilities**: ASP.NET Core 3 provides built-in defense mechanisms for cross-site scripting (XSS), cross-site request forgery (CSRF), and SQL injection attacks, helping developers adhere to security best practices with minimal configuration.
- **Data Encryption and HTTPS Support**: ASP.NET Core 3 has native support for HTTPS redirection and HSTS (HTTP Strict Transport Security), enforcing secure connections by default. Sensitive data can be encrypted, and certificate management is simplified for deployment in production environments.
- **Policy-Based Authorization**: The framework offers role-based, claims-based, and policy-based authorization, allowing fine-grained control over access rights within an application. This flexibility enables developers to create complex access policies that reflect real-world business requirements.

4. Versatile Tooling and Developer Productivity

ASP.NET Core 3 is designed to enhance developer productivity, providing a comprehensive suite of tools and streamlined workflows that accelerate development without compromising quality.

- **Integration with Visual Studio and Visual Studio Code**: ASP.NET Core 3 is tightly integrated with Visual Studio (for Windows and macOS) and Visual Studio Code, providing a rich development experience across platforms. Developers can take advantage of features like IntelliSense, integrated debugging, and live unit testing, making it easier to build, test, and troubleshoot applications.
- **Command-Line Interface (CLI)**: The .NET Core CLI enables developers to create, build, and deploy applications directly from the command line, facilitating automation in CI/CD pipelines. The

CLI is particularly useful for developers working in non-Windows environments or those looking to automate routine tasks.
- **Blazor for Full-Stack C# Development**: Blazor allows developers to write client-side code in C#, eliminating the need for JavaScript in certain scenarios. This feature is beneficial for teams with deep C# expertise, allowing them to create fully interactive applications with shared codebases across client and server.
- **Razor Components and Reusable UI Elements**: ASP.NET Core 3 introduces Razor Components, a new approach to creating reusable UI components that can be easily embedded in different parts of an application. This approach not only speeds up development but also ensures UI consistency and reduces redundancy.

5. Robust Support for Modern API Development

ASP.NET Core 3 is well-suited for developing RESTful APIs, which are critical in modern applications, especially those following microservices and serverless architectures.

- **gRPC for High-Performance APIs**: In addition to REST APIs, ASP.NET Core 3 supports gRPC, a framework for building high-performance, cross-platform remote procedure calls. gRPC is particularly beneficial for microservices, as it enables efficient, low-latency communication between services using HTTP/2.
- **OpenAPI and Swagger Integration**: ASP.NET Core 3 makes it easy to document APIs with OpenAPI/Swagger, allowing developers to automatically generate and share API documentation. This documentation is invaluable for client developers and teams integrating with the API, providing clarity on available endpoints, parameters, and response formats.
- **API Versioning**: ASP.NET Core 3 includes built-in support for API versioning, making it easier to manage and evolve APIs over time. This feature is essential in maintaining backward compatibility as applications grow and change.

- **Middleware for Custom Processing**: The middleware pipeline in ASP.NET Core 3 allows developers to implement custom logic, such as logging, authentication, and exception handling, for every API request. Middleware is highly configurable and can be applied selectively to specific endpoints or conditions, offering fine-grained control over API behavior.

6. Simplified Dependency Injection and Modularity

ASP.NET Core 3 fully embraces Dependency Injection (DI) as a core feature, allowing developers to build modular, testable code by injecting services into their components.

- **Built-In Dependency Injection Container**: ASP.NET Core 3 includes a lightweight DI container that handles service lifetimes (transient, scoped, singleton), making it straightforward to register and manage dependencies across the application.
- **Simplified Configuration and Service Setup**: The configuration model in ASP.NET Core 3 has been streamlined, making it easier to add and configure services in the Startup class. This is particularly helpful for setting up complex services like database connections, caching, and logging.
- **Custom Middleware and Extensibility**: The modular architecture allows developers to build custom middleware components that can be added to the request pipeline, giving them complete control over the flow of HTTP requests. This flexibility makes ASP.NET Core 3 ideal for building both monolithic applications and distributed systems.

7. Comprehensive Diagnostics and Monitoring Tools

ASP.NET Core 3 provides extensive support for diagnostics and monitoring, making it easier to detect and resolve issues in production.

- **Integrated Logging Framework**: ASP.NET Core 3 has a built-in

logging system that supports multiple providers (e.g., Console, Debug, EventLog, Azure Application Insights), enabling developers to capture detailed logs across all components.
- **Health Checks for Monitoring Services**: ASP.NET Core 3 includes a health check API that allows developers to monitor the status of various services, such as databases, caches, and external dependencies. These checks can be configured to trigger alerts or restart processes, making them essential for high-availability applications.
- **Distributed Tracing with OpenTelemetry**: ASP.NET Core 3 can integrate with distributed tracing systems using OpenTelemetry, allowing developers to track request flow across multiple services. This is especially useful in microservices architectures, where it can be challenging to trace errors across interconnected services.
- **Application Insights for Real-Time Monitoring**: With support for Azure Application Insights, ASP.NET Core 3 allows developers to monitor application performance, exceptions, and user interactions in real-time. This provides valuable insights into application behavior, helping teams optimize performance and improve user experience.

8. Comprehensive Support for C# 8 and Language Features

ASP.NET Core 3, targeting .NET Core 3, allows developers to take full advantage of C# 8, which introduces several language features that enhance readability, safety, and performance.

- **Nullable Reference Types**: Nullable reference types in C# 8 help developers prevent null reference exceptions by explicitly defining nullable variables, reducing the potential for runtime errors.
- **Async Streams**: Async streams allow developers to work with asynchronous data sequences, enabling more efficient processing of large datasets or real-time data streams.
- **Pattern Matching Enhancements**: The expanded pattern matching capabilities in C# 8 allow for cleaner, more concise code, especially when dealing with complex conditional logic.

INTRODUCTION TO ASP.NET CORE 3 AND MODERN C# WEB DEVELOPMENT

ASP.NET Core 3 delivers a versatile, high-performance, and secure platform for modern web development, suited to a wide range of application architectures. By embracing cross-platform compatibility, optimizing performance, and introducing features like Blazor, gRPC, and integrated health checks, ASP.NET Core 3 meets the demands of cloud-native, scalable, and interactive web applications. With these benefits, ASP.NET Core 3 stands out as an ideal choice for developers looking to build applications that are ready for the future, leveraging the latest in web technology and developer tools. As you continue through this book, you'll gain hands-on knowledge and insights on how to use ASP.NET Core 3's powerful features to their fullest potential, ensuring that your applications are performant, secure, and maintainable.

Overview of the .NET Core Ecosystem and Compatibility with .NET Standard

The .NET Core ecosystem is a modular, open-source framework designed to support cross-platform development and deployment of high-performance applications. It represents Microsoft's shift toward an ecosystem that addresses the demands of modern software development—primarily cross-platform support, cloud integration, and microservices architecture. This overview explores the key components of the .NET Core ecosystem and how they relate to ASP.NET Core 3, alongside compatibility considerations with .NET Standard, which facilitates code sharing across different .NET implementations.

The .NET Core Ecosystem: Key Components

.NET Core serves as the foundation for a variety of application types, from web applications to cloud services, command-line tools, and desktop applications. It is designed to be lightweight and flexible, supporting multiple workloads and scenarios. Here's a breakdown of some core components within the .NET Core ecosystem:

.NET Runtime (CoreCLR)

At the heart of .NET Core is the CoreCLR, the runtime responsible for executing .NET applications. It includes key features such as Just-In-Time (JIT) compilation, garbage collection, and native interoperability. CoreCLR is optimized for performance, making it suitable for applications with demanding resource and performance requirements.

ASP.NET Core

ASP.NET Core is the web framework built on .NET Core for creating scalable and high-performance web applications. Its lightweight, cross-platform nature supports modern web application architectures, such as microservices and serverless computing, and it is widely used for APIs, MVC applications, and real-time web applications with SignalR.

Entity Framework Core (EF Core)

EF Core is the data access library in the .NET Core ecosystem, offering an object-relational mapper (ORM) that simplifies database interactions. EF Core supports a range of databases, from SQL Server to PostgreSQL and MySQL, and provides capabilities for modeling, querying, and managing database schemas within .NET applications.

Blazor

Blazor enables web UI development in C#, replacing JavaScript for client-side code. It has two main modes: Blazor Server, where components run on the server with SignalR handling UI updates, and Blazor WebAssembly, where code runs in the browser on WebAssembly. This is significant for .NET developers aiming to create rich client-side applications without leaving the .NET ecosystem.

ML.NET

ML.NET is Microsoft's machine learning library for .NET applications. It provides tools for integrating machine learning models into .NET Core applications, allowing developers to create applications that include predictive analytics, recommendations, and other machine learning-powered features without relying on external ML frameworks.

Xamarin

Xamarin enables cross-platform mobile application development for Android, iOS, and Windows. Although it's more tightly aligned with .NET 6, Xamarin remains an integral part of the .NET ecosystem, allowing mobile developers to share code between platforms using C#.

Command-Line Interface (CLI)

The .NET Core CLI is a command-line tool that developers can use to create, build, and manage .NET Core projects. This tool is particularly beneficial for developers working in cross-platform environments, as it allows for project management without depending on a particular IDE.

NuGet Package Ecosystem

NuGet is the package manager for .NET, providing access to a vast library of third-party packages, from UI components to logging frameworks. NuGet helps modularize applications, allowing developers to incorporate pre-built functionality and reduce development time.

.NET Standard: A Unifying Specification for .NET Platforms

.NET Standard is a formal specification that defines a common set of APIs across different .NET implementations, such as .NET Core, .NET Framework, and Xamarin. Its purpose is to enable code sharing across these platforms by creating a consistent API surface that all .NET platforms can implement. .NET Standard has been particularly important in facilitating code reuse across desktop, web, mobile, and IoT applications.

- **Unified API Surface**: .NET Standard includes APIs that are implemented in both .NET Core and .NET Framework, providing a baseline for cross-platform development. Libraries targeting .NET Standard can be reused across multiple .NET runtimes, which is invaluable for

teams maintaining large, multi-platform projects.
- **Versioning of .NET Standard**: .NET Standard is versioned to accommodate the growing set of APIs across .NET platforms. Higher versions of .NET Standard include more APIs but may not be supported by older platforms. For instance, .NET Standard 2.0 is widely supported by .NET Core, .NET Framework (4.6.1 and above), Xamarin, and UWP, while .NET Standard 2.1 is supported only by .NET Core 3 and newer platforms.
- **Backward Compatibility**: Libraries targeting .NET Standard can run on both .NET Framework and .NET Core, giving developers flexibility and backward compatibility. This is particularly useful for enterprises transitioning from .NET Framework to .NET Core, as they can leverage their existing libraries and gradually adopt .NET Core.

Compatibility between ASP.NET Core 3 and .NET Standard

ASP.NET Core 3 and .NET Standard complement each other in enabling cross-platform and cross-application compatibility. However, there are some considerations to keep in mind when building libraries and applications that need to be compatible with both.

- **.NET Core-Specific Optimizations**: ASP.NET Core 3 is fully optimized for .NET Core 3, which means it benefits from .NET Core 3's performance improvements, dependency injection, and asynchronous processing features. However, these optimizations are specific to .NET Core and may not be available in libraries targeting .NET Standard.
- **Compatibility Constraints**: While ASP.NET Core 3 supports libraries targeting .NET Standard 2.0 and 2.1, not all features in ASP.NET Core 3 are compatible with .NET Standard libraries. For example, gRPC and some advanced diagnostics features are specific to .NET Core 3 and above. This means that while general-purpose libraries can target .NET Standard, more specialized libraries may

need to target .NET Core 3 directly.
- **Transition to .NET 5 and Beyond**: Microsoft's unification of .NET with .NET 5 and .NET 6 builds on the cross-platform and cross-compatibility approach of .NET Core 3 and .NET Standard. Libraries built for .NET Standard 2.0 and 2.1 remain compatible with .NET 5 and .NET 6, providing a smooth upgrade path for ASP.NET Core 3 applications to the newer unified .NET platform.

Benefits of .NET Standard Compatibility in the .NET Core Ecosystem

1. Library Reusability Across Projects

.NET Standard's unifying API surface allows developers to create libraries that work across different .NET platforms. This promotes code reuse, saving development time and ensuring consistency in business logic and functionality.

2. Simplified Migration from .NET Framework

.NET Standard serves as a bridge for developers transitioning from .NET Framework to .NET Core. By targeting .NET Standard, libraries that were initially built for .NET Framework can be used in .NET Core applications, enabling a gradual migration path without requiring a complete rewrite.

3. Interoperability with Legacy Systems

For organizations with applications built on .NET Framework that cannot be easily moved to .NET Core, .NET Standard provides a way to create shared libraries that can be used across new and legacy applications. This allows developers to modernize portions of their systems incrementally.

4. Future-Proofing Applications

Since .NET Standard is designed to be compatible with future versions of .NET, libraries targeting .NET Standard are more adaptable to future changes within the ecosystem. Developers benefit from long-term compatibility as Microsoft continues to evolve .NET.

Choosing Between .NET Core and .NET Standard for ASP.NET Core

3 Projects

When developing with ASP.NET Core 3, developers may wonder whether to target .NET Core 3 or .NET Standard for libraries within their projects. Here are some guidelines to help decide:

- **Target .NET Core 3 for Maximum Performance**: Libraries targeting .NET Core 3 can take full advantage of features and optimizations specific to this runtime, such as async streams and improved JSON serialization. For applications that do not need to run on .NET Framework, targeting .NET Core 3 is generally preferable.
- **Use .NET Standard for Cross-Platform and Multi-Framework Compatibility**: If a library needs to support both .NET Core and .NET Framework, targeting .NET Standard (preferably 2.0 or 2.1) ensures broad compatibility. This is particularly useful for libraries intended to be reused across multiple projects and environments.
- **Consider the Future with .NET 5 and .NET 6**: With .NET 5 and .NET 6 unifying .NET Core and .NET Framework under a single runtime, libraries targeting .NET Standard 2.1 will remain compatible. However, if the library requires .NET 5/6-specific features, it should target .NET 5 or later directly.

The .NET Core ecosystem, with its focus on performance, cross-platform flexibility, and modularity, empowers developers to build modern applications that are scalable, efficient, and adaptable. Compatibility with .NET Standard plays a crucial role in this ecosystem by enabling code sharing and reuse across different .NET platforms. For ASP.NET Core 3 developers, understanding the advantages and compatibility considerations between .NET Core and .NET Standard helps in building robust, future-proof applications that can evolve alongside the .NET platform. As we continue, this book will provide a detailed look into building applications with ASP.NET Core 3, leveraging the strengths of

.NET Core, and optimizing compatibility with .NET Standard where needed.

Setting up the Development Environment

Building modern web applications with ASP.NET Core 3 requires an efficient and well-configured development environment. Setting up this environment involves installing the necessary software, configuring key tools, and establishing best practices that streamline coding, testing, and deployment. In this section, we'll go over each step to ensure your development environment is optimized for building ASP.NET Core 3 applications, covering IDE setup, command-line tools, and configuring your first ASP.NET Core 3 project.

1. Installing .NET Core SDK

The .NET Core SDK is the essential toolkit for building .NET Core applications, including ASP.NET Core 3. It contains the libraries, runtime, and command-line interface required to create, build, and run .NET Core applications.

Download the SDK:

Visit the .NET download page and select the .NET Core 3.1 SDK (or later if available and compatible with ASP.NET Core 3). Choose the installer based on your operating system: Windows, macOS, or Linux.

Verify Installation:

After installation, open a terminal or command prompt and run:

```bash
Copy code
dotnet --version
```

This command should output the installed version of the .NET Core SDK, confirming that the SDK is correctly installed and accessible in your environment.

Update Path Variables (Linux and macOS):
If the SDK is not immediately recognized in your terminal on Linux or macOS, you may need to add the SDK's installation path to your system's PATH variable. This ensures that dotnet commands are available globally.

2. Choosing an Integrated Development Environment (IDE)
.NET Core is supported by multiple IDEs, each offering a range of features. Here are the primary options:

Visual Studio (Windows and macOS):
Visual Studio is the most feature-rich IDE for .NET development, offering robust debugging, code navigation, IntelliSense, and integrated tools for managing projects. For ASP.NET Core 3, ensure you have Visual Studio 2019 (version 16.3 or later), as it includes full support for .NET Core 3.

- **Workloads**: During installation, select the **ASP.NET and web development** workload to ensure that all necessary components, including tools for web applications, Entity Framework Core, and other web essentials, are installed.

Visual Studio Code (Windows, macOS, Linux):
Visual Studio Code (VS Code) is a lightweight, cross-platform code editor that, with the right extensions, provides a powerful development environment for ASP.NET Core 3. It's particularly suitable for developers who prefer a fast, customizable setup or are working on non-Windows platforms.

- **Extensions**: Install the following extensions in VS Code for ASP.NET Core 3 development:
- **C# Extension**: Provides C# IntelliSense, debugging, and support for

.NET Core projects.
- **REST Client**: Useful for testing HTTP requests directly from VS Code, which is helpful when building APIs.
- **Debugger for Chrome**: For developers working on full-stack applications with Blazor or JavaScript-heavy front ends.

JetBrains Rider (Windows, macOS, Linux):

Rider is a cross-platform IDE that offers full support for .NET development, including ASP.NET Core 3. It's known for its powerful code analysis tools, fast performance, and seamless Git integration.

Command-Line Tools and Project Scaffolding

.NET Core includes a Command-Line Interface (CLI) that enables project creation, building, and running from the terminal. This is especially useful for quickly generating project templates or for use in CI/CD pipelines.

Creating a New ASP.NET Core Project:

Open a terminal or command prompt, navigate to the desired directory, and run:

```bash
Copy code
dotnet new webapp -o MyFirstAspNetCoreApp
```

This command creates a new Razor Pages web application in a folder named MyFirstAspNetCoreApp. The -o flag specifies the output directory. For MVC or API projects, replace webapp with mvc or webapi, respectively.

Basic CLI Commands:

- **dotnet run**: Runs the application. Use this command to start the development server.

- **dotnet build**: Compiles the application, checking for errors and generating executable files.
- **dotnet test**: Runs unit tests for the project (if any are set up).
- **dotnet publish**: Prepares the application for deployment, creating a package in the publish folder.

Using the .NET Core CLI for Scaffolding:
Scaffolding generates boilerplate code for controllers, views, and models. Use the dotnet-aspnet-codegenerator tool, which is part of the ASP.NET Core CLI. For instance, to scaffold a controller for an existing model, run:

```bash
Copy code
dotnet aspnet-codegenerator controller -name MyController -model MyModel -dataContext MyDbContext
```

4. Configuring the Development Environment for First-Time Setup

After installing the SDK and IDE, configure the project for efficient development.

Setting Up the Launch Profile:
ASP.NET Core applications use launch profiles for development and production. Edit the launchSettings.json file in the Properties folder to configure settings like URLs, environment variables, and debug options.

Adding Application Configuration Files:
ASP.NET Core uses configuration files (appsettings.json and appsettings.Development.json) for managing settings. Store environment-specific configurations in separate files and leverage IConfiguration to access settings in your application.

Environment Variables:
Set ASPNETCORE_ENVIRONMENT to "Development" for

INTRODUCTION TO ASP.NET CORE 3 AND MODERN C# WEB DEVELOPMENT

development-specific configurations. This can be done in the launchSettings.json file or through system-level environment variables.

NuGet Package Management:
ASP.NET Core 3 projects can include various packages for added functionality. In Visual Studio, right-click the project and select **Manage NuGet Packages** to install packages like Swashbuckle.AspNetCore for Swagger or Dapper for simplified data access.

Setting Up Git for Version Control:
Use Git for version control, which is integrated into most IDEs. Initialize Git in your project directory:

```bash
Copy code
git init
git add .
git commit -m "Initial commit"
```

Commit regularly and use branches to manage different features or bug fixes.

5. Running and Debugging the Application

Debugging is a critical aspect of ASP.NET Core development. Setting up a robust debugging process helps identify issues early and streamline development.

Running the Application in Debug Mode:
In Visual Studio, press F5 to start the application in debug mode. Breakpoints, step-through debugging, and real-time variable inspection are available. In VS Code, open the Debug panel, select .NET Core, and click Start Debugging.

Configuring Breakpoints and Watch Variables:
Set breakpoints in your code by clicking to the left of the line number

in the IDE. Use the Watch panel to monitor specific variables, allowing for close inspection of application state.

Hot Reload and Live Reloading:
ASP.NET Core 3 supports hot reload, allowing for changes to be reflected without restarting the application. This feature speeds up development by eliminating the need for constant rebuilds, particularly useful for frontend changes in Razor views or Blazor components.

6. Testing the Environment with a Sample Application
To ensure everything is configured correctly, create a small sample application that incorporates various elements of ASP.NET Core 3, such as MVC, Razor Pages, or Web API.

Creating a Simple API:
Create a new Web API project using the CLI:

```bash
Copy code
dotnet new webapi -o MyApiApp
```

Open the project and add a sample controller in the Controllers folder, then run the project to test the API.

Testing with Swagger:
ASP.NET Core 3 includes integrated support for Swagger through the Swashbuckle package, which automatically generates API documentation. Install Swashbuckle:

```bash
Copy code
dotnet add package Swashbuckle.AspNetCore
```

INTRODUCTION TO ASP.NET CORE 3 AND MODERN C# WEB DEVELOPMENT

Configure Swagger in Startup.cs, then navigate to /swagger in your browser to see your API documentation.

Running Unit Tests:

For a complete environment setup, create unit tests using xUnit or NUnit. Install a test framework via NuGet and add test classes in a separate Tests project to verify application functionality.

By following these steps, you'll have a fully configured development environment optimized for ASP.NET Core 3. From installing the .NET Core SDK and choosing the right IDE to setting up the CLI and configuring debugging tools, these foundational steps ensure you're ready to build robust, scalable applications. Each setup component contributes to a smooth development experience, enabling you to focus on writing high-quality code and managing projects effectively. As we proceed, you'll dive into the core concepts and features of ASP.NET Core 3, applying them within this well-configured development environment to build powerful, modern web applications.

Understanding the Project Structure of ASP.NET Core 3 Applications

ASP.NET Core 3 applications have a modular and organized project structure that aids in the maintainability, scalability, and readability of the code. The structure of an ASP.NET Core project is designed to separate concerns, making it easier for developers to navigate and expand upon. Understanding the purpose of each directory and file within the default structure allows you to make the most out of ASP.NET Core's organization and leverage its architecture effectively.

In this section, we'll examine the main components of an ASP.NET Core 3 project structure, including the purpose of each file and folder, and discuss how they fit into the development, testing, and deployment processes.

1. Root-Level Files and Folders

When you create a new ASP.NET Core 3 project, the following files and folders are generated at the root level:
- **Program.cs**
- The Program.cs file contains the entry point for the application. This is where the ASP.NET Core application is configured and launched. In Program.cs, the CreateHostBuilder method is called, which sets up the host environment, loads configurations, and specifies which Startup class to use.
- **Startup.cs**
- The Startup.cs file defines the startup logic for the application, including service configuration and middleware pipeline setup. It contains two main methods:
- ConfigureServices: Used to register services with the dependency injection (DI) container.
- Configure: Used to define the HTTP request pipeline, where middleware components like routing, authentication, and logging are specified.
- **appsettings.json and appsettings.Development.json**
- These files store configuration settings for the application. appsettings.json contains general configuration, while appsettings.Development.json is used to override settings specifically for the development environment. Settings like database connection strings, API keys, and logging configurations are typically stored here. The configurations are accessed through the IConfiguration interface, which reads these settings at runtime.
- **Properties/launchSettings.json**
- The launchSettings.json file is used to configure launch profiles for different environments (e.g., Development, Production). It specifies environment variables, the URL the application should use during debugging, and other settings related to launching the

application. Visual Studio and Visual Studio Code use this file to manage environment-specific launch configurations.

2. The Controllers Folder

In ASP.NET Core applications that follow the MVC or API pattern, the Controllers folder houses controller classes. Controllers are responsible for handling HTTP requests, processing incoming data, and returning responses. There are two main types of controllers in ASP.NET Core:

- **MVC Controllers**: These handle web requests and render views (HTML) for the browser. An MVC controller might have methods (actions) that return IActionResult types like View() (to render a Razor view) or RedirectToAction() (to redirect to another action).
- **API Controllers**: These are used for building RESTful services and often return data in JSON format. API controllers generally inherit from ControllerBase instead of Controller to avoid the overhead of MVC-specific features, focusing solely on JSON data.

Example:

```csharp
csharp
Copy code
public class ProductsController : ControllerBase
{
    [HttpGet("{id}")]
    public IActionResult GetProduct(int id)
    {
        var product = _productService.GetById(id);
        if (product == null) return NotFound();
        return Ok(product);
    }
}
```

3. The Models Folder

The Models folder holds classes that represent the data structure and business logic of the application. Models are used to define the shape of data in the application and can include validation rules and data annotations. Common types of models include:

- **Domain Models**: Represent the core entities in the application, such as Product, Customer, or Order.
- **View Models**: Contain data specifically tailored for views, often combining data from multiple entities.
- **DTOs (Data Transfer Objects)**: Used to transfer data between layers or services without exposing full domain models.

Example:

```csharp
Copy code
public class Product
{
    public int Id { get; set; }
    public string Name { get; set; }
    public decimal Price { get; set; }
}
```

4. The Views Folder (MVC Projects)

The Views folder contains Razor view files (.cshtml files) in MVC applications. These files are responsible for rendering HTML content and are structured around the MVC pattern. Typically, the Views folder has subfolders for each controller, and within each subfolder, there are view files corresponding to different actions.

- **_ViewStart.cshtml**: This file is executed before each view is rendered. It is commonly used to set the layout for views.
- **_ViewImports.cshtml**: Contains directives (such as @using and @addTagHelper) that are applied across views in the project.
- **Layouts**: Layout files (e.g., _Layout.cshtml) define a consistent look and feel across the application. Individual views reference the layout

to inherit common elements like headers, footers, and navigation.

Example of a Razor view file (Index.cshtml):

```html
Copy code
@model IEnumerable<Product>

<h1>Product List</h1>
<ul>
    @foreach (var product in Model)
    {
        <li>@product.Name - $@product.Price</li>
    }
</ul>
```

5. The wwwroot Folder

The wwwroot folder is the root directory for static files in an ASP.NET Core application. Files in wwwroot are directly accessible via HTTP requests, making this the ideal location for content like images, CSS, JavaScript, and custom fonts.

- **Static Files**: Any files placed here can be accessed with a URL that maps to the file structure in wwwroot. For example, a file at wwwroot/images/logo.png is accessible at /images/logo.png.
- **Bundling and Minification**: ASP.NET Core provides support for bundling and minifying CSS and JavaScript files to improve performance. Tools like gulp and webpack can be integrated for advanced bundling needs.

6. The Data Folder (Optional)

In projects that use Entity Framework Core (EF Core) for database interactions, the Data folder often contains the database context class and migration files.

- **DbContext**: The context class (e.g., ApplicationDbContext) represents a session with the database, allowing CRUD operations on entities. It includes DbSet<T> properties for each entity model, mapping classes to database tables.
- **Migrations**: If using code-first migrations, the Migrations folder holds migration files that track schema changes over time. These files can be generated using the command dotnet ef migrations add MigrationName.

Example of a DbContext:

```csharp
Copy code
public class ApplicationDbContext : DbContext
{
    public ApplicationDbContext(DbContextOptions<ApplicationDbContext> options)
        : base(options)
    {
    }

    public DbSet<Product> Products { get; set; }
}
```

7. The Services Folder (Optional)

The Services folder is used to implement business logic that can be injected into controllers or other parts of the application. Services are classes that encapsulate specific tasks, making them reusable and promoting a clean separation of concerns.

- **Dependency Injection**: ASP.NET Core uses dependency injection (DI) natively, making it easy to inject services into controllers. Services are registered in the ConfigureServices method in Startup.cs.

Example of a service interface and implementation:

```csharp
Copy code
public interface IProductService
{
    Product GetById(int id);
}

public class ProductService : IProductService
{
    public Product GetById(int id)
    {
        // Implementation logic here
    }
}
```

8. Additional Folders (Optional)

ASP.NET Core is flexible, allowing you to create additional folders as needed to organize your application's code. Common optional folders include:

- **Repositories**: For implementing the repository pattern, where data access logic is encapsulated.
- **Helpers**: For utility classes and functions that are used across the application.
- **Middlewares**: For custom middleware components, enhancing the HTTP request pipeline with custom logic.

Summary of the Project Structure

The modular structure of ASP.NET Core 3 applications aids in organizing code by purpose, promoting best practices such as the separation of concerns, reusability, and maintainability. Here's a quick recap:

- **Program.cs and Startup.cs**: The main entry point and configuration files.

- **Controllers**: Handles HTTP requests and generates responses.
- **Models**: Represents data structures and business logic.
- **Views**: Renders HTML in MVC applications.
- **wwwroot**: Contains static files like CSS and JavaScript.
- **Optional Folders**: Data, Services, Repositories, Helpers, etc., which add flexibility to accommodate different application architectures.

Understanding the structure of an ASP.NET Core 3 project is essential to effectively building and maintaining scalable web applications. Each folder and file has a specific role, promoting organization, separation of concerns, and ease of navigation. With a clear grasp of the project structure, you are well-equipped to begin coding, structuring services, handling requests, and delivering a streamlined experience to users. As you continue building applications in ASP.NET Core 3, this structured approach will enable you to maintain and expand your codebase with confidence and clarity.

Getting Started - Building Your First ASP.NET Core 3 Project

Creating a New Project from Scratch
Building your first ASP.NET Core 3 project is a straightforward process, especially with the robust tooling and template support provided by .NET Core. Starting from scratch allows you to learn the essential configurations, understand project structure, and set up foundational components that are critical for a real-world ASP.NET Core 3 web application. In this section, we'll go through the step-by-step process of creating a new project, exploring various templates, and configuring initial settings for a smooth development experience.

1. Setting Up the Project Directory
Before creating a new project, start by organizing your workspace. It's helpful to establish a folder structure that can accommodate multiple projects, especially if you plan to build supporting libraries or related applications.

Create a Main Folder:
Organize all project files under a single main directory to keep your workspace clean. For example, create a folder named ASPNetCoreProjects where you can save different applications in the future.

Open a Terminal or Command Prompt:

Launch your terminal (or command prompt on Windows), and navigate to the main folder. If you're using an IDE like Visual Studio or Visual Studio Code, you can use the integrated terminal for easier navigation.

2. Choosing a Project Template

ASP.NET Core 3 offers a variety of templates tailored for different types of applications. Choosing the right template at the start provides a strong foundation for your project, aligning it with your specific requirements. Here are the main project templates available in ASP.NET Core 3:

- **Web Application (MVC)**: For applications following the Model-View-Controller pattern, best suited for web applications that render HTML.
- **Web API**: For building RESTful services, used primarily when your application needs to serve data to other applications or frontends.
- **Razor Pages**: A simplified alternative to MVC, which combines logic and markup in a single file, aimed at page-centric web applications.

To create a new project, use either Visual Studio's GUI or the .NET Core CLI, which offers a flexible way to generate projects from the terminal.

3. Creating a New Project with Visual Studio

Using Visual Studio is one of the most popular ways to create and manage ASP.NET Core projects. Here's how to create a new project:

Open Visual Studio: Launch Visual Studio (ensure you're using Visual Studio 2019 version 16.3 or later for full ASP.NET Core 3 support).

Select "Create a new project": From the welcome screen, choose the "Create a new project" option.

Choose Project Template:
In the template selection screen:

- For a web application with MVC, select **ASP.NET Core Web Application**.
- For a web API, select **ASP.NET Core Web API**.
- For a Razor Pages application, select **ASP.NET Core Web Application** and choose the **Razor Pages** option in the following steps.

Configure Project Settings:

- **Project Name**: Give your project a descriptive name, e.g., MyFirstAspNetCoreApp.
- **Location**: Choose the directory where the project should be saved.
- **Solution Name**: If you're creating multiple projects, grouping them in a solution is helpful. You can use the same name as your project or something broader if you plan to add more projects later.
- **Framework**: Select **.NET Core** as the target framework, and make sure **ASP.NET Core 3.1** is selected as the version.

Additional Settings:
Depending on your application type, you may have additional options:

- **Authentication**: Choose an authentication type (None, Individual Accounts, etc.) depending on your application's security needs. You can modify authentication settings later if needed.
- **Docker Support**: If you're planning to containerize your application, enable Docker support here.

Create Project: Click "Create" to generate the project. Visual Studio will scaffold the necessary files and dependencies automatically.

4. Creating a New Project Using the .NET Core CLI

The .NET Core Command-Line Interface (CLI) offers a flexible, platform-independent way to create ASP.NET Core projects. Using the CLI is especially useful for developers working outside Visual Studio or those who prefer a command-line setup.

Open Terminal or Command Prompt:
Navigate to your desired folder where you want to create the project.

Run the dotnet new Command:
Use the following commands based on the application type you wish to create:

- **For MVC**:

```bash
Copy code
dotnet new mvc -o MyFirstAspNetCoreApp
```

- **For Web API**:

```bash
Copy code
dotnet new webapi -o MyFirstAspNetCoreApp
```

- **For Razor Pages**:

```bash
Copy code
dotnet new webapp -o MyFirstAspNetCoreApp
```

The -o option specifies the output directory name. Replace MyFirstAsp-

GETTING STARTED - BUILDING YOUR FIRST ASP.NET CORE 3 PROJECT

NetCoreApp with your preferred project name.

Navigate to the Project Directory:
After the project is created, move into the project folder:

```bash
Copy code
cd MyFirstAspNetCoreApp
```

Run the Project:
Start the application to verify everything is set up correctly:

```bash
Copy code
dotnet run
```

The application will start, and you should see a message indicating it's running on https://localhost:5001 and http://localhost:5000 by default.

5. Configuring the Project

Once the project is created, configuring it to suit your development needs is essential. Here are some key initial setup tasks:

Configure Launch Settings:
Open the launchSettings.json file located in Properties. Here, you can set up different profiles, define environment variables, and customize the launch URL.

Example entry in launchSettings.json:

```json
Copy code
{
  "profiles": {
```

```json
    "IIS Express": {
      "commandName": "IISExpress",
      "launchBrowser": true,
      "launchUrl": "weatherforecast",
      "environmentVariables": {
        "ASPNETCORE_ENVIRONMENT": "Development"
      }
    },
    "MyFirstAspNetCoreApp": {
      "commandName": "Project",
      "dotnetRunMessages": true,
      "launchBrowser": true,
      "launchUrl": "weatherforecast",
      "environmentVariables": {
        "ASPNETCORE_ENVIRONMENT": "Development"
      }
    }
  }
}
```

The environment variable ASPNETCORE_ENVIRONMENT can be set to Development, Staging, or Production, depending on your setup.

Install Necessary NuGet Packages:

ASP.NET Core projects often require additional libraries. You can install packages using the dotnet add package command or through Visual Studio's **NuGet Package Manager**.

Initialize Source Control:

Version control is vital for tracking code changes. Initialize a Git repository within the project folder:

```bash
Copy code
git init
git add .
```

```
git commit -m "Initial commit"
```

6. Exploring the Default Project Structure

The new project comes with a default folder and file structure, tailored to your chosen template. Key folders and files include:

- **Controllers**: Contains controller classes for handling HTTP requests.
- **Models**: Houses model classes representing data.
- **Views** (MVC or Razor Pages): Contains .cshtml files for views in Razor syntax.
- **wwwroot**: Holds static files such as CSS, JavaScript, and images.
- **appsettings.json**: Configures application settings.

Understanding this structure is critical, as each folder serves a specific purpose in ASP.NET Core's architecture.

7. Running and Testing the Application

With your project created and configured, it's time to run it and verify that everything works as expected.

Run the Application in Development Mode:
Start the application in development mode to ensure the project is set up correctly. In Visual Studio, press F5 to start the application with debugging, or use dotnet run in the CLI. Open a browser and navigate to the default launch URL, typically https://localhost:5001.

Verify the Default Content:
Depending on the project template, you may see a welcome page (Razor Pages), a simple JSON output (Web API), or a basic MVC layout. This confirms that the project has been set up successfully.

Basic Debugging:
Place breakpoints in Startup.cs or controller files to test debugging

capabilities. This helps you verify that Visual Studio or your chosen IDE is configured correctly for handling breakpoints, watches, and variable inspections.

8. Making Initial Customizations

Finally, to make the project your own, consider making a few initial customizations:

- **Modify the Home Page**:
- Replace default content with something relevant to your project by editing the .cshtml files in the Views/Home folder (for MVC) or Pages folder (for Razor Pages).
- **Add Sample Data and API Endpoints**:
- If you're using the Web API template, create a simple controller method to return mock data. This will help you verify the API setup and ensure endpoints are functioning as expected.

Example:

```csharp
Copy code
[Route("api/[controller]")]
public class SampleController : ControllerBase
{
    [HttpGet]
    public IActionResult Get()
    {
        return Ok(new { Message = "Hello, ASP.NET Core 3!" });
    }
}
```

Update appsettings.json:

- Add essential configuration items, such as a connection string or custom settings, which will support the upcoming development stages.

GETTING STARTED - BUILDING YOUR FIRST ASP.NET CORE 3 PROJECT

Creating a new ASP.NET Core 3 project from scratch is a simple process that sets the stage for building powerful, scalable applications. By understanding the available templates, configuring your development environment, and familiarizing yourself with the project's structure, you've laid a strong foundation for development.

Exploring Templates: Razor Pages vs. MVC

ASP.NET Core 3 offers multiple templates, with Razor Pages and MVC (Model-View-Controller) being two of the most popular options for building web applications. Both provide efficient ways to handle requests, present data, and structure application logic, but they are suited to slightly different development scenarios. Understanding the strengths and intended use cases for each can help you decide which template best meets the needs of your project.

In this section, we'll break down the core concepts behind Razor Pages and MVC, highlight their differences, and explore specific scenarios where one might be more advantageous than the other.

1. Overview of Razor Pages

Razor Pages is a relatively recent addition to the ASP.NET Core ecosystem, introduced as an alternative to the MVC framework. It simplifies the development process by consolidating both the logic and the UI for a single page into one file, which can reduce complexity for page-centric applications. Razor Pages follow a "page-based" approach, meaning each page is self-contained and handles its own data interactions, making it a natural fit for simpler web applications or projects that don't require full MVC structure.

Key Features of Razor Pages:
- **Page-Focused Structure**: Razor Pages are organized around individual pages, each with its own .cshtml file and a corresponding .cshtml.cs code-behind file where business logic is implemented.

- **Separation of Logic and View**: Business logic resides in the code-behind file, while HTML markup remains in the .cshtml file.
- **Simplified Routing**: Razor Pages simplify routing by automatically mapping URL paths to the page files. For instance, a file located at Pages/Products.cshtml would automatically be accessible at /Products.
- **Enhanced Performance for Simple Pages**: Since each page can handle its own data binding, Razor Pages can be more efficient for applications that don't need the overhead of MVC.

Example Structure of a Razor Page:

```plaintext
Copy code
- Pages/
    - Products/
        - Index.cshtml
        - Index.cshtml.cs
```

In the above structure, Index.cshtml handles the HTML and view presentation, while Index.cshtml.cs contains the page model and server-side logic for data binding, processing requests, and managing the page's lifecycle.

When to Use Razor Pages:

- Single-purpose pages, like forms, dashboards, or static content pages.
- Page-centric applications that don't require complex data interactions across multiple controllers.
- Scenarios where simplicity and speed of development are prioritized.

2. Overview of MVC (Model-View-Controller)

MVC is a powerful, well-established design pattern in ASP.NET Core, organizing applications into three main components: Model, View, and Controller. MVC is highly modular and promotes separation of concerns, which is ideal for complex applications with extensive data processing, business logic, and multiple user interactions. In MVC, each of the three components has a dedicated role, making it easier to manage, test, and scale the application as it grows.

Key Components of MVC:

- **Model**: Represents the data structure of the application. Models are often directly mapped to database tables and can include validation rules, relationships, and business logic.
- **View**: The HTML templates (or Razor views) that define what users see on the front end. Views are tightly integrated with MVC, allowing dynamic data binding and rendering.
- **Controller**: Handles HTTP requests and processes them by interacting with the Model, then passing data to the View. Controllers are responsible for routing and determining what content should be displayed to the user.

Example of an MVC Controller:

```csharp
Copy code
public class ProductsController : Controller
{
    public IActionResult Index()
    {
        var products = _productService.GetAll();
        return View(products);
    }
}
```

When to Use MVC:

- Applications that require complex data management, processing, or custom workflows.
- Projects that benefit from a structured architecture, where each component can be developed, tested, and maintained independently.

- Scenarios that involve many views or endpoints sharing data models and controllers.

MVC's separation of data, presentation, and logic allows for fine-grained control over each component, making it ideal for large applications with multiple team members working on different parts of the application.

3. Key Differences Between Razor Pages and MVC

While both Razor Pages and MVC offer robust features, they differ in structure, setup, and usage. Here's a breakdown of the major distinctions:

Feature	Razor Pages	MVC
Architecture	Page-centric (individual pages)	Component-based (separate Model, View, Controller)
Routing	Automatic routing based on file structure	Customizable, route definitions in controllers
Complexity	Simpler, with less overhead	More complex but allows greater control
Use Case	Single-purpose pages or small apps	Large-scale apps with complex workflows
Learning Curve	Easier for beginners	Steeper but provides more flexibility
File Organization	Combined logic and view in `PageModel` files	Separation of business logic (Controller) and views

Razor Pages simplify routing by mapping URL paths directly to file paths, which reduces the need for manual route configuration. MVC, on the other hand, allows for more detailed routing and control over URL patterns, making it a better choice when extensive route customization is needed.

4. Choosing Between Razor Pages and MVC

The decision between Razor Pages and MVC largely depends on the type and complexity of your application. Here are some scenarios to guide your choice:

- **Razor Pages** is ideal if:
- You're building a small or medium-sized application with a straightforward page structure.
- Your application is primarily form-based or data entry-focused.
- Simplicity and development speed are more critical than complex routing or modularity.
- **MVC** is more suitable if:
- You're working on a large-scale application with multiple components, complex data relationships, or workflows.
- You require a highly modular approach that separates business logic, data, and presentation.
- You need fine-grained control over routing, security, and middleware components.

Ultimately, ASP.NET Core is flexible enough to allow mixing both Razor Pages and MVC in the same project. This hybrid approach can be beneficial if you want to use MVC for core application areas while leveraging Razor Pages for simpler, self-contained pages.

5. Practical Example: Building the Same Page in Razor Pages vs. MVC

To understand how Razor Pages and MVC handle similar tasks differently, consider a simple example: displaying a list of products.

Razor Pages Implementation:

1. Create a new Razor Page in the Pages/Products folder called Index.cshtml.
2. In Index.cshtml.cs, add code to retrieve the list of products and bind it to the page.
3. Display the products in Index.cshtml using Razor syntax.

Index.cshtml.cs (Razor Page Model):

```csharp
Copy code
public class IndexModel : PageModel
{
    private readonly IProductService _productService;

    public List<Product> Products { get; private set; }

    public IndexModel(IProductService productService)
    {
        _productService = productService;
    }

    public void OnGet()
    {
        Products = _productService.GetAllProducts();
    }
}
```

Index.cshtml (View):

```html
Copy code
@page
@model IndexModel

<h1>Product List</h1>
<ul>
    @foreach (var product in Model.Products)
    {
        <li>@product.Name - $@product.Price</li>
    }
</ul>
```

MVC Implementation:

1. Create a new controller called ProductsController with an Index action method.

GETTING STARTED - BUILDING YOUR FIRST ASP.NET CORE 3 PROJECT

2. In Index action, retrieve the product list and pass it to the view.
3. In the Views/Products/Index.cshtml file, display the products list.

ProductsController.cs:

```csharp
Copy code
public class ProductsController : Controller
{
    private readonly IProductService _productService;

    public ProductsController(IProductService productService)
    {
        _productService = productService;
    }

    public IActionResult Index()
    {
        var products = _productService.GetAllProducts();
        return View(products);
    }
}
```

Views/Products/Index.cshtml (View):

```html
Copy code
@model IEnumerable<Product>

<h1>Product List</h1>
<ul>
    @foreach (var product in Model)
    {
        <li>@product.Name - $@product.Price</li>
    }
</ul>
```

In this example:

- Razor Pages consolidates the page logic and view in a single folder, while MVC separates them across controllers and views.
- Razor Pages automatically maps Index.cshtml to /Products, while MVC requires route configuration in the controller.

Both Razor Pages and MVC offer robust templates for building ASP.NET Core applications. Razor Pages provides simplicity and a page-focused approach, making it ideal for small to medium applications with minimal complexity. MVC offers modularity and control, making it better suited for large-scale applications where fine-grained control over each component is necessary. By understanding the strengths and ideal use cases for each, you can choose the template that best aligns with your project's needs and complexity level.

Understanding the Program and Startup Files

In ASP.NET Core 3 applications, the **Program.cs** and **Startup.cs** files are foundational to configuring and launching the web application. Together, these files manage the application's lifecycle from initialization to handling requests. They define the application's configuration, set up services, and control how the app responds to HTTP requests. Understanding how these files work is essential for configuring custom services, middleware, and dependencies that make up your web application's architecture.

1. Overview of Program.cs

The **Program.cs** file serves as the entry point of an ASP.NET Core application. It's responsible for setting up the application's host, configuring the environment, and ultimately calling the Startup class to initialize the rest of the application. The Main method, which executes when the application starts, creates and configures a web host—a server environment that will manage the application's lifetime.

GETTING STARTED - BUILDING YOUR FIRST ASP.NET CORE 3 PROJECT

Key points about Program.cs:
- It defines the **Host Builder** pattern, which allows the configuration of essential services, including dependency injection, configuration sources, and logging.
- Program.cs integrates the **Generic Host** model in ASP.NET Core 3, which enables both web and non-web workloads, making it flexible enough for a wide range of applications.

A typical Program.cs file looks like this:

```csharp
Copy code
public class Program
{
    public static void Main(string[] args)
    {
        CreateHostBuilder(args).Build().Run();
    }

    public static IHostBuilder CreateHostBuilder(string[] args) =>
        Host.CreateDefaultBuilder(args)
            .ConfigureWebHostDefaults(webBuilder =>
            {
                webBuilder.UseStartup<Startup>();
            });
}
```

Breaking Down the Key Components

- **Main Method**: This is the entry point of the application. It creates the host, builds it, and then runs it.
- **CreateHostBuilder**: This method configures and returns an IHostBuilder instance, which defines the app's host (server) settings.
- **Host.CreateDefaultBuilder**: This default builder configures several critical services:

- **Configuration**: Loads app settings (from appsettings.json, environment variables, etc.).
- **Logging**: Sets up logging services, often configured in the appsettings.json file.
- **Dependency Injection (DI)**: Registers core DI services so that components can be injected throughout the app.

The **webBuilder.UseStartup<Startup>()** line is particularly important as it specifies that Startup should handle additional configurations, such as middleware setup, service registrations, and routing.

2. Overview of Startup.cs

The **Startup.cs** file is where you define the application's behavior, specifying configurations, services, and middleware that handle requests and responses. The Startup class contains two key methods: ConfigureServices and Configure.

Startup Class Structure:

```csharp
Copy code
public class Startup
{
    public Startup(IConfiguration configuration)
    {
        Configuration = configuration;
    }

    public IConfiguration Configuration { get; }

    public void ConfigureServices(IServiceCollection services)
    {
        // Register services and dependencies here
    }

    public void Configure(IApplicationBuilder app,
    IWebHostEnvironment env)
```

GETTING STARTED - BUILDING YOUR FIRST ASP.NET CORE 3 PROJECT

```
    {
        // Define middleware pipeline here
    }
}
```

Key Components
Startup Constructor:

- The constructor receives an IConfiguration object, which represents application configuration settings (like those in appsettings.json or environment variables).
- By assigning it to the Configuration property, the application gains easy access to settings throughout the Startup class.

ConfigureServices Method:

- This method is responsible for registering services with the **Dependency Injection (DI) container**. In ASP.NET Core, services are configured here to be injected into different components of the app.
- Services can include database contexts, authentication schemes, MVC services, custom services (e.g., email providers, repositories), and more.
- ASP.NET Core's DI system will then manage these services and their lifetimes (e.g., Singleton, Scoped, Transient).

Example of **ConfigureServices** method:

```csharp
Copy code
public void ConfigureServices(IServiceCollection services)
{
    services.AddControllersWithViews();
    services.AddDbContext<MyDbContext>(options =>
```

```
        options.UseSqlServer(Configuration.
GetConnectionString("DefaultConnection")));
    services.AddRazorPages();
}
```

- **AddControllersWithViews**: Registers MVC services for an application using controllers and views.
- **AddDbContext**: Configures a database context (MyDbContext) to be used with Entity Framework, pulling the connection string from configuration.
- **AddRazorPages**: Enables Razor Pages, making them accessible in the application.

Configure Method:

- The Configure method defines the **HTTP request pipeline**, which dictates how requests are handled from start to finish.
- Middleware components are added in sequence, and each can process requests, modify responses, or terminate request handling.
- Common middleware includes error handling, routing, static files, and authentication.

Example of **Configure** method:

```csharp
Copy code
public void Configure(IApplicationBuilder app, IWebHostEnvironment env)
{
    if (env.IsDevelopment())
    {
        app.UseDeveloperExceptionPage();
    }
```

GETTING STARTED - BUILDING YOUR FIRST ASP.NET CORE 3 PROJECT

```
    else
    {
        app.UseExceptionHandler("/Home/Error");
        app.UseHsts();
    }

    app.UseHttpsRedirection();
    app.UseStaticFiles();
    app.UseRouting();

    app.UseAuthentication();
    app.UseAuthorization();

    app.UseEndpoints(endpoints =>
    {
        endpoints.MapControllerRoute(
            name: "default",
            pattern: "{controller=Home}/{action=Index}/{id?}");
        endpoints.MapRazorPages();
    });
}
```

- **UseDeveloperExceptionPage**: Shows detailed error information during development.
- **UseExceptionHandler**: Configures a custom error page for production.
- **UseHsts**: Enforces HTTP Strict Transport Security for secure connections.
- **UseHttpsRedirection**: Redirects HTTP requests to HTTPS.
- **UseStaticFiles**: Serves static files (like CSS, JavaScript, images) from the wwwroot directory.
- **UseRouting**: Enables routing to match incoming requests to endpoints.
- **UseAuthentication/UseAuthorization**: Adds authentication and authorization capabilities.

- **UseEndpoints**: Specifies the endpoints the app should support, such as controllers and Razor Pages.

3. Customizing Program and Startup Files

Both the **Program.cs** and **Startup.cs** files offer extensive customization options to tailor your application's setup:

- **Adding Custom Configuration Sources**: In Program.cs, you can add custom configuration providers, like JSON files or environment variables.
- Example:

```csharp
Copy code
Host.CreateDefaultBuilder(args)
    .ConfigureAppConfiguration((hostingContext, config) =>
    {
        config.AddJsonFile("customsettings.json", optional: true, reloadOnChange: true);
    });
```

- **Extending Services**: In Startup.cs, ConfigureServices allows you to add custom services, such as third-party libraries for logging or telemetry.
- Example:

```csharp
Copy code
public void ConfigureServices(IServiceCollection services)
{
```

```
    services.AddSingleton<IMyService,
MyServiceImplementation>();
}
```

- **Adding Custom Middleware**: You can create and add custom middleware in the Configure method to handle requests in a unique way. Custom middleware is useful for implementing custom logging, error handling, or specific security checks.

4. The Execution Flow

To understand how the **Program.cs** and **Startup.cs** files work together, it's essential to follow the typical execution flow:

1. **Program.cs** initializes and configures the host, determining the environment and loading the Startup class.
2. Startup.ConfigureServices registers the required services for the application, making them available through dependency injection.
3. Startup.Configure sets up the middleware pipeline, defining how requests are handled.
4. The host begins listening for HTTP requests, and requests are processed through the middleware pipeline configured in Startup.Configure.

Each step in the execution flow is crucial, from starting the host to configuring services and the request pipeline. Together, these steps create a cohesive and flexible environment for handling requests, providing a seamless experience for the end user.

The **Program.cs** and **Startup.cs** files form the backbone of any ASP.NET Core 3 application, setting up the host, configuring services, and managing the request pipeline. Understanding how these files interact, and knowing when and where to make customizations, enables you to build applications that are not only highly functional but also scalable and easy to maintain. Whether you're adding new services, configuring middleware, or customizing your application's behavior, mastery of these files is essential for building professional, production-ready ASP.NET Core applications.

Running and Debugging Your Application

Once your ASP.NET Core 3 application is set up, the next step is to run and debug it to verify that everything works as expected. The debugging process helps you identify and fix issues early, ensuring a smooth development experience and improving code quality. In this section, we'll cover the essentials of running your application, setting up debugging sessions, and using debugging tools effectively in Visual Studio.

1. Running Your ASP.NET Core Application

ASP.NET Core applications can be run in multiple ways, depending on your development environment and requirements.

Running the Application in Visual Studio

Visual Studio provides a straightforward way to run ASP.NET Core applications:

Start the Application:
- In the Solution Explorer, ensure that your project is set as the startup project.
- Click the green **Run** button (or press F5).

Select the Hosting Environment:

GETTING STARTED - BUILDING YOUR FIRST ASP.NET CORE 3 PROJECT

- By default, Visual Studio will run the application in **IIS Express** if installed, or in a standalone **Kestrel** server otherwise.
- Select the desired environment from the drop-down list next to the Run button.

View the Application in a Browser:

- Once the application is running, a browser will open, navigating to http://localhost:<port>, where <port> is the port number assigned to the application.

Running from the Command Line

If you're not using Visual Studio or prefer the command line, you can run the application using the .NET CLI:

Open a terminal in your project's root directory.

Execute the command:

```bash
Copy code
dotnet run
```

Once the application is running, access it in a browser at http://localhost:<port>, where <port> is assigned dynamically or specified in launchSettings.json.

This command starts the application using the **Kestrel** web server, which is lightweight and suitable for development purposes.

2. Debugging Essentials

Effective debugging in ASP.NET Core involves a mix of breakpoints, watch windows, and diagnostic tools. In Visual Studio, debugging is fully integrated, providing a streamlined experience for identifying issues.

Using Breakpoints

Breakpoints are a fundamental tool for debugging. They allow you to pause the execution of your application at specific lines of code, enabling you to inspect variable values and program flow.

Setting a Breakpoint:

- In Visual Studio, open the file where you want to set a breakpoint.
- Click to the left of the line number or press F9 to add a breakpoint.

Running the Application in Debug Mode:

- Start the application in Debug mode by clicking **Start Debugging** (or pressing F5).
- The application will run until it reaches a breakpoint, at which point it will pause, allowing you to examine the current state.

Inspecting Variables:

- Hover over variables in the code to see their current values.
- Use the **Locals** or **Autos** window to view all variables in the current scope.

Stepping Through Code:

- Use the **Step Into (F11)**, **Step Over (F10)**, and **Step Out (Shift+F11)** options to navigate through your code line by line.

Conditional Breakpoints

Conditional breakpoints allow you to pause execution only when specific conditions are met, which can be helpful when debugging loops or repetitive actions:

1. Right-click on a breakpoint and select **Conditions**.
2. Define a condition, such as a specific variable value (e.g., count ==

10).
3. The application will pause at this breakpoint only when the condition is true.

3. Watch Windows and Immediate Window

The **Watch** and **Immediate** windows in Visual Studio allow you to track variables and evaluate expressions as your application runs.

Watch Windows

The Watch window lets you track specific variables or expressions:

1. Open the **Watch** window by going to **Debug > Windows > Watch**.
2. Add variables or expressions you want to monitor by typing them directly in the Watch window.
3. As you step through your code, the values will update automatically.

This is particularly useful for monitoring the state of key variables or expressions across different code segments.

Immediate Window

The **Immediate** window allows you to evaluate expressions or execute code while debugging:

1. Open the **Immediate** window by selecting **Debug > Windows > Immediate**.
2. Type expressions, variable names, or methods to evaluate them in real time.

For instance, you could type myVariable.ToString() to see its value or even call methods if you need additional context while debugging.

4. Inspecting the Call Stack

The **Call Stack** window shows the sequence of method calls that led to the current point in the application, making it easier to trace back through your code. This is particularly useful for diagnosing errors that occur deep within a chain of methods.

1. Open the Call Stack by going to **Debug > Windows > Call Stack**.
2. Review each frame (method call) to understand the execution path.
3. Double-click on any frame to jump directly to that line of code.

The Call Stack window can be helpful for understanding complex workflows and for pinpointing issues that may be arising from specific method calls or dependencies.

5. Debugging Middleware and Request Pipeline

In ASP.NET Core, requests pass through a series of middleware components. Debugging the request pipeline can help identify issues with request handling, routing, or response generation.

Set Breakpoints in Middleware:

- Open your Startup.cs file and set breakpoints in the Configure method where middleware is registered (e.g., app.UseRouting();, app.UseAuthentication();).
- Run the application in Debug mode.

Trace Request Flow:

- Step through each middleware component to observe how requests are processed.
- Inspect the HttpContext object to examine headers, routes, and other request details.

This approach helps troubleshoot authentication, authorization, and routing issues by allowing you to follow the entire request flow.

6. Exception Handling and Logging

ASP.NET Core provides integrated exception handling and logging, which can be helpful for diagnosing errors in both development and production.

Viewing Exceptions in Development

In the development environment, the **Developer Exception Page** displays detailed exception information, including stack traces and request details. To enable it:

- In Startup.cs, ensure you call app.UseDeveloperExceptionPage() inside the Configure method, wrapped in an environment check:

```csharp
Copy code
if (env.IsDevelopment())
{
    app.UseDeveloperExceptionPage();
}
```

Global Exception Handling for Production

In production, configure a custom error handler to prevent exposing detailed errors to end users:

- Add app.UseExceptionHandler("/Home/Error") in Configure, where "/Home/Error" is a route to a custom error page.

Logging with ASP.NET Core

ASP.NET Core has built-in logging support. To log exceptions and other information:

Inject the ILogger service into your class:

```csharp
Copy code
```

```
private readonly ILogger<YourClassName> _logger;
public YourClassName(ILogger<YourClassName> logger)
{
    _logger = logger;
}
```

Log messages using various log levels:

```
csharp
Copy code
_logger.LogError("An error occurred in YourClassName.");
```

These logs can be viewed in the **Output** window in Visual Studio or directed to a logging provider (e.g., files, databases, external services) as configured in appsettings.json.

7. Debugging with Browser DevTools

For front-end debugging, modern browsers offer Developer Tools that can help troubleshoot client-side code.

Inspect Elements:

- Open the **Elements** tab to view HTML, CSS, and inspect DOM structure.

Console:

- The **Console** tab shows JavaScript errors, warnings, and logs, which can help track down issues in front-end scripts.

Network:

- The **Network** tab allows you to examine requests and responses between the browser and server. This is useful for verifying API calls and debugging issues related to loading resources.

These tools are invaluable for debugging front-end code and ensuring that your ASP.NET Core application is interacting correctly with the client side.

Running and debugging an ASP.NET Core 3 application is a streamlined experience thanks to Visual Studio's integrated tools. By understanding how to use breakpoints, watch windows, the Immediate window, and browser dev tools, you'll be well-equipped to identify and resolve issues. This systematic debugging approach can save time, enhance code quality, and help you understand the inner workings of your application's lifecycle and architecture.

Structuring Your Project for Scalability

Structuring an ASP.NET Core project for scalability is crucial for developing applications that can grow over time, handle increased traffic, and accommodate new features without requiring major rewrites. By organizing your codebase into logical layers, following best practices for modularity, and using design patterns that promote separation of concerns, you create an application that is easier to maintain and expand.

A scalable structure generally includes multiple layers, each responsible for a different part of the application's functionality, such as presentation, business logic, and data access. The following sections outline the key principles and practices for structuring a scalable ASP.NET Core 3 project.

1. Use a Layered Architecture

A layered architecture helps separate concerns, making each part of your application more manageable and testable. Common layers include:
- **Presentation Layer**: Handles user interactions, typically through controllers, views, and Razor Pages.

- **Business Logic Layer (BLL)**: Contains the core functionality and rules of the application, often organized through services that process data and enforce rules.
- **Data Access Layer (DAL)**: Manages interactions with the database, typically through repositories or an ORM like Entity Framework Core.
- **Infrastructure Layer**: Manages cross-cutting concerns like logging, caching, or external services.

This layered approach allows each part of your application to evolve independently and promotes a clear separation of responsibilities.

Example of a Layered Folder Structure

A typical ASP.NET Core project structured for scalability might look like this:

```bash
Copy code
/MyApp
 /Controllers           # Presentation layer (Web API or MVC controllers)
 /Views                 # Razor Views (if using MVC)
 /Pages                 # Razor Pages (if using Razor Pages)
 /Services              # Business Logic layer (application-specific services)
 /Data
    /Repositories       # Data access layer (e.g., repository classes)
    MyDbContext.cs      # EF Core database context
 /Models                # Domain models and view models
 /Infrastructure        # Cross-cutting concerns (e.g., logging, caching)
 /wwwroot               # Static files (e.g., CSS, JS, images)
```

Each folder represents a distinct layer, with folders like Controllers,

Services, and Repositories containing classes that adhere to specific roles within the architecture.

2. Implement the Repository Pattern for Data Access

The **Repository Pattern** abstracts data access logic, making it easier to switch between data sources and facilitating testing by allowing for mock repositories. By implementing a repository pattern, you encapsulate the database access layer in one place, isolating it from the rest of the application.

Example repository interface and implementation:

```csharp
Copy code
// IProductRepository.cs
public interface IProductRepository
{
    Task<IEnumerable<Product>> GetAllAsync();
    Task<Product> GetByIdAsync(int id);
    Task AddAsync(Product product);
    Task UpdateAsync(Product product);
    Task DeleteAsync(int id);
}

// ProductRepository.cs
public class ProductRepository : IProductRepository
{
    private readonly MyDbContext _context;

    public ProductRepository(MyDbContext context)
    {
        _context = context;
    }

    public async Task<IEnumerable<Product>> GetAllAsync() =>
        await _context.Products.ToListAsync();

    public async Task<Product> GetByIdAsync(int id) =>
```

```csharp
        await _context.Products.FindAsync(id);

    public async Task AddAsync(Product product)
    {
        await _context.Products.AddAsync(product);
        await _context.SaveChangesAsync();
    }

    public async Task UpdateAsync(Product product)
    {
        _context.Products.Update(product);
        await _context.SaveChangesAsync();
    }

    public async Task DeleteAsync(int id)
    {
        var product = await _context.Products.FindAsync(id);
        if (product != null)
        {
            _context.Products.Remove(product);
            await _context.SaveChangesAsync();
        }
    }
}
```

With this pattern, the data access layer becomes flexible and easy to modify or replace without impacting other parts of the application.

3. Use Dependency Injection (DI) for Better Modularization

ASP.NET Core has built-in dependency injection, which allows you to inject dependencies such as services, repositories, or configuration settings into controllers, services, or other classes. This enables loose coupling, as each component depends on interfaces rather than specific implementations.

In Startup.cs, register your services and repositories:

```csharp
// Copy code
public void ConfigureServices
(IServiceCollection services)
{
    services.AddScoped<IProductRepository, ProductRepository>();
    services.AddScoped<IProductService, ProductService>(); // Business logic
    services.AddControllersWithViews();
}
```

With DI, you can easily swap out implementations, making the application more modular and adaptable to change.

4. Implement a Service Layer for Business Logic

The **Service Layer** provides a central place for business logic, keeping it separate from controllers and repositories. By encapsulating business rules within services, you reduce redundancy and ensure that the logic is consistent across the application.

Example service interface and implementation:

```csharp
// Copy code
// IProductService.cs
public interface IProductService
{
    Task<IEnumerable<Product>> GetAllProductsAsync();
    Task<Product> GetProductByIdAsync(int id);
}

// ProductService.cs
public class ProductService : IProductService
{
    private readonly IProductRepository _productRepository;

    public ProductService
```

```
(IProductRepository productRepository)
    {
        _productRepository = productRepository;
    }

    public async Task<IEnumerable<Product>> 
GetAllProductsAsync() =>
        await _productRepository
.GetAllAsync();

    public async Task<Product> 
GetProductByIdAsync(int id) =>
        await _productRepository.GetByIdAsync(id);
}
```

By implementing a service layer, controllers can focus on handling HTTP requests and responses, while the service layer handles business rules and processes. This separation promotes scalability and makes it easier to apply changes to business rules without affecting the presentation layer.

5. Use DTOs and View Models for Data Transfer

In a scalable project, it's important to separate **domain models** (used in business logic and data access layers) from **Data Transfer Objects (DTOs)** and **View Models** (used in the presentation layer). This separation allows you to control which data is exposed in the API or UI, protecting sensitive information and reducing payload size.

Example of a ViewModel for a Product:

```
csharp
Copy code
public class ProductViewModel
{
    public int Id { get; set; }
    public string Name { get; set; }
    public decimal Price { get; set; }
```

```
    public string Description { get; set; }
}
```

When data moves between layers, you can map domain models to DTOs or View Models using tools like **AutoMapper**:

```csharp
Copy code
var productViewModel = _mapper.
Map<ProductViewModel>(product);
```

6. Use Middleware for Cross-Cutting Concerns

Middleware in ASP.NET Core provides a clean way to handle cross-cutting concerns (e.g., logging, error handling, authentication) in the request pipeline. Middleware components are executed sequentially, so you can customize the behavior of incoming requests.

Example of custom middleware for request logging:

```csharp
Copy code
public class RequestLoggingMiddleware
{
    private readonly RequestDelegate _next;

    public RequestLoggingMiddleware
(RequestDelegate next)
    {
        _next = next;
    }

    public async Task InvokeAsync(HttpContext context)
    {
        // Log request details
        Console.WriteLine($"Request Path: {context.Request.Path}");
        await _next(context); // Call the next middleware
    }
```

Register the middleware in Startup.cs:

```csharp
public void Configure(IApplicationBuilder app,
 IWebHostEnvironment env)
{
    app.UseMiddleware<RequestLoggingMiddleware>();
    app.UseRouting();
    app.UseAuthorization();
    app.UseEndpoints(endpoints =>
{ endpoints.MapControllers(); });
}
```

Using middleware for cross-cutting concerns keeps your codebase clean and centralizes common logic.

7. Organize Configuration Settings

A scalable ASP.NET Core application often relies on numerous configuration settings, such as connection strings, API keys, and feature flags. ASP.NET Core's **Options Pattern** makes it easy to organize and manage these configurations.

Define Configuration Classes:

```csharp
public class DatabaseSettings
{
    public string ConnectionString { get; set; }
}
```

Bind Configuration in Startup:

GETTING STARTED - BUILDING YOUR FIRST ASP.NET CORE 3 PROJECT

```csharp
Copy code
public void ConfigureServices
(IServiceCollection services)
{
    services.Configure<
DatabaseSettings>(Configuration.
GetSection("DatabaseSettings"));
}
```

Inject Configuration: In any class, inject IOptions <DatabaseSettings> to access configuration values:

```csharp
Copy code
public class MyService
{
    private readonly DatabaseSettings _settings;

    public MyService(IOptions<DatabaseSettings> settings)
    {
        _settings = settings.Value;
    }
}
```

This approach centralizes configuration management, making it easier to scale and maintain your application as settings change.

Structuring your ASP.NET Core 3 application for scalability involves using a layered architecture, employing the repository and service patterns, separating domain models from view models, leveraging middleware, and managing configurations effectively. With these practices in place, your application becomes modular, testable, and capable of handling growth. This approach not only simplifies the development process but also ensures that your application remains manageable and adaptable as requirements evolve.

Deep Dive into Razor Pages and MVC Architectur

Comparison of Razor Pages and MVC in ASP.NET Core 3
ASP.NET Core 3 offers two primary approaches for building web applications: **Razor Pages** and **MVC (Model-View-Controller)**. Both are powerful frameworks built on top of ASP.NET Core, sharing many foundational elements but differing in structure, workflow, and intended use cases. Choosing between Razor Pages and MVC depends largely on the application's complexity, development team preferences, and specific project needs. This section compares Razor Pages and MVC in detail, covering their architectures, advantages, and optimal use cases.

1. Overview of Razor Pages and MVC
Razor Pages

Introduced in ASP.NET Core 2.0, **Razor Pages** is a page-based framework built on top of MVC. It simplifies the development of web applications by focusing on individual pages rather than a controller-centric approach. Each Razor Page is self-contained with its own model, view, and logic, which makes it ideal for smaller applications or individual, specific pages in larger applications.

- **File Structure**: Razor Pages are organized as individual .cshtml files

in a Pages directory. Each page can have an associated PageModel class (similar to a controller) that handles request logic.
- **URL Mapping**: URLs map directly to individual pages, such as /Products or /Contact, making them user-friendly and intuitive.
- **Two-Way Data Binding**: Razor Pages provide simple mechanisms for data binding, where data can be easily passed between the model and view.

MVC (Model-View-Controller)

ASP.NET Core MVC is a well-established architectural pattern that divides an application into three main components:

- **Model**: Represents the application data and business logic.
- **View**: Handles the UI layer, presenting data to the user.
- **Controller**: Manages the flow of the application, processing incoming requests and sending appropriate responses.

MVC is a more robust and flexible approach, suitable for large-scale applications that require complex interactions and structured request handling. With MVC, controllers handle multiple views and actions, allowing for highly customizable routing and separation of concerns.

2. Architecture and Structure Differences

The core architectural difference between Razor Pages and MVC lies in the handling of requests and organization of files.

Razor Pages Structure

Razor Pages structure revolves around individual pages, each with an associated PageModel that encapsulates the page-specific logic. Razor Pages automatically separate code and UI within the same file path, which simplifies development and helps keep related files organized.

- **Pages Directory**: By default, Razor Pages are located in the /Pages directory. Each .cshtml file represents a single page.

DEEP DIVE INTO RAZOR PAGES AND MVC ARCHITECTUR

- **PageModel Classes**: Razor Pages rely on a PageModel class for handling page-specific logic. This model typically sits beside the .cshtml file in the same directory.
- **Simplified Routing**: URLs correspond directly to the page structure in the /Pages directory, reducing the need for custom route configuration.

Example Folder Structure for Razor Pages:

```bash
Copy code
/Pages
  Index.cshtml          # Homepage Razor Page
  Index.cshtml.cs       # PageModel for Index
  Products.cshtml       # Products Razor Page
  Products.cshtml.cs    # PageModel for Products
```

MVC Structure

MVC structures applications with clear separations between models, views, and controllers, each organized in their respective folders. This separation promotes modularity and is especially beneficial in large applications where each component may be extensively customized.

- **Controllers Directory**: Each controller manages requests for specific application modules and typically defines multiple actions corresponding to different views or requests.
- **Views Directory**: Views are organized by controller names, keeping the UI layer closely related to the corresponding controller.
- **Models Directory**: Models are placed in a separate folder to centralize application data and logic, making them accessible to both controllers and views.

Example Folder Structure for MVC:

```bash
Copy code
/Controllers
  HomeController.cs        # Controller for home-related actions
  ProductsController.cs    # Controller for product-related actions
/Views
  Home
    Index.cshtml           # View for HomeController.Index action
    About.cshtml           # View for HomeController.About action
  Products
    Details.cshtml         # View for ProductsController.Details action
/Models
  Product.cs               # Product model accessible by both controllers and views
```

3. Differences in Routing and URL Structure

Routing determines how URLs map to application code, and both Razor Pages and **MVC handle routing differently.**

Razor Pages Routing

Razor Pages uses **convention-based routing**, where URLs match the page file path within the /Pages directory. This convention simplifies routing by automatically mapping URLs to Razor Pages without requiring explicit routing configurations.

- **File-Based Routing**: For example, a Pages/Products.cshtml page would be accessible at /Products.
- **Folder-Based Nesting**: Subfolders within /Pages translate to URL segments. For instance, Pages/Products/Details.cshtml is accessible at /Products/Details.
- **Custom Routes**: Razor Pages supports custom routing using the

@page directive. For example, @page "{id:int}" within a Razor Page file can define URL patterns with parameters.

MVC Routing

MVC uses a more traditional routing mechanism with **attribute routing** or **convention-based routing** defined in Startup.cs. Routes are mapped to controllers and actions, providing finer control over URL patterns and allowing complex routing scenarios.

- **Route Attributes**: Routes can be configured using attributes above controller actions, such as [Route("products/details/{id}")].
- **Startup Configuration**: In Startup.cs, the MapControllerRoute method defines a global route pattern that matches controller names, actions, and optional parameters.
- **Complex Routing**: MVC routing is highly customizable, making it suitable for complex applications requiring advanced URL structures.

Example of MVC Route Configuration:

```csharp
Copy code
app.UseEndpoints(endpoints =>
{
    endpoints.MapControllerRoute(
        name: "default",
        pattern: "{controller=Home}/{action=Index}/{id?}");
});
```

4. Data Binding and Form Handling

Data binding and form handling are critical for web applications. Razor Pages and MVC approach this in slightly different ways.

Razor Pages

Razor Pages use **two-way data binding** with properties defined in the PageModel class. This approach simplifies binding data to UI components and handling form submissions.

- **Automatic Property Binding**: Properties in the PageModel can automatically bind to form fields.
- **OnGet and OnPost Handlers**: Razor Pages use handler methods, such as OnGet and OnPost, to handle GET and POST requests. Each handler can target a specific user action, like OnPostSubmit for form submissions.
- **Model Binding Simplified**: Data is automatically bound to properties without needing parameterized method signatures.

MVC

MVC relies on **model binding** within action methods to manage form data. Controllers can receive data through parameters or model objects, and actions can handle multiple request types.

- **Parameterized Actions**: Action methods accept parameters for binding data from request URLs or forms.
- **Explicit Binding**: MVC often requires explicit binding in controllers, allowing more control over input validation and form processing.
- **ViewModels for Binding**: MVC applications commonly use **ViewModels** to pass data between the controller and view, providing structure and validation for form data.

5. Use Cases: When to Choose Razor Pages or MVC

Both Razor Pages and MVC are powerful frameworks within ASP.NET Core 3, and choosing one over the other depends on the application's needs and complexity.

When to Use Razor Pages

Razor Pages is best suited for simpler applications or individual pages within a larger application. Scenarios where Razor Pages excel include:

- **Single-Page Applications (SPA)**: For applications focused on individual pages, such as a landing page, blog, or e-commerce product page.

- **Small to Medium Projects**: Razor Pages offer a more streamlined approach with less boilerplate code, ideal for projects that don't require a highly structured architecture.
- **Page-Focused Design**: If the application's design revolves around individual pages with minimal shared components, Razor Pages simplify development and maintenance.

When to Use MVC

MVC is ideal for complex, large-scale applications requiring a highly organized structure, robust routing, and granular control over request handling. Scenarios for MVC include:

- **Enterprise-Level Applications**: MVC's separation of concerns and ability to handle complex routing make it suitable for large, modular applications with multiple interrelated components.
- **Applications with Complex Business Logic**: MVC supports structured service layers and business logic, making it easier to manage complex workflows and interactions.
- **Highly Interactive Applications**: Applications that require frequent API calls, advanced routing, or a modular approach often benefit from MVC's flexibility and architecture.

6. Performance and Scalability

Both Razor Pages and MVC are built on top of ASP.NET Core, so they share similar performance capabilities. However, project structure and complexity impact performance in practice.

- **Razor Pages**: Due to its page-based focus and minimalistic routing, Razor Pages can be more lightweight and potentially faster for smaller, page-centric applications.
- **MVC**: For applications with complex workflows or interdependent components, MVC offers scalability by allowing services, models, and controllers to scale independently. This structure can improve

performance for large applications through optimized routing and modular design.

Choosing Between Razor Pages and MVC for Different Project Needs

When embarking on a web development project using ASP.NET Core 3, one of the critical decisions to make is whether to use Razor Pages or MVC (Model-View-Controller) architecture. Each approach has its strengths and weaknesses, and the choice largely depends on the specific requirements and goals of the project. This section delves into the factors that influence the decision, including project size, complexity, team skills, and specific application needs.

1. Project Size and Complexity
Small Projects

For smaller projects, such as personal blogs, portfolios, or simple business websites, Razor Pages often emerges as the more suitable choice. The following points highlight why Razor Pages may be preferred in such scenarios:

- **Simplified Structure**: Razor Pages promote a more straightforward project structure, making it easier to get started without the overhead of configuring multiple controllers and views.
- **Rapid Development**: The page-centric model allows developers to create and deploy pages quickly, with less boilerplate code required. This is especially beneficial for projects with tight deadlines or minimal feature sets.
- **Ease of Use**: Developers can easily bind data to the page, handle forms, and manage page-specific logic in one place, reducing the cognitive load during development.

Example Use Cases for Small Projects:

- Landing pages
- Basic e-commerce sites with limited product offerings
- Portfolio or personal websites

Large Projects

For larger applications that require extensive features, complex interactions, or sophisticated data management, MVC is often the better choice. Key considerations include:

- **Separation of Concerns**: MVC's architecture naturally separates business logic, data, and presentation layers, making it easier to manage large codebases and allowing teams to work on different parts of the application independently.
- **Scalability**: The modularity of MVC allows for easy scaling of individual components, which is crucial for large applications that may experience variable traffic and require robust load handling.
- **Complex Routing Needs**: Applications with intricate routing requirements benefit from MVC's customizable routing capabilities, enabling tailored URL patterns and improved SEO strategies.

Example Use Cases for Large Projects:

- Enterprise applications with complex workflows
- Social networking platforms with numerous features and interactions
- Multi-tiered applications requiring APIs for mobile or desktop clients

2. Development Team Skills

The experience and skill set of the development team can heavily influence the choice between Razor Pages and MVC.

Familiarity with MVC

If the development team has a strong background in traditional MVC frameworks (e.g., ASP.NET MVC or other MVC-based frameworks), they may find the MVC approach more comfortable. Teams that understand how to effectively implement controller actions, manage routing, and handle models are well-equipped to leverage the full potential of MVC in ASP.NET Core.

Newer Developers

For teams with less experience or those new to web development, Razor Pages may be the better starting point. The straightforward page model reduces the complexity of learning the MVC pattern, allowing newer developers to grasp web development concepts without getting overwhelmed by the additional layers of abstraction that MVC introduces.

3. Specific Application Needs

Certain project requirements can tilt the balance toward one framework or the other. Understanding the specific needs of the application can guide the decision-making process.

Applications with Heavy Form Handling

For applications that focus on user input and form handling, such as content management systems or data entry applications, Razor Pages can provide a more streamlined experience. The two-way data binding capabilities and page-centric architecture facilitate easier management of form submissions and validations.

- **Example**: A survey application where users fill out forms on different pages can be efficiently developed using Razor Pages, minimizing the complexity involved in managing multiple controller actions and views.

APIs and Rich Interactions

If the application requires extensive use of APIs or involves rich client-side interactions, MVC may be more suitable due to its flexibility in handling multiple views, actions, and data sources. Additionally, MVC's structured approach makes it easier to implement RESTful services alongside traditional views.

- **Example**: A web application that serves as both a front-end for users and an API for mobile clients would benefit from the modular nature of MVC, allowing developers to build and maintain the API and UI components independently.

4. Testing and Maintenance

Considerations around testing and maintenance practices can also influence the decision between Razor Pages and MVC.

Testing

Both Razor Pages and MVC support testing, but the structured nature of MVC often makes it easier to write unit tests for controllers and services due to their clear separation of concerns.

- **Unit Testing in MVC**: With distinct controllers and service layers, unit tests can be created to independently validate the functionality of each component.
- **Integration Testing**: MVC applications can employ integration tests that cover multiple components interacting together, providing assurance that the application functions correctly as a whole.

In contrast, while Razor Pages can be tested effectively, the tight coupling of page models and views may require more complex testing setups in some scenarios.

Maintenance

For applications expected to evolve over time, MVC's architecture is often better suited for long-term maintenance. The clear separation of models, views, and controllers allows teams to make updates or refactor parts of the application without affecting unrelated components.

- **Modular Updates**: When changes or new features are needed, developers can focus on specific controllers or services, minimizing the impact on the overall application.
- **Feature Addition**: Adding new features can often be accomplished by creating new controllers and views, while Razor Pages may require adjustments to existing page models, which could lead to tighter coupling of functionality.

Choosing between Razor Pages and MVC in ASP.NET Core 3 is a decision that should be informed by the project's size, complexity, team expertise, specific application needs, and considerations around testing and maintenance.

- **Razor Pages**: Best for smaller, simpler applications with a focus on individual pages, rapid development needs, and straightforward form handling.
- **MVC**: Ideal for larger, more complex applications requiring modularity, extensive routing customization, and a robust structure for long-term maintenance.

Ultimately, both approaches can be highly effective, and understanding their unique strengths allows developers to make the best choice for their projects, ensuring a solid foundation for future growth and success. By carefully considering the specific context and requirements of the application, teams can harness the capabilities of ASP.NET Core to deliver efficient, scalable web solutions.

Advanced Features in Razor Pages and MVC Controllers

ASP.NET Core 3 offers a wealth of advanced features in both Razor Pages and MVC Controllers that enable developers to create robust, efficient, and scalable web applications. These features not only enhance the capabilities of the frameworks but also improve developer productivity and user experience. In this section, we will explore several advanced features available in Razor Pages and MVC Controllers, including dependency injection, middleware, model binding, validation, custom tag helpers, and more.

1. Dependency Injection

Dependency Injection (DI) is a core feature of ASP.NET Core, facilitating the management of dependencies in both Razor Pages and MVC Controllers. By allowing developers to inject services into their classes, DI promotes loose coupling and improves the testability of applications.

Razor Pages

In Razor Pages, DI can be utilized within the PageModel classes. Developers can inject services directly into the constructors of these models, enabling easy access to application services, such as repositories or logging mechanisms.

Example of DI in Razor Pages:

```csharp
Copy code
public class ProductsModel : PageModel
{
    private readonly IProductService _productService;

    public ProductsModel(IProductService productService)
    {
        _productService = productService;
    }

    public IList<Product> Products { get; private set; }

    public void OnGet()
    {
        Products = _productService.GetAllProducts();
    }
}
```

MVC Controllers

MVC Controllers also benefit from DI. Services can be injected through the controller's constructor, making them readily available to action methods.

Example of DI in MVC:

```csharp
Copy code
public class ProductsController : Controller
{
    private readonly IProductService _productService;

    public ProductsController
(IProductService productService)
    {
        _productService = productService;
    }

    public IActionResult Index()
    {
        var products = _productService.GetAllProducts();
        return View(products);
    }
}
```

Benefits of DI:

- Reduces the need for hard-coded dependencies, improving flexibility and maintainability.
- Facilitates unit testing by allowing mocks or stubs to be injected during tests.

2. Middleware

Middleware components are a critical aspect of the ASP.NET Core request pipeline, enabling developers to handle requests and responses at various stages. Both Razor Pages and MVC applications can leverage middleware for cross-cutting concerns such as authentication, logging, and error handling.

Implementing Middleware

Middleware can be added to the application in the Startup.cs file using the Configure method. Here's how to set up a simple logging middleware:

Example of Custom Middleware:

```csharp
Copy code
public class RequestLoggingMiddleware
{
    private readonly RequestDelegate _next;

    public RequestLoggingMiddleware (RequestDelegate next)
    {
        _next = next;
    }

    public async Task InvokeAsync (HttpContext context)
    {
        Console.WriteLine($"Request: {context.Request.Method} {context.Request.Path}");
        await _next(context);
    }
}

// In Startup.cs
public void Configure(IApplicationBuilder app, IWebHostEnvironment env)
{
    app.UseMiddleware<RequestLoggingMiddleware>();
    app.UseRouting();
    app.UseEndpoints(endpoints =>
    {
        endpoints.MapRazorPages();
        endpoints.MapControllers();
    });
```

}

Benefits of Middleware:

- Provides a mechanism to process requests and responses before they reach the application.
- Supports modular development by allowing developers to add or remove functionality easily.

3. Model Binding

Model Binding in ASP.NET Core is a powerful feature that simplifies the process of mapping incoming request data to C# objects. Both Razor Pages and MVC leverage this feature to handle user input efficiently.

Razor Pages

In Razor Pages, model binding occurs automatically based on the property names of the PageModel. This feature allows developers to work with complex data models seamlessly.

Example of Model Binding in Razor Pages:

```csharp
csharp
Copy code
public class CreateProductModel : PageModel
{
    [BindProperty]
    public Product Product { get; set; }

    public void OnGet() { }

    public IActionResult OnPost()
    {
        if (!ModelState.IsValid)
        {
            return Page();
        }
```

```
        // Save product to database
        return RedirectToPage("Index");
    }
}
```

MVC Controllers

MVC Controllers utilize model binding in a similar way. Incoming data from forms or query strings is automatically mapped to the action method parameters or model objects.

Example of Model Binding in MVC:

```csharp
Copy code
public class ProductsController : Controller
{
    [HttpPost]
    public IActionResult Create(Product product)
    {
        if (!ModelState.IsValid)
        {
            return View(product);
        }

        // Save product to database
        return RedirectToAction("Index");
    }
}
```

Benefits of Model Binding:

- Simplifies data handling, allowing developers to work with strongly typed objects directly.
- Supports automatic validation based on data annotations, ensuring data integrity.

4. Validation

ASP.NET Core provides built-in support for **validation,** allowing developers to ensure that user input meets certain criteria before processing. Both Razor Pages and MVC utilize data annotations for model validation.

Razor Pages

Validation in Razor Pages can be easily implemented using data annotations on properties within the PageModel. ASP.NET Core automatically performs validation during model binding.

Example of Validation in Razor Pages:

```csharp
Copy code
public class Product
{
    [Required]
    [StringLength(100)]
    public string Name { get; set; }

    [Range(0, 1000)]
    public decimal Price { get; set; }
}

public class CreateProductModel : PageModel
{
    [BindProperty]
    public Product Product { get; set; }

    public void OnGet() { }

    public IActionResult OnPost()
    {
        if (!ModelState.IsValid)
        {
            return Page();
        }

        // Save product to database
        return RedirectToPage("Index");
    }
```

}

MVC Controllers

In MVC, validation works similarly, with data annotations applied to model properties. The framework checks model state automatically and provides error messages when validation fails.

Example of Validation in MVC:

```csharp
Copy code
public class Product
{
    [Required]
    [StringLength(100)]
    public string Name { get; set; }

    [Range(0, 1000)]
    public decimal Price { get; set; }
}

public class ProductsController : Controller
{
    [HttpPost]
    public IActionResult Create(Product product)
    {
        if (!ModelState.IsValid)
        {
            return View(product);
        }

        // Save product to database
        return RedirectToAction("Index");
    }
}
```

Benefits of Validation:

- Ensures data integrity and provides immediate feedback to users

about input errors.
- Reduces the need for manual error handling by utilizing built-in validation features.

5. Custom Tag Helpers

Tag Helpers are a feature of ASP.NET Core that allow developers to create reusable components for rendering HTML in Razor views. Custom Tag Helpers can simplify the markup in Razor Pages and MVC views, making them more readable and maintainable.

Creating Custom Tag Helpers

Developers can create custom Tag Helpers by creating a class that inherits from TagHelper. The Tag Helper can then be applied in Razor markup.

Example of a Custom Tag Helper:

```csharp
Copy code
[HtmlTargetElement("my-greeting")]
public class GreetingTagHelper : TagHelper
{
    public string Name { get; set; }

    public override void Process
(TagHelperContext context, TagHelperOutput output)
    {
output.Content.SetContent($"Hello, {Name}!");
    }
}


// In a Razor view
<my-greeting name="Alice"></my-greeting>
```

Benefits of Custom Tag Helpers:

- Simplifies Razor markup by encapsulating logic within reusable components.

- Encourages the use of semantic HTML while providing flexibility for dynamic content.

6. Filters

Filters are another powerful feature of ASP.NET Core that can be applied to both Razor Pages and MVC controllers to add cross-cutting concerns such as authorization, logging, or caching.

Types of Filters

- **Authorization Filters**: Check user permissions before executing an action.
- **Action Filters**: Run code before and after an action method executes.
- **Result Filters**: Modify the result returned by an action method before sending it to the client.
- **Exception Filters**: Handle exceptions thrown during the execution of an action.

Example of an Action Filter

```csharp
csharp
Copy code
public class LogActionFilter : ActionFilterAttribute
{
    public override void OnActionExecuting(ActionExecutingContext context)
    {
        Console.WriteLine($"Action {context.ActionDescriptor.DisplayName} is executing.");
    }
}

// Applying the filter to a controller
[ServiceFilter(typeof(LogActionFilter))]
```

```
public class ProductsController : Controller
{
    public IActionResult Index()
    {
        return View();
    }
}
```

Benefits of Filters:

- Centralizes cross-cutting concerns, reducing repetitive code in action methods.
- Provides a clear structure for handling actions at various stages of execution.

ASP.NET Core 3 equips developers with a robust set of advanced features in both Razor Pages and MVC Controllers. From dependency injection and middleware to model binding and validation, these capabilities enhance application architecture, improve developer productivity, and facilitate the creation of high-quality web applications.

By leveraging these advanced features, developers can build more maintainable, testable, and scalable applications that meet the demands of modern web development. Understanding how to effectively utilize these features in Razor Pages and MVC will empower developers to deliver solutions that not only perform well but also provide an exceptional user experience. As the web development landscape continues to evolve, embracing these advanced features will remain essential for staying competitive and innovative.

Customizing Views with Razor Syntax

Razor syntax is a powerful feature of ASP.NET Core that allows developers to create dynamic web pages with ease. It enables a seamless blend of HTML and C# code, providing an efficient way to generate dynamic content. This section explores how to customize views using Razor syntax, including how to use expressions, directives, helpers, and layouts to create rich, interactive web pages.

1. Razor Syntax Basics

Razor syntax uses the @ character to transition from HTML to C#. This allows developers to embed C# code within HTML markup. Here are some key aspects of Razor syntax:
- **Inline Expressions**: Simple expressions can be used to output values directly in HTML.
- **Code Blocks**: Enclosed in @{ }, code blocks allow for the execution of multiple statements or more complex logic.

Example of Inline Expression

```html
Copy code
<p>Hello, @Model.Name!</p>
```

Example of Code Block

```html
Copy code
@{
    var currentDate = DateTime.Now;
}

<p>Today's date is @currentDate.ToShortDateString()</p>
```

2. Using Razor Directives

Razor directives are special commands that modify how the Razor view is processed. Common directives include @model, @using, and @inherits.

The @model Directive

The @model directive specifies the type of the model that the view will use. This strongly typed model allows access to properties and methods in the view.

Example:

```csharp
Copy code
@model MyApp.Models.Product

<h2>@Model.Name</h2>
<p>Price: @Model.Price.ToString("C")</p>
```

The @using Directive

The @using directive is used to import namespaces, enabling access to classes without fully qualifying their names.

Example:

```csharp
Copy code
@using MyApp.Models

@model Product

<h1>Product Details</h1>
<p>Name: @Model.Name</p>
```

The @inherits Directive

This directive allows the view to inherit from a specific base class. This is useful for creating custom base views that include shared functionality.

Example:

```csharp
Copy code
@inherits MyBaseView
```

```
<p>This view inherits methods and
properties from MyBaseView.</p>
```

3. Conditional Logic and Loops

Razor syntax makes it easy to incorporate conditional logic and loops directly within views. This is crucial for rendering content dynamically based on the model's state or other conditions.

Conditional Logic

Razor uses standard C# syntax for conditional statements. The if, else if, and else statements can be utilized directly within the markup.

Example of Conditional Logic:

```html
Copy code
@if (Model.IsAvailable)
{
    <p>This product is available for purchase.</p>
}
else
{
    <p>This product is currently out of stock.</p>
}
```

Loops

The foreach statement is commonly used to iterate over collections. This allows developers to render lists or tables of items dynamically.

Example of a Loop:

```html
Copy code
<ul>
@foreach (var item in Model.ProductList)
{
    <li>@item.Name - @item.Price.ToString("C")</li>
```

```
}
</ul>
```

4. HTML Helpers

ASP.NET Core includes several built-in HTML helpers that simplify the creation of common HTML elements while providing strong typing and validation support.

Creating Forms with HTML Helpers

HTML helpers like Html.BeginForm(), Html.TextBoxFor(), and Html.ValidationMessageFor() streamline form creation.

Example of a Form Using HTML Helpers:

```html
Copy code
@using (Html.BeginForm("Create",
 "Products", FormMethod.Post))
{
    <div>
        @Html.LabelFor(m => m.Product.Name)
        @Html.TextBoxFor(m => m.Product.Name)
        @Html.ValidationMessageFor
(m => m.Product.Name)
    </div>
    <div>
        @Html.LabelFor(m => m.Product.Price)
        @Html.TextBoxFor(m => m.Product.Price)
        @Html.ValidationMessageFor
(m => m.Product.Price)
    </div>
    <input type="submit" value="Create" />
}
```

Custom HTML Helpers

Developers can create custom HTML helpers to encapsulate reusable logic or HTML structures.

Example of a Custom HTML Helper:

```csharp
Copy code
public static class HtmlHelpers
{
    public static IHtmlContent CustomButton(this IHtmlHelper htmlHelper, string text, string cssClass)
    {
        var button = new TagBuilder("button");
        button.InnerHtml.Append(text);
        button.AddCssClass(cssClass);
        return new HtmlString(button.RenderStartTag() + button.RenderEndTag());
    }
}

// Using the custom helper in a Razor view
@Html.CustomButton("Click Me", "btn btn-primary")
```

5. Layouts and Sections

Razor provides a powerful layout feature that allows developers to define a common structure for multiple views, promoting DRY (Don't Repeat Yourself) principles. Layouts can include headers, footers, and shared navigation.

Defining a Layout

A layout is typically defined in the _Layout.cshtml file. It can contain sections where individual views can insert content.

Example of a Layout:

```html
Copy code
<!DOCTYPE html>
<html>
<head>
    <title>@ViewData["Title"]</title>
```

```
</head>
<body>
    <header>
        <h1>My Application</h1>
    </header>
    <div>
        @RenderBody()
    </div>
    <footer>
        <p>&copy; 2024 My Application</p>
    </footer>
</body>
</html>
```

Using Sections

Sections can be defined in the layout and filled in by views. This allows for flexible content insertion.

Example of Defining and Using a Section: In _Layout.cshtml:

```
html
Copy code
@RenderSection("Scripts", required: false)
```

In a view:

```
html
Copy code
@section Scripts {
    <script src="~/js/custom.js"></script>
}
```

6. Partial Views

Partial Views allow developers to break down complex views into smaller, reusable components. This promotes reusability and helps manage large codebases more effectively.

Creating and Using Partial Views

Partial views are typically placed in a Shared folder or a dedicated folder for a specific feature. They can be rendered in any parent view using Html.Partial() or Html.RenderPartial().

Example of a Partial View:

```html
Copy code
<!-- _ProductCard.cshtml -->
@model MyApp.Models.Product

<div class="product-card">
    <h3>@Model.Name</h3>
    <p>Price: @Model.Price.ToString("C")</p>
</div>
```

Rendering a Partial View:

```html
Copy code
@foreach (var product in Model.Products)
{
    @Html.Partial("_ProductCard", product)
}
```

Customizing views with Razor syntax in ASP.NET Core provides developers with a robust toolkit for creating dynamic, maintainable web applications. By leveraging Razor's capabilities—such as inline expressions, directives, conditional logic, HTML helpers, layouts, sections, and partial views—developers can create rich, interactive user interfaces with minimal effort.

These features not only enhance the developer experience but also lead to more structured and efficient code, allowing teams to build applications that are easier to maintain and extend over time. Mastering Razor syntax and its advanced features will empower developers to create engaging web experiences that meet the diverse needs of users and stakeholders alike.

Implementing Dependency Injection within Controllers and Pages

Dependency Injection (DI) is a fundamental design pattern used in ASP.NET Core that promotes better software architecture by allowing for more maintainable, testable, and scalable code. In this section, we will explore how to implement dependency injection within MVC Controllers and Razor Pages, emphasizing the steps required to configure services, inject dependencies, and utilize them effectively.

1. Understanding Dependency Injection

Dependency Injection involves providing an object with its dependencies rather than having the object create them itself. In ASP.NET Core, DI is a first-class citizen, integrated into the framework's architecture. This design pattern allows developers to:

- Decouple classes, making them easier to test and maintain.
- Promote the reuse of components through interfaces.
- Easily switch implementations, which is particularly useful in testing scenarios.

In ASP.NET Core, services are registered in the Startup.cs class and resolved at runtime by the framework's built-in dependency injection container.

2. Configuring Services in Startup.cs

To implement dependency injection, the first step is to register your services in the ConfigureServices method of the Startup class. ASP.NET Core supports various service lifetimes, including:

- **Transient**: A new instance is created each time the service is requested.

- **Scoped**: A new instance is created for each HTTP request.
- **Singleton**: A single instance is created and shared throughout the application's lifetime.

Example of Service Registration

In Startup.cs, you can register services as follows:

```csharp
Copy code
public class Startup
{
    public void ConfigureServices(IServiceCollection services)
    {
        // Registering a service with transient lifetime
        services.AddTransient<IProductService, ProductService>();

        // Registering a service with scoped lifetime
        services.AddScoped<IOrderService, OrderService>();

        // Registering a service with singleton lifetime
        services.AddSingleton<ILogger, ConsoleLogger>();

        services.AddControllersWithViews();
        services.AddRazorPages();
    }

    // ... other methods
}
```

In this example, IProductService, IOrderService, and ILogger are interfaces, while ProductService, OrderService, and ConsoleLogger are their respective implementations.

3. Injecting Dependencies in MVC Controllers

Once services are registered, they can be injected into MVC Controllers through constructor injection. This is the preferred method for acquiring dependencies, as it promotes immutability and ensures that all required dependencies are provided when the controller is created.

Example of Dependency Injection in a Controller

```csharp
Copy code
public class ProductsController : Controller
{
    private readonly IProductService _productService;

    // Constructor injection
    public ProductsController
(IProductService productService)
    {
        _productService = productService;
    }

    public IActionResult Index()
    {
        var products = _productService.GetAllProducts();
        return View(products);
    }

    public IActionResult Details(int id)
    {
        var product = _productService.GetProductById(id);
        if (product == null)
        {
            return NotFound();
        }
        return View(product);
    }
}
```

In this example, IProductService is injected into the ProductsController, allowing the controller to utilize the service methods without directly instantiating the service.

4. Injecting Dependencies in Razor Pages

In Razor Pages, dependency injection is similarly straightforward. The services can be injected into the PageModel classes, enabling the use of the registered services in page handlers.

Example of Dependency Injection in a Razor Page

```csharp
Copy code
public class ProductsModel : PageModel
{
    private readonly IProductService _productService;

    // Constructor injection
    public ProductsModel(IProductService productService)
    {
        _productService = productService;
    }

    public IList<Product> Products { get; private set; }

    public void OnGet()
    {
        Products = _productService.GetAllProducts();
    }

    public IActionResult OnPostCreate(Product product)
    {
        if (!ModelState.IsValid)
        {
            return Page();
        }

        _productService.CreateProduct(product);
        return RedirectToPage("Index");
    }
```

}

In this example, the ProductsModel class uses constructor injection to obtain an instance of IProductService, allowing it to access product-related methods for both GET and POST requests.

5. Managing the Lifetime of Services

Understanding and managing the lifetime of services is crucial in dependency injection. The chosen lifetime affects the application's memory consumption, performance, and behavior. Here are some considerations for each service lifetime:

- **Transient**: Use transient services when you want to ensure a new instance is created for each request. This is suitable for lightweight services that do not maintain state.
- **Scoped**: Scoped services are ideal for services that should maintain state during a single request but be recreated for each new request. This is common for services that deal with database context or user sessions.
- **Singleton**: Use singleton services when a single instance is sufficient and shared state is acceptable. This is often suitable for services that do not change state or hold configuration settings.

Example of Scoped Service

Consider a scenario where you have a database context that should be scoped to a single request:

```csharp
csharp
Copy code
public class ApplicationDbContext : DbContext
{
    public ApplicationDbContext
(DbContextOptions
```

DEEP DIVE INTO RAZOR PAGES AND MVC ARCHITECTUR

```
<ApplicationDbContext>
options) : base(options)
    {
    }

    public DbSet<Product> Products { get; set; }
}

// In Startup.cs
services.AddDbContext<
ApplicationDbContext>(options =>
    options
.UseSqlServer(Configuration.
GetConnectionString("DefaultConnection")));
```

In this case, ApplicationDbContext is registered as a scoped service, ensuring that each HTTP request gets its own instance.

6. Resolving Dependencies in Views

While controller and page model constructors are the primary means of injecting dependencies, you might encounter scenarios where you need to resolve dependencies directly within Razor views. This can be achieved using the @inject directive.

Example of Using @inject in a Razor View

```html
Copy code
@page
@model ProductsModel

@inject IProductService ProductService

<h1>Product List</h1>

<ul>
@foreach (var product in ProductService.GetAllProducts())
```

```
{
    <li>@product.Name - @product.Price.ToString("C")</li>
}
</ul>
```

In this example, the @inject directive allows the view to access IProductService, demonstrating another method to incorporate dependencies without direct constructor injection.

7. Testing Controllers and Pages with Dependency Injection

One of the key benefits of dependency injection is that it simplifies unit testing. Since dependencies are injected rather than hardcoded, you can easily substitute them with mock implementations during tests.

Example of Testing a Controller

Using a mocking framework like Moq, you can create unit tests for your controllers:

```csharp
Copy code
public class ProductsControllerTests
{
    [Fact]
    public void Index_ReturnsViewResult_WithListOfProducts()
    {
        // Arrange
var mockService = new Mock<IProductService>();
        mockService.Setup(service => service.GetAllProducts())
                   .Returns(GetTestProducts());

        var controller = new ProductsController(mockService.Object);

        // Act
        var result = controller.Index();
```

```
        // Assert
        var viewResult = Assert.
IsType<ViewResult>(result);
        var model = Assert.
IsAssignableFrom<List<Product>>
(viewResult.ViewData.Model);
        Assert.Equal(3, model.Count);
    }

    private List<Product> GetTestProducts()
    {
        return new List<Product>
        {
            new Product { Name = "Product 1", Price = 10 },
            new Product { Name = "Product 2", Price = 20 },
            new Product { Name = "Product 3", Price = 30 }
        };
    }
}
```

In this unit test, the IProductService is mocked to return a predetermined list of products, allowing you to verify that the Index action method behaves as expected.

Implementing dependency injection within ASP.NET Core MVC Controllers and Razor Pages is essential for creating maintainable and testable applications. By registering services, injecting dependencies through constructors, and managing service lifetimes, developers can leverage the full potential of dependency injection to build scalable and flexible web applications.

Additionally, dependency injection facilitates unit testing by allowing for easy substitution of services with mocks or stubs, ensuring that each component can be tested in isolation. Mastering dependency injection in ASP.NET Core will significantly enhance your ability to design and develop modern web applications that are both robust and adaptable.

Chapter 4: Entity Framework Core - Mastering Data Access and Management

Introduction to Entity Framework Core and Code-First Migrations

Entity Framework Core (EF Core) is Microsoft's modern Object-Relational Mapper (ORM) for .NET, designed to simplify data access and management within applications. Built as a leaner, faster, and more modular version of the original Entity Framework, EF Core provides a high level of flexibility and compatibility with various databases. This chapter will introduce you to EF Core, its benefits, and how to implement code-first migrations—a powerful feature that enables you to define and manage your database schema directly from your C# code.

1. Overview of Entity Framework Core

EF Core serves as a bridge between the domain models in your application and the underlying database. It allows developers to interact with databases using C# code rather than SQL, making data handling more intuitive and reducing the need for manual query writing. As an ORM, EF Core maps classes in your C# application to database tables, and each object instance corresponds to a database row. This approach is highly efficient for handling complex data relationships, streamlining CRUD (Create, Read, Update, Delete) operations, and ensuring a more maintainable codebase.

Key Benefits of Using EF Core:

- **Cross-platform compatibility**: EF Core works on Windows, macOS, and Linux, supporting a variety of databases such as SQL Server, SQLite, MySQL, PostgreSQL, and even NoSQL databases like Cosmos DB.
- **Modularity**: EF Core's lightweight architecture allows developers to pick only the components needed, optimizing application performance.
- **Strongly-typed LINQ queries**: EF Core leverages LINQ (Language Integrated Query) for querying databases, enabling developers to use strongly-typed expressions in their code.
- **Flexible schema management**: Through code-first migrations, EF Core enables schema evolution within the code itself, making database updates seamless.

EF Core can work with two main approaches for database design:

- **Code-first**: The database schema is generated based on the C# classes and their relationships, allowing developers to start with the code and create the database afterward.
- **Database-first**: An existing database is used to generate classes in C#, which is useful for applications with pre-existing schemas.

In this chapter, we focus on the code-first approach, which offers flexibility in defining and updating the database schema as your application evolves.

2. Understanding Code-First Approach

In the code-first approach, developers define entities and relationships directly in C# code. These classes serve as the blueprint for the database tables. When the application is run, EF Core uses these definitions to automatically create or update the database schema through migrations.

Benefits of the Code-First Approach:

- **Flexibility and agility**: Developers can define, update, and manage

CHAPTER 4: ENTITY FRAMEWORK CORE - MASTERING DATA ACCESS AND...

database schema from within the application code without needing a separate database design tool.
- **Consistency**: The model classes, or entities, in your code are always in sync with the database schema, minimizing potential mismatches between the code and database.
- **Version control**: Database migrations can be version-controlled alongside the code, making it easier to track and manage schema changes over time.

In the code-first model, your DbContext class and entity classes (representing database tables) form the basis of your schema.

3. Defining the DbContext and Entities

The DbContext class in EF Core represents the session with the database, allowing you to query and save data. It provides access to the entity collections, which map to the tables in your database.

Example: Creating a DbContext Class

```csharp
Copy code
public class ApplicationDbContext : DbContext
{
    public ApplicationDbContext
(DbContextOptions<ApplicationDbContext> options)
        : base(options)
    {
    }

    // DbSet properties represent tables in the database
    public DbSet<Product> Products { get; set; }
    public DbSet<Category> Categories { get; set; }

    protected override void OnModelCreating(ModelBuilder modelBuilder)
    {
        // Additional configurations can be done here
```

        }
    }

In this example, ApplicationDbContext represents the database context, with Products and Categories as DbSet properties. Each DbSet represents a database table, with each instance of an entity corresponding to a row in the table.

Example: Defining Entity Classes

Entities are the classes representing the structure of database tables. Each property in an entity class maps to a column in the database.

```csharp
Copy code
public class Product
{
    public int ProductId { get; set; }   // Primary Key
    public string Name { get; set; }
    public decimal Price { get; set; }

    // Navigation property for relationship with Category
    public int CategoryId { get; set; }
    public Category Category { get; set; }
}

public class Category
{
    public int CategoryId { get; set; }
    public string CategoryName { get; set; }

    // Navigation property to enable reverse navigation
    public ICollection<Product> Products { get; set; }
}
```

In this example, the Product and Category classes represent two tables. The Product class has a foreign key (CategoryId) that links it to the Category table, demonstrating a one-to-many relationship.

CHAPTER 4: ENTITY FRAMEWORK CORE - MASTERING DATA ACCESS AND...

4. Configuring the Database Connection

To connect your application to a database, specify the database provider (e.g., SQL Server, SQLite) and provide the connection string in your application's configuration file (e.g., appsettings.json).

```json
Copy code
{
  "ConnectionStrings": {
    "DefaultConnection":
    "Server=(localdb)\\mssqllocaldb;Database=MyDatabase;
Trusted_Connection=True;"
  }
}
```

Then, configure the connection in Startup.cs:

```csharp
Copy code
public class Startup
{
    public void ConfigureServices(IServiceCollection services)
    {
        services.AddDbContext<ApplicationDbContext>(options =>
            options.UseSqlServer(Configuration.GetConnectionString("DefaultConnection")));
        services.AddControllersWithViews();
    }
}
```

This configuration tells EF Core to use SQL Server as the database provider and to connect using the specified connection string.

5. Code-First Migrations

Migrations in EF Core are a way to incrementally update the database schema as the application evolves. They track changes in the entity classes and apply them to the database. This approach is ideal for applications in active development, where schema changes are frequent.

Creating an Initial Migration

To create a migration, use the following commands in the Package Manager Console or terminal:

```bash
Copy code
dotnet ef migrations add InitialCreate
dotnet ef database update
```

The add command generates the migration file, which includes SQL commands for creating the database schema. The update command applies the migration to the database.

6. Managing Schema Changes with Migrations

When you make changes to the entity classes, you'll need to create a new migration to reflect these changes in the database. For example, if you add a new property to the Product entity, EF Core detects this modification and includes it in the next migration.

```csharp
Copy code
public class Product
{
    public int ProductId { get; set; }
    public string Name { get; set; }
    public decimal Price { get; set; }
    public DateTime CreatedDate { get; set; }  //
// New property added
}
```

To apply this change:

Run dotnet ef migrations add AddCreatedDateToProduct to create a new migration.

Run dotnet ef database update to apply the new migration.

CHAPTER 4: ENTITY FRAMEWORK CORE - MASTERING DATA ACCESS AND...

7. Reviewing Migration Files

Each migration file contains two main methods:

- **Up**: Defines the changes to apply to the database.
- **Down**: Defines the rollback operations, allowing you to revert the changes if needed.

An example migration file might look like this:

```csharp
Copy code
public partial class InitialCreate : Migration
{
    protected override void Up(MigrationBuilder migrationBuilder)
    {
        migrationBuilder.CreateTable(
            name: "Categories",
            columns: table => new
            {
CategoryId = table.Column<int>(nullable: false)
.Annotation("SqlServer:Identity", "1, 1"),
CategoryName = table.Column<string>(nullable: true)
            },
            constraints: table =>
            {
                table.PrimaryKey("PK_Categories",
x => x.CategoryId);
            });

        migrationBuilder.CreateTable(
            name: "Products",
            columns: table => new
            {
ProductId = table.Column<int>(nullable: false)
.Annotation("SqlServer:Identity", "1, 1"),
Name = table.Column<string>(nullable: true),
Price = table.Column<decimal>(nullable: false),
```

```
                CategoryId = table.Column<int>(nullable: false)
                    },
                    constraints: table =>
                    {
table.PrimaryKey("PK_Products", x => x.ProductId);
                        table.ForeignKey(
name: "FK_Products_Categories_CategoryId",
                            column: x => x.CategoryId,
                            principalTable: "Categories",
                            principalColumn: "CategoryId",
onDelete: ReferentialAction.Cascade);
                    });
            }

            protected override void Down
(MigrationBuilder migrationBuilder)
            {
                migrationBuilder.DropTable(name: "Products");
                migrationBuilder.DropTable(name: "Categories");
            }
}
```

Entity Framework Core and code-first migrations offer a powerful and flexible approach to data access and schema management in ASP.NET Core applications. By defining entities and relationships in code, you can easily maintain a synchronized and up-to-date database schema without manual intervention. Additionally, code-first migrations enable seamless updates to the database structure, providing an efficient workflow for applications that evolve over time.

Creating and Managing Models, DbContext, and Relationships

Entity Framework Core (EF Core) simplifies database interactions by enabling developers to work directly with .NET objects to create, retrieve, update, and delete data. Models, DbContext, and relationships among

CHAPTER 4: ENTITY FRAMEWORK CORE - MASTERING DATA ACCESS AND...

entities form the backbone of this functionality, making it essential to understand how to define and manage them effectively. This section explores creating models, configuring DbContext, and establishing relationships to build robust, maintainable data layers for your ASP.NET Core applications.

1. Defining Models in EF Core

In EF Core, models (or entities) are classes that represent tables in your database, where each property maps to a column, and each instance represents a row. Properly defining models is key to accurately structuring your data and enabling EF Core to work seamlessly with your schema.

Example: Creating Basic Models

Suppose you are building an e-commerce application. You could start by defining Product and Category models as follows:

```csharp
Copy code
public class Product
{
    public int ProductId { get; set; }
  // Primary key
    public string Name { get; set; }
    public decimal Price { get; set; }
    public int StockQuantity { get; set; }
    public int CategoryId { get; set; }
  // Foreign key
    public Category Category { get; set; }
 // Navigation property
}

public class Category
{
    public int CategoryId { get; set; }
 // Primary key
    public string CategoryName { get; set; }
    public ICollection<Product> Products
```

```
{ get; set; } // Navigation property
for one-to-many relationship
}
```

In this example:

- Product has properties for ProductId, Name, Price, StockQuantity, and CategoryId. The Category navigation property links it to a category, establishing a relationship.
- Category contains a collection of Products, signifying that one category can contain many products (one-to-many relationship).

2. Configuring the DbContext

The DbContext class in EF Core represents a session with the database and acts as a bridge between your entity models and the database. It tracks changes, manages transactions, and performs CRUD operations.

Example: Creating a DbContext Class

The DbContext configuration involves defining DbSet properties for each entity and optionally using the OnModelCreating method to fine-tune relationships and constraints.

```csharp
Copy code
public class ApplicationDbContext : DbContext
{
    public ApplicationDbContext(DbContextOptions
<ApplicationDbContext> options) : base(options)
    {
    }

    public DbSet<Product> Products { get; set; }
    public DbSet<Category> Categories { get; set; }

    protected override void OnModelCreating(ModelBuilder
    modelBuilder)
```

CHAPTER 4: ENTITY FRAMEWORK CORE - MASTERING DATA ACCESS AND...

```
    {
        // Additional configurations can be done here if necessary
        base.OnModelCreating(modelBuilder);
    }
}
```

In this example:

- Products and Categories are DbSet properties, representing tables in the database.
- OnModelCreating can be used to configure relationships, constraints, or complex mappings.

In your Startup.cs or equivalent configuration file, you must also specify the database provider and connection string in the ConfigureServices method:

```csharp
Copy code
public class Startup
{
    public void ConfigureServices(IServiceCollection services)
    {
        services.AddDbContext<ApplicationDbContext>(options =>
            options.UseSqlServer(Configuration.GetConnectionString("DefaultConnection")));
        services.AddControllersWithViews();
    }
}
```

3. Establishing Relationships Between Models

Relationships in EF Core define how entities are associated with each other. They play a critical role in structuring data and affect how you query, insert, update, and delete data. EF Core supports three primary types of relationships:

- **One-to-many**: A single entity relates to many entities of another type.
- **One-to-one**: One entity relates to only one entity of another type.
- **Many-to-many**: Multiple entities relate to multiple entities of another type.

One-to-Many Relationships

One-to-many relationships are the most common and are easy to configure in EF Core. For example, a Category can have many Products, but each Product belongs to only one Category.

In the example above:

- The Product model includes a CategoryId foreign key and a Category navigation property.
- The Category model has a Products collection to enable reverse navigation.

EF Core automatically infers the one-to-many relationship based on the navigation properties and foreign key. However, you can also explicitly configure it in OnModelCreating:

```csharp
Copy code
protected override void OnModelCreating (ModelBuilder modelBuilder)
{
    modelBuilder.Entity<Product>()
        .HasOne(p => p.Category)
        .WithMany(c => c.Products)
        .HasForeignKey(p => p.CategoryId);
}
```

CHAPTER 4: ENTITY FRAMEWORK CORE - MASTERING DATA ACCESS AND...

This configuration is useful if you want to add further constraints or clarify the relationship explicitly.

One-to-One Relationships

A one-to-one relationship is less common and requires configuring both entities to ensure each has only one corresponding entity in the other.

For example, consider Product and ProductDetail models, where each product has a single detailed record:

```csharp
Copy code
public class Product
{
    public int ProductId { get; set; }
    public string Name { get; set; }
    public ProductDetail ProductDetail { get; set; }
}

public class ProductDetail
{
    public int ProductDetailId { get; set; }
    public string Description { get; set; }
    public DateTime ManufactureDate { get; set; }
    public Product Product { get; set; }
    public int ProductId { get; set; }
}
```

To configure this in OnModelCreating:

```csharp
Copy code
protected override void OnModelCreating(ModelBuilder modelBuilder)
{
    modelBuilder.Entity<Product>()
        .HasOne(p => p.ProductDetail)
```

```
            .WithOne(d => d.Product)
            .HasForeignKey<ProductDetail>(d => d.ProductId);
}
```

This mapping defines a one-to-one relationship where ProductDetail references Product with a unique foreign key.

Many-to-Many Relationships

EF Core 5 and above supports many-to-many relationships natively, allowing for straightforward configurations. For example, if you have a Product and Tag entity, and each product can have multiple tags, while each tag can belong to multiple products, you can set up the relationship without a joining entity.

```csharp
Copy code
public class Product
{
    public int ProductId { get; set; }
    public string Name { get; set; }
    public ICollection<Tag> Tags { get; set; }
}

public class Tag
{
    public int TagId { get; set; }
    public string TagName { get; set; }
    public ICollection<Product> Products { get; set; }
}
```

EF Core will automatically create an intermediate table to manage this many-to-many relationship. However, if you need to add properties to the relationship, you would define an explicit joining entity.

4. Fluent API and Data Annotations for Model Configuration

EF Core offers two main ways to configure models:

CHAPTER 4: ENTITY FRAMEWORK CORE - MASTERING DATA ACCESS AND...

- **Data annotations**: Apply attributes directly in the model classes.
- **Fluent API**: Use the OnModelCreating method in DbContext for more granular configurations.

Example of Data Annotations

Data annotations provide a simple, in-line way to define properties and constraints.

```csharp
Copy code
public class Product
{
    [Key]
    public int ProductId { get; set; }

    [Required]
    [MaxLength(100)]
    public string Name { get; set; }

    [Column(TypeName = "decimal(18, 2)")]
    public decimal Price { get; set; }
}
```

In this example:

- [Key] defines the primary key.
- [Required] specifies that Name cannot be null.
- [Column(TypeName = "decimal(18, 2)")] configures the column type in the database.

Example of Fluent API

The Fluent API allows for more detailed configurations, especially for relationships and constraints not easily defined with data annotations.

```
csharp
Copy code
protected override void OnModelCreating
(ModelBuilder modelBuilder)
{
    modelBuilder.Entity<Product>()
        .Property(p => p.Name)
        .IsRequired()
        .HasMaxLength(100);

    modelBuilder.Entity<Product>()
        .Property(p => p.Price)
        .HasColumnType("decimal(18, 2)");
}
```

Both approaches achieve the same goal, so the choice depends on your preference or the complexity of the configuration.

5. Loading Related Data

When working with relationships, you often need to load related data along with the main entities. EF Core provides several strategies for this purpose:

- **Eager loading**: Loads related data as part of the initial query using Include.
- **Explicit loading**: Loads related data separately, on-demand.
- **Lazy loading**: Loads related data automatically when accessed (requires special configuration).

Example of Eager Loading

Eager loading is accomplished with the Include method, useful when you know in advance that related data is needed.

```
csharp
Copy code
var productsWithCategories = context.Products.Include(p =>
p.Category).ToList();
```

This query retrieves all products along with their associated categories.

Example of Explicit Loading

Explicit loading is used when you want to load related data conditionally.

```
csharp
Copy code
var product = context.Products.Find(1);
context.Entry(product).Reference(p => p.Category).Load();
```

Explicit loading is beneficial when you only need related data in specific cases, helping reduce unnecessary data loading.

Setting up models, DbContext, and relationships in EF Core is foundational to building scalable data-driven applications. By effectively defining entities, configuring relationships, and choosing the right loading strategy, you ensure your data layer is optimized for maintainability, performance, and flexibility.

Advanced Querying Techniques with LINQ and Lambda Expressions

LINQ (Language Integrated Query) and lambda expressions are powerful tools in .NET that enable developers to perform complex queries against collections, including database entities through Entity Framework Core (EF Core). By mastering these techniques, you can build efficient, expressive, and highly readable queries to retrieve, filter, transform, and aggregate data in your ASP.NET Core 3 applications. This section dives into advanced querying with LINQ and lambda expressions, covering filtering, sorting, projections, aggregations, joins, and performance optimization tips for working with EF Core.

1. Overview of LINQ and Lambda Expressions

LINQ offers a declarative way to query collections, including in-memory collections (like arrays and lists) as well as databases when used with EF Core. LINQ has two main syntax styles:
- **Query syntax**: A SQL-like syntax that is easy to read and understand.
- **Method syntax (or lambda expressions)**: Chainable methods with lambda expressions, offering more flexibility.

While both styles are functional, lambda expressions are more commonly used for advanced operations and are generally preferred in EF Core for complex queries.

Example of Basic LINQ Query

A simple query using query syntax to retrieve products costing more than $50:

```csharp
Copy code
var expensiveProducts = from product in context.Products
                       where product.Price > 50
                       select product;
```

The same query can be written with lambda expressions:

```csharp
Copy code
var expensiveProducts = context.Products.Where(p => p.Price > 50).ToList();
```

Both queries achieve the same result, but lambda expressions provide more options for advanced querying.

2. Filtering and Sorting with Lambda Expressions

Filtering and sorting are core components of data retrieval, allowing you to precisely target data based on conditions and order the results.

Advanced Filtering with Where

The Where method in lambda expressions enables you to specify complex conditions by chaining multiple filters together.

```csharp
Copy code
var filteredProducts = context.Products
    .Where(p => p.Price > 50 && p.CategoryId == 2)
    .ToList();
```

In this example, only products with a Price greater than $50 and a CategoryId of 2 are returned.

Sorting with OrderBy and OrderByDescending

To sort data, use OrderBy for ascending order or OrderByDescending for descending order. You can also chain multiple ThenBy clauses for secondary sorting.

```csharp
Copy code
var sortedProducts = context.Products
    .Where(p => p.Price > 50)
    .OrderBy(p => p.Price)
    .ThenByDescending(p => p.Name)
    .ToList();
```

Here, products are first sorted by price in ascending order, then by name in descending order within each price group.

3. Selecting Specific Data with Select (Projection)

Projection with Select is useful when you only need specific fields instead of the entire entity. This can improve performance by reducing the amount of data retrieved from the database.

Selecting Specific Fields

```csharp
Copy code
var productNames = context.Products
    .Where(p => p.Price > 50)
    .Select(p => new { p.Name, p.Price })
    .ToList();
```

This query retrieves only the Name and Price properties of products, reducing the data footprint.

Anonymous Types and Custom Types

You can project results into anonymous types (as above) or custom DTO (Data Transfer Object) types to structure the data in specific ways.

```csharp
Copy code
public class ProductSummary
{
    public string Name { get; set; }
    public decimal Price { get; set; }
}

var productSummaries = context.Products
    .Where(p => p.Price > 50)
    .Select(p => new ProductSummary
{ Name = p.Name, Price = p.Price })
    .ToList();
```

Using custom types can make the code more readable and organized, especially for complex data structures.

4. Aggregation Functions

LINQ and lambda expressions support aggregation functions like Count, Sum, Average, Min, and Max, which allow you to summarize

CHAPTER 4: ENTITY FRAMEWORK CORE - MASTERING DATA ACCESS AND...

data efficiently.

Counting Records with Count

```csharp
Copy code
int productCount = context.Products
    .Where(p => p.Price > 50)
    .Count();
```

This query counts the number of products with a price greater than $50.

Summing Values with Sum

```csharp
Copy code
decimal totalInventoryValue = context.Products
    .Sum(p => p.Price * p.StockQuantity);
```

Here, the total value of all products in stock is calculated by multiplying Price and StockQuantity for each product and summing the results.

Calculating Averages with Average

```csharp
Copy code
decimal averagePrice = context.Products
    .Where(p => p.CategoryId == 1)
    .Average(p => p.Price);
```

This query calculates the average price of products in a specific category.

5. Working with Joins in LINQ and EF Core

Joins are essential for retrieving data across multiple tables. LINQ supports different types of joins, with Include being particularly helpful in EF Core for related entities.

Inner Join Example

Suppose you want to join Products with Categories to list each product along with its category name:

```csharp
Copy code
var productsWithCategories = from product in context.Products
            join category in context.Categories
        on product.CategoryId equals category.CategoryId
                    select new
                    {
                        ProductName = product.Name,
                        CategoryName =
                        category.CategoryName,
                        Price = product.Price
                    };
```

Join with Lambda Expressions

Lambda expressions can also perform joins using SelectMany:

```csharp
Copy code
var productsWithCategories = context.Products
    .Join(context.Categories,
        product => product.CategoryId,
        category => category.CategoryId,
        (product, category) => new
        {
            ProductName = product.Name,
            CategoryName = category.CategoryName,
            Price = product.Price
        })
    .ToList();
```

6. Eager Loading, Explicit Loading, and Lazy Loading

Efficiently loading related data is vital in optimizing application performance. EF Core offers several loading strategies:

- **Eager loading**: Loads related entities with the main entity using Include.
- **Explicit loading**: Loads related data on demand, useful for perfor-

mance optimization.
- **Lazy loading**: Automatically loads related data when accessed.

Eager Loading with Include

```csharp
Copy code
var productsWithCategories = context.Products
    .Include(p => p.Category)
    .Where(p => p.Price > 50)
    .ToList();
```

Using Include to retrieve related data avoids multiple database calls, which is beneficial when the related data is always needed.

Explicit Loading

Explicit loading is helpful when related data is needed conditionally:

```csharp
Copy code
var product = context.Products.Find(1);
context.Entry(product).Reference(p => p.Category).Load();
```

Lazy Loading

With lazy loading, related data is loaded only when accessed. This requires enabling lazy loading in your DbContext configuration.

7. Performance Optimization Tips for LINQ Queries

To keep queries efficient, consider the following best practices:

- **Filter Early**: Apply filters before loading related data to reduce data retrieved from the database.
- **Limit Data Retrieval**: Use Select to load only the necessary fields, especially when working with large datasets.
- **Use AsNoTracking for Read-Only Data**: Disabling change tracking with AsNoTracking improves performance for read-only queries.

```csharp
Copy code
var readOnlyProducts = context.Products
    .AsNoTracking()
    .Where(p => p.Price > 50)
    .ToList();
```

- **Consider Stored Procedures for Complex Queries**: For complex operations involving multiple joins or extensive aggregation, consider using stored procedures to improve performance.

Advanced querying techniques with LINQ and lambda expressions allow developers to build highly flexible, efficient, and expressive data access layers in ASP.NET Core applications. By understanding how to use filtering, sorting, projections, joins, and aggregations, you can effectively manage and query your data to meet the needs of complex business applications while ensuring optimal performance.

Handling Data Seeding and Configuring Database Providers

Data seeding and configuring database providers are foundational aspects of database management in ASP.NET Core applications using Entity Framework Core (EF Core). Data seeding is the process of preloading initial data into a database, which can be essential for setting up testing environments, defining reference data, or populating default values. Meanwhile, selecting and configuring the right database provider ensures compatibility and optimal performance for your application's specific requirements.

This section will provide a detailed guide on data seeding techniques, configuring multiple database providers, and making your application flexible enough to adapt to different data storage solutions.

1. Overview of Database Providers in EF Core

Entity Framework Core supports multiple database providers that enable compatibility with various relational and non-relational databases. Some of the commonly used providers include:

- **Microsoft SQL Server**: The most commonly used relational database provider for .NET applications.
- **SQLite**: A lightweight, file-based database often used for local development, testing, and small-scale applications.
- **PostgreSQL**: A robust, open-source relational database with strong support for advanced data types.
- **MySQL**: A popular open-source relational database often used in web applications.
- **In-Memory Database**: A non-persistent, memory-based database useful for unit testing and development.

Each database provider offers specific features and configurations tailored to its underlying storage mechanism. EF Core includes built-in support for these providers, enabling a seamless integration of database-specific capabilities.

Example: Setting Up SQL Server Provider

In the Startup class, configure the SQL Server provider by calling UseSqlServer on the DbContext in the ConfigureServices method:

```csharp
Copy code
public class Startup
{
    public void ConfigureServices(IServiceCollection services)
    {
        services.AddDbContext<ApplicationDbContext>(options =>
            options.UseSqlServer(Configuration.GetConnectionString("DefaultConnection")));
```

```
        services.AddControllersWithViews();
    }
}
```

Ensure that your appsettings.json includes the correct connection string:

```json
Copy code
{
  "ConnectionStrings": {
    "DefaultConnection":
    "Server=your_server_name;Database=your_database_name;User
    Id=your_user;Password=your_password;"
  }
}
```

This configuration connects your application to a SQL Server database, but similar configurations can be applied for other providers by swapping out UseSqlServer with the respective method (e.g., UseSqlite, UseNpgsql for PostgreSQL, etc.).

2. Configuring Multiple Database Providers

In some applications, you may need to support multiple database providers. EF Core enables this flexibility through configuration settings or dependency injection.

Example: Switching Between SQL Server and SQLite

To allow switching between SQL Server and SQLite, you could create a conditional configuration based on an environment variable or application setting:

```csharp
Copy code
public void ConfigureServices(IServiceCollection services)
{
    var useSqlite = Configuration.
```

CHAPTER 4: ENTITY FRAMEWORK CORE - MASTERING DATA ACCESS AND...

```
GetValue<bool>("UseSqlite");

    if (useSqlite)
    {
        services.AddDbContext<
ApplicationDbContext>(options =>
            options.UseSqlite(Configuration.
GetConnectionString("SqliteConnection")));
    }
    else
    {
        services.AddDbContext<
ApplicationDbContext>(options =>
            options.UseSqlServer(Configuration
.GetConnectionString("DefaultConnection")));
    }

    services.AddControllersWithViews();
}
```

With this setup, your application can dynamically use SQL Server or SQLite based on the configuration value. This is particularly useful for development environments where SQLite can serve as a lightweight alternative to SQL Server.

3. Introduction to Data Seeding

Data seeding in EF Core provides a way to insert initial data into a database when it is first created or updated. Seed data can populate reference tables, initialize default settings, or support testing scenarios. EF Core allows for fluent API configurations or model data annotations for data seeding.

Simple Data Seeding with the ModelBuilder

To seed data, use the HasData method in the OnModelCreating method within your DbContext. For example, to populate a Category table with default values:

```csharp
Copy code
public class ApplicationDbContext : DbContext
{
    public DbSet<Category> Categories { get; set; }

    protected override void OnModelCreating(ModelBuilder
    modelBuilder)
    {
        modelBuilder.Entity<Category>().HasData(
            new Category { CategoryId = 1, CategoryName =
            "Electronics" },
            new Category { CategoryId = 2,
CategoryName = "Books" },
            new Category { CategoryId = 3,
CategoryName = "Clothing" }
        );

        base.OnModelCreating(modelBuilder);
    }
}
```

In this example:

- The HasData method seeds the Category table with predefined entries.
- When the database is created or updated via migrations, EF Core will insert this data into the table, provided that these entries do not already exist.

4. Seeding Complex Data with Relationships

In scenarios where seeded data includes relationships between entities, such as foreign keys, EF Core's seeding mechanism requires defining the foreign keys manually.

Example: Seeding Products with Categories

If you have a Product model that references Category, seeding both entities with a relationship would look like this:

CHAPTER 4: ENTITY FRAMEWORK CORE - MASTERING DATA ACCESS AND...

```csharp
Copy code
public class ApplicationDbContext : DbContext
{
    public DbSet<Product> Products { get; set; }
    public DbSet<Category> Categories { get; set; }

    protected override void OnModelCreating(ModelBuilder modelBuilder)
    {
        modelBuilder.Entity<Category>().HasData(
            new Category { CategoryId = 1, CategoryName = "Electronics" },
            new Category { CategoryId = 2, CategoryName = "Books" }
        );

        modelBuilder.Entity<Product>().HasData(
            new Product { ProductId = 1, Name = "Laptop", Price = 999.99M, CategoryId = 1 },
            new Product { ProductId = 2, Name = "Smartphone", Price = 499.99M, CategoryId = 1 },
            new Product { ProductId = 3, Name = "Novel", Price = 19.99M, CategoryId = 2 }
        );

        base.OnModelCreating(modelBuilder);
    }
}
```

Here, Product entries reference CategoryId, establishing a relationship between products and categories. EF Core inserts this data in the correct order to maintain the integrity of foreign key constraints.

5. Data Seeding in Migrations

Data seeding often works in conjunction with EF Core migrations. Once you add or update seed data, generate a new migration to apply these changes to the database:

```bash
Copy code
dotnet ef migrations add SeedInitialData
dotnet ef database update
```

EF Core tracks seeded data via migrations, so it only inserts new entries that don't already exist in the database. However, modifying seeded data after the initial migration requires either updating the migration or writing custom logic, as EF Core does not automatically update existing rows.

6. Advanced Data Seeding Techniques

In addition to the basic data seeding with HasData, more advanced seeding may involve executing SQL scripts or leveraging EF Core's raw SQL queries for complex scenarios.

Executing SQL Scripts

You can execute raw SQL commands to seed data that requires more control than HasData provides, such as using stored procedures or custom data logic.

```csharp
Copy code
protected override void OnModelCreating
(ModelBuilder modelBuilder)
{
    modelBuilder.Entity<Category>().HasData(
        new Category { CategoryId = 1, 
CategoryName = "Electronics" },
        new Category { CategoryId = 2, 
 CategoryName = "Books" }
    );

    base.OnModelCreating(modelBuilder);
}
```

CHAPTER 4: ENTITY FRAMEWORK CORE - MASTERING DATA ACCESS AND...

```csharp
public void SeedWithRawSql()
{
    Database.ExecuteSqlRaw(
"INSERT INTO Categories (CategoryId, CategoryName) VALUES (3,
'Furniture')");
}
```

Executing raw SQL can also handle data updates or modifications that the EF Core seeding mechanism does not support directly.

7. Using In-Memory Database for Testing

The In-Memory database provider in EF Core is valuable for testing scenarios. It simulates database behavior without persisting data, allowing you to test data operations, seed test data, and isolate test environments.

Setting Up the In-Memory Database for Tests

To configure an In-Memory database, specify the provider in your test setup:

```csharp
csharp
Copy code
var options = new DbContextOptionsBuilder
<ApplicationDbContext>()
    .UseInMemoryDatabase("TestDatabase")
    .Options;

using var context = new ApplicationDbContext(options);
context.Database.EnsureCreated();

// Seed test data
context.Categories.Add(new Category
 CategoryId = 1, CategoryName = "Test Category" });
context.SaveChanges();
```

This configuration is useful for unit tests, enabling you to verify CRUD operations and query logic without requiring an actual database server.

Data seeding and configuring database providers in EF Core allow you to set up robust, adaptable database connections while providing a way to initialize data for application startup, testing, or default values. By understanding how to use HasData, configure providers, and set up advanced seeding strategies, you build a foundation that supports flexibility, testing, and deployment readiness for ASP.NET Core applications.

Performance Optimization Techniques in EF Core

Efficient data access is essential for high-performance applications, especially when dealing with complex data models or high transaction volumes. EF Core provides several built-in mechanisms to optimize data access and query execution, reducing latency and improving responsiveness. This section covers essential techniques for performance optimization in EF Core, including efficient querying practices, managing tracking behaviors, caching strategies, batching commands, and more.

1. Use of AsNoTracking for Read-Only Data

By default, EF Core tracks all entities retrieved from the database to monitor changes for updates. However, for read-only operations where you do not intend to modify entities, tracking is unnecessary and consumes memory and processing power. Using AsNoTracking significantly boosts performance in such cases by disabling tracking.

```csharp
Copy code
var products = context.Products
    .AsNoTracking()
    .Where(p => p.Price > 50)
    .ToList();
```

In this example, EF Core retrieves Product entities without tracking, reducing overhead for read-only queries.

When to Use: Apply AsNoTracking in scenarios where data is only viewed and not modified, such as data displayed on read-only dashboards or lists.

2. Limiting Data Retrieval with Projections (Select)

Loading only necessary fields instead of entire entities minimizes data retrieval and optimizes query performance. Using the Select method allows for projection, retrieving only specific fields rather than full entities.

Example: Selecting Specific Fields

```csharp
Copy code
var productSummaries = context.Products
    .Where(p => p.Price > 50)
    .Select(p => new { p.Name, p.Price })
    .ToList();
```

By selecting only Name and Price, EF Core reduces the amount of data transferred from the database.

When to Use: Use projections when you need only a subset of an entity's properties to reduce network and memory overhead.

3. Batching Commands with SaveChanges

EF Core allows multiple changes to be saved to the database in a single call to SaveChanges, which reduces the number of database round trips. However, each call to SaveChanges results in a separate transaction by default. Grouping related updates or inserts together before calling SaveChanges minimizes network latency and transaction overhead.

```csharp
Copy code
var product1 = new Product
{ Name = "Product A", Price = 30 };
var product2 = new Product
```

```
{ Name = "Product B", Price = 50 };

context.Products.Add(product1);
context.Products.Add(product2);

// Saving both entries in a single transaction
context.SaveChanges();
```

When to Use: Use this approach to batch multiple inserts, updates, or deletes for optimized transaction handling.

4. Efficient Loading with Include, ThenInclude, and Lazy Loading

Loading related data is a common requirement, but it can impact performance if not managed carefully. EF Core offers several strategies for loading related data efficiently:

- **Eager loading**: Retrieves related data with the primary query using Include and ThenInclude. This reduces round trips but can lead to larger datasets if used indiscriminately.
- **Explicit loading**: Loads related data on demand by explicitly specifying navigation properties.
- **Lazy loading**: Automatically retrieves related data when accessed, reducing upfront loading but increasing potential round trips.

Example of Eager Loading with Include

```csharp
Copy code
var ordersWithDetails = context.Orders
    .Include(o => o.OrderDetails)
    .Where(o => o.CustomerId == customerId)
    .ToList();
```

In this query, related OrderDetails are loaded with each Order, reducing the need for additional queries.

CHAPTER 4: ENTITY FRAMEWORK CORE - MASTERING DATA ACCESS AND...

When to Use: Use eager loading when related data is essential to the primary entity and will be accessed immediately. Use explicit loading or lazy loading for optional data.

5. Avoiding N + 1 Query Problems

The N + 1 problem occurs when an application issues one query to retrieve a collection of entities (N) and then performs additional queries for each entity in the result. This is commonly seen with improperly configured lazy loading or missing Include statements.

Solution: Using Include to Avoid N + 1

```csharp
Copy code
var customersWithOrders = context.Customers
    .Include(c => c.Orders)
    .ToList();
```

By including Orders in the query, EF Core retrieves all orders related to each customer in a single query rather than issuing separate queries per customer.

When to Use: Always review query plans to check for N + 1 issues, especially when dealing with related collections. Use Include or explicit joins as needed.

6. Caching Strategies

Caching frequently accessed data is a powerful optimization, especially for data that does not change often. EF Core can be used alongside caching solutions like MemoryCache, Redis, or third-party caching libraries to store frequently accessed data, reducing repetitive database queries.

Example: Using MemoryCache for Simple Caching

```csharp
Copy code
```

```csharp
private readonly IMemoryCache _cache;

public ProductService(IMemoryCache cache)
{
    _cache = cache;
}

public List<Product> GetProducts()
{
    if (!_cache.TryGetValue("productList", out List<Product>
    products))
    {
        products = context.Products.AsNoTracking().ToList();

        var cacheOptions = new MemoryCacheEntryOptions
            .SetSlidingExpiration(TimeSpan.FromMinutes(30));

        _cache.Set("productList", products, cacheOptions);
    }

    return products;
}
```

In this example, the product list is cached for 30 minutes, reducing database queries for repeat access.

When to Use: Implement caching for frequently accessed data that remains static or changes infrequently.

7. Optimizing Query Execution with Compiled Queries

EF Core allows for compiled queries, which can significantly boost performance by precompiling frequently executed queries. This approach is especially useful for complex or repetitive queries.

Example: Compiling a Query

```
csharp
Copy code
```

```csharp
public static readonly Func<ApplicationDbContext, decimal,
IEnumerable<Product>> GetProductsByPrice =
    EF.CompileQuery
((ApplicationDbContext context, decimal price) =>
        context.Products.Where
(p => p.Price >= price));
```

Now, calling GetProductsByPrice(context, 50) will execute a compiled query, reducing the overhead of query parsing and compilation at runtime.

When to Use: Use compiled queries for high-traffic queries, especially those with parameters and complex logic.

8. Controlling Database Connections and Command Timeouts

EF Core supports configuring command timeouts, which define the maximum duration for a database operation before it times out. Adjusting command timeouts can prevent blocking issues in scenarios with long-running queries.

Example: Setting Command Timeout

```
csharp
Copy code
services.AddDbContext<ApplicationDbContext>(options =>
    options.UseSqlServer(Configuration.
GetConnectionString("DefaultConnection"),
        sqlOptions => sqlOptions.CommandTimeout(60)));
```

Here, the command timeout is set to 60 seconds, which can be helpful in managing performance for resource-intensive operations.

When to Use: Adjust command timeouts for operations that may require longer processing, such as data migrations or batch updates.

9. Using Raw SQL for Complex Queries

For complex queries or operations requiring highly optimized SQL, using raw SQL can be more efficient than LINQ. EF Core supports executing raw SQL queries and mapping results directly to entity types.

```csharp
Copy code
var expensiveProducts = context.Products
    .FromSqlRaw("SELECT * FROM Products WHERE Price > 100")
    .ToList();
```

Raw SQL provides more control over the query and can incorporate database-specific optimizations or hints, but lacks EF Core's LINQ-based safety checks.

When to Use: Consider raw SQL for complex joins, data aggregations, or operations where LINQ syntax may be less efficient or impractical.

By implementing these optimization techniques in EF Core, you can achieve significant performance gains, reducing memory consumption, network latency, and query execution time. The use of AsNoTracking, efficient loading strategies, caching, compiled queries, and batch operations ensures that your ASP.NET Core application remains responsive and scalable, even under heavy loads or with large datasets. Optimizing EF Core requires an awareness of query behavior, memory management, and database configurations, but the payoff is substantial in creating fast and efficient data-driven applications.

Advanced Authentication and Authorization Techniques

Overview of ASP.NET Core Identity

ASP.NET Core Identity is the framework's built-in membership system that provides a comprehensive set of tools for managing user authentication and authorization. It enables secure, customizable, and extensible identity management in web applications. ASP.NET Core Identity supports essential security features such as password hashing, multi-factor authentication, role-based and policy-based authorization, external logins, and token-based authentication, making it highly suitable for modern web applications that prioritize user security and data integrity.

In this section, we'll cover the core components of ASP.NET Core Identity, the architecture that underpins it, and its customizable aspects, setting the stage for advanced authentication and authorization techniques.

1. Key Features of ASP.NET Core Identity

ASP.NET Core Identity offers a range of features that simplify the process of managing users and securing applications. Here are some of the key features:

- **User Authentication**: Handles user login, logout, and registration.
- **Role-Based Authorization**: Supports assigning users to roles and

enforcing role-based access control (RBAC).
- **Policy-Based Authorization**: Offers fine-grained control over access by defining policies and claims.
- **Password Management**: Provides robust password hashing and configuration options for complexity requirements, expiration, and history.
- **Multi-Factor Authentication (MFA)**: Enables MFA options to enhance security.
- **External Login Providers**: Integrates with social login providers like Google, Facebook, Twitter, and Microsoft.
- **Token-Based Authentication**: Supports generating and validating JWT (JSON Web Tokens) for API authentication.
- **User Lockout and Security Stamps**: Includes mechanisms to handle account lockout for repeated failed login attempts and to validate security stamps for user session integrity.

These features make ASP.NET Core Identity a comprehensive solution for managing and securing user identities in modern web applications.

2. ASP.NET Core Identity Architecture and Core Concepts

Understanding the architecture of ASP.NET Core Identity is essential for leveraging its full potential. The framework uses a modular, extensible design that includes several core components:

- **IdentityDbContext**: A specialized DbContext provided by Entity Framework Core (EF Core) that stores user and role data in a SQL database.
- **UserManager and RoleManager**: High-level APIs for managing users and roles. UserManager handles user-specific tasks, such as creating users, setting passwords, and managing claims. RoleManager manages role-related tasks.
- **SignInManager**: Handles authentication tasks, such as signing users in and out, and supports multi-factor authentication and external

logins.
- **IdentityUser and IdentityRole**: Base classes representing users and roles. Both can be extended to include additional properties or behaviors as needed.
- **Claims and Tokens**: ASP.NET Core Identity supports claims-based identity, where users are authenticated and authorized based on their claims. Tokens, especially JWTs, are commonly used in API scenarios.

Together, these components form the backbone of ASP.NET Core Identity, enabling applications to handle user management and access control seamlessly.

3. Setting Up ASP.NET Core Identity

Setting up ASP.NET Core Identity requires configuring services and modifying the application's data layer to include Identity tables. By default, Identity includes tables for managing users, roles, claims, and tokens, which are required to support the complete identity lifecycle.

Step-by-Step Guide to Initial Setup

Add Identity Service in Startup.cs:

In the Startup.cs file, add ASP.NET Core Identity services in the ConfigureServices method. If your application uses Entity Framework Core, configure it to use a database, such as SQL Server, for persisting identity information.

```csharp
csharp
Copy code
public class Startup
{
    public void ConfigureServices(IServiceCollection services)
    {
        services.AddDbContext<ApplicationDbContext>(options =>
            options.UseSqlServer(Configuration.GetConnectionString("DefaultConnection")));
```

```
        services.AddIdentity<IdentityUser, IdentityRole>()
            .AddEntityFrameworkStores<ApplicationDbContext>()
            .AddDefaultTokenProviders();

        services.AddControllersWithViews();
    }
}
```

This code configures Identity to use IdentityUser and IdentityRole by default and registers ApplicationDbContext as the storage context.

Configure Identity Options:

Identity provides configurable options for password requirements, lockout settings, and sign-in options. For instance, you may want to enforce strong passwords and limit lockout attempts for security reasons.

```csharp
Copy code
services.Configure<IdentityOptions>(options =>
{
    options.Password.RequireDigit = true;
    options.Password.RequiredLength = 8;
    options.Password.RequireNonAlphanumeric = false;
    options.Password.RequireUppercase = true;
    options.Password.RequireLowercase = true;

    options.Lockout.DefaultLockoutTimeSpan = TimeSpan.FromMinutes(5);
    options.Lockout.MaxFailedAccessAttempts = 5;
    options.SignIn.RequireConfirmedEmail = true;
});
```

These settings help enforce password complexity and account lockout policies, enhancing security and reducing the risk of brute-force attacks.

Run Initial Migrations:

ADVANCED AUTHENTICATION AND AUTHORIZATION TECHNIQUES

After configuring Identity, run the initial migrations to create the Identity tables in your database. Use the following commands in the terminal:

```bash
Copy code
dotnet ef migrations add InitialIdentitySetup
dotnet ef database update
```

This step creates tables like AspNetUsers, AspNetRoles, AspNetUserRoles, AspNetUserClaims, and others required by ASP.NET Core Identity.

4. Identity User and Role Management

ASP.NET Core Identity provides several classes and methods to manage users and roles efficiently.

Creating and Managing Users

The UserManager class offers methods for creating, updating, and deleting users, as well as managing user-specific settings like passwords and claims. Here's an example of how to create a new user:

```csharp
Copy code
var user = new IdentityUser { UserName = "user@example.com",
Email = "user@example.com" };
var result = await userManager.CreateAsync(user,
"SecurePassword123!");

if (result.Succeeded)
{
    // User created successfully
}
```

The CreateAsync method adds a user with a specified password, and the result will indicate if the operation succeeded.

Role Management with RoleManager

The RoleManager class allows for the creation, deletion, and modification of roles. Roles can simplify authorization by grouping permissions, allowing you to assign a set of permissions to users at once.

```csharp
Copy code
var roleExists = await roleManager.RoleExistsAsync("Admin");
if (!roleExists)
{
    var roleResult = await roleManager.CreateAsync(new
    IdentityRole("Admin"));
    // Role created successfully
}
```

Roles like "Admin" or "Editor" can then be assigned to users, making it easy to define broad access permissions.

5. Authentication Flows in ASP.NET Core Identity

Authentication is the process of verifying user identity, and ASP.NET Core Identity simplifies common authentication flows through its SignInManager and other built-in methods.

Password-Based Authentication

Password authentication is the most straightforward method. SignInManager handles the complexities, ensuring that password hashing, validation, and login attempts are securely managed.

```csharp
Copy code
var signInResult = await
signInManager.PasswordSignInAsync("user@example.com",
"SecurePassword123!", isPersistent: false,
lockoutOnFailure: true);

if (signInResult.Succeeded)
{
```

ADVANCED AUTHENTICATION AND AUTHORIZATION TECHNIQUES

```
    // User signed in successfully
}
```

In this example, PasswordSignInAsync takes care of verifying the credentials and managing any lockout policies.

Two-Factor Authentication (2FA)

ASP.NET Core Identity supports two-factor authentication (2FA), which adds an extra layer of security by requiring users to verify their identity with a second factor, such as an SMS code or email confirmation.

To enable 2FA, set up token providers and use the SignInManager to generate a 2FA code during sign-in.

```
csharp
Copy code
var code = await userManager
 .GenerateTwoFactorTokenAsync(user, "Email");
await emailService.SendAsync(user.Email,
 "Your verification code", code);
```

Upon receiving the code, the user must input it to complete the authentication process, further securing their account.

6. Authorization Models in ASP.NET Core Identity

Authorization in ASP.NET Core can be managed at various levels to restrict user access to specific resources or operations based on their role or claims. The framework supports both **role-based** and **policy-based** authorization models.

Role-Based Authorization

Role-based authorization grants access to resources based on assigned roles. For instance, only users with the "Admin" role might access certain areas of an application.

```csharp
Copy code
[Authorize(Roles = "Admin")]
public IActionResult AdminDashboard()
{
    return View();
}
```

In this example, only users assigned to the "Admin" role can access the AdminDashboard action.

Policy-Based Authorization

Policy-based authorization offers finer control by allowing complex access requirements, such as claims-based or custom rules. Policies are defined in the Startup class and can incorporate multiple claims or conditions.

```csharp
Copy code
services.AddAuthorization(options =>
{
    options.AddPolicy("MustBeOver18", policy =>
        policy.RequireClaim("Age", "18"));
});
```

Policies provide flexibility in defining custom authorization logic, enabling advanced access control scenarios.

ASP.NET Core Identity is a powerful, feature-rich solution for managing authentication and authorization in ASP.NET Core applications. Its flexibility allows for secure, scalable identity management, offering everything from user and role management to policy-based authorization and 2FA. By understanding the underlying architecture and capabilities of

ASP.NET Core Identity, you can create secure and robust authentication flows tailored to your application's needs. In the following sections, we'll explore advanced techniques for extending and customizing ASP.NET Core.

Implementing Role-Based, Policy-Based, and Claims-Based Authorization

In modern web applications, authorization is crucial for determining what resources and functionalities a user can access. ASP.NET Core Identity provides a robust framework for implementing various authorization strategies, including role-based, policy-based, and claims-based authorization. Understanding these authorization models allows developers to tailor access control to the specific needs of their applications, enhancing security and user experience.

1. Role-Based Authorization

Role-based authorization is a straightforward method for managing user access based on their assigned roles. In this model, users are granted permissions to access resources or execute actions based on their role membership. This is particularly useful in applications where users fall into distinct categories, such as "Admin," "Editor," or "Viewer."

Setting Up Role-Based Authorization
Step 1: Define Roles

First, you need to define the roles in your application. This can be done during application startup or through a management interface. Below is an example of how to create roles programmatically:

```csharp
Copy code
public class SeedData
{
    public static async Task Initialize(IServiceProvider
```

```csharp
    serviceProvider)
{
    var roleManager =
    serviceProvider.GetRequiredService<RoleManager<IdentityRole>>();

    string[] roleNames = { "Admin", "Editor", "Viewer" };
    IdentityResult roleResult;

    foreach (var roleName in roleNames)
    {
        var roleExists = await
        roleManager.RoleExistsAsync(roleName);
        if (!roleExists)
        {
            roleResult = await roleManager.CreateAsync(new
            IdentityRole(roleName));
        }
    }
}
}
```

In this example, the roles "Admin," "Editor," and "Viewer" are created if they do not already exist.

Step 2: Assign Roles to Users

Once roles are defined, you can assign them to users using the UserManager class:

```
csharp
Copy code
var user = await userManager.
FindByEmailAsync("user@example.com");
await userManager.AddToRoleAsync(user, "Admin");
```

Step 3: Protecting Resources with Role-Based Authorization

To protect resources or actions, use the [Authorize] attribute in your controllers or actions, specifying the required roles:

ADVANCED AUTHENTICATION AND AUTHORIZATION TECHNIQUES

```csharp
Copy code
[Authorize(Roles = "Admin")]
public IActionResult AdminDashboard()
{
    return View();
}
```

In this example, only users who are members of the "Admin" role can access the AdminDashboard action.

2. Policy-Based Authorization

Policy-based authorization provides a more flexible approach compared to role-based authorization. It allows developers to define complex rules that determine whether a user can access a resource based on multiple criteria. Policies can incorporate claims, roles, and other conditions.

Setting Up Policy-Based Authorization
Step 1: Define Authorization Policies

Define your policies in the Startup.cs file within the ConfigureServices method. For example, you can create a policy that requires users to have a specific claim:

```csharp
Copy code
services.AddAuthorization(options =>
{
    options.AddPolicy("RequireAdminRole", policy =>
        policy.RequireRole("Admin"));

    options.AddPolicy("Over18", policy =>
        policy.RequireClaim("Age", "18"));
});
```

In this example, the policy RequireAdminRole checks if a user has the "Admin" role, while the Over18 policy ensures that users have an "Age" claim equal to 18.

Step 2: Applying Policies to Actions

Use the [Authorize] attribute to apply policies to specific actions or controllers:

```csharp
Copy code
[Authorize(Policy = "RequireAdminRole")]
public IActionResult AdminOnly()
{
    return View();
}

[Authorize(Policy = "Over18")]
public IActionResult AdultContent()
{
    return View();
}
```

These actions can now only be accessed by users who meet the policy requirements.

3. Claims-Based Authorization

Claims-based authorization allows for a fine-grained access control mechanism by evaluating user claims. A claim is a key-value pair associated with a user, representing user attributes or privileges. This method is especially powerful when you need to make authorization decisions based on user data beyond roles.

Working with Claims

Step 1: Adding Claims to Users

You can add claims to users using the UserManager class. Here's how to add a claim:

ADVANCED AUTHENTICATION AND AUTHORIZATION TECHNIQUES

```csharp
Copy code
var user = await userManager.
FindByEmailAsync("user@example.com");
await userManager.AddClaimAsync
(user, new Claim("Permission", "CanEdit"));
```

In this example, a claim is added to the user, indicating that they have permission to edit content.

Step 2: Define Claims Policies

You can define policies that require specific claims in the Startup.cs file:

```csharp
Copy code
services.AddAuthorization(options =>
{
    options.AddPolicy("EditPolicy", policy =>
        policy.RequireClaim("Permission", "CanEdit"));
});
```

Step 3: Applying Claims Policies

Similar to role and policy-based authorization, you can use the [Authorize] attribute to enforce claims-based policies:

```csharp
Copy code
[Authorize(Policy = "EditPolicy")]
public IActionResult EditContent()
{
    return View();
}
```

In this case, only users with the "CanEdit" permission claim can access the EditContent action.

4. Combining Authorization Models

ASP.NET Core allows you to combine authorization models for more complex scenarios. For instance, you can define a policy that requires both a specific role and a claim.

Example of Combined Authorization

```csharp
Copy code
services.AddAuthorization(options =>
{
    options.AddPolicy("AdminAndEditPolicy", policy =>
        policy.RequireRole("Admin").
RequireClaim("Permission", "CanEdit"));
});
```

You can then apply this policy to actions in your controllers:

```csharp
Copy code
[Authorize(Policy = "AdminAndEditPolicy")]
public IActionResult AdminEdit()
{
    return View();
}
```

In this example, only users who are both "Admin" and have the "CanEdit" permission can access the AdminEdit action.

5. Custom Authorization Handlers

For even more complex scenarios, you can implement custom authorization handlers. This allows you to define your own logic for determining whether a user meets the requirements of a specific policy.

Step 1: Create a Custom Authorization Requirement

First, create a class that implements IAuthorizationRequirement:

ADVANCED AUTHENTICATION AND AUTHORIZATION TECHNIQUES

```csharp
Copy code
public class CustomRequirement : IAuthorizationRequirement
{
    public string RequiredClaim { get; }

    public CustomRequirement(string requiredClaim)
    {
        RequiredClaim = requiredClaim;
    }
}
```

Step 2: Implement the Authorization Handler

Next, implement the handler that will validate the requirement:

```csharp
Copy code
public class CustomAuthorizationHandler : AuthorizationHandler<CustomRequirement>
{
    protected override Task HandleRequirementAsync(AuthorizationHandlerContext context, CustomRequirement requirement)
    {
        if (context.User.HasClaim(c => c.Type == requirement.RequiredClaim))
        {
            context.Succeed(requirement);
        }

        return Task.CompletedTask;
    }
}
```

Step 3: Register the Handler

Register the custom handler in the Startup.cs:

```csharp
Copy code
services.AddSingleton<IAuthorizationHandler,
CustomAuthorizationHandler>();
```

Step 4: Define the Policy Using the Custom Requirement

You can now define a policy that uses your custom requirement:

```csharp
Copy code
services.AddAuthorization(options =>
{
    options.AddPolicy("CustomClaimPolicy", policy =>
        policy.Requirements.Add(new
        CustomRequirement("CustomClaimType")));
});
```

Step 5: Applying the Custom Policy

Finally, apply the custom policy in your controller actions:

```csharp
Copy code
[Authorize(Policy = "CustomClaimPolicy")]
public IActionResult CustomClaimAction()
{
    return View();
}
```

This approach provides complete control over how authorization is processed, allowing you to implement complex business rules effectively.

ADVANCED AUTHENTICATION AND AUTHORIZATION TECHNIQUES

ASP.NET Core Identity provides a robust framework for implementing authorization in web applications, allowing developers to leverage role-based, policy-based, and claims-based models. By understanding these authorization strategies, you can create secure applications that enforce access control according to the specific requirements of your user base. Furthermore, the ability to combine these models and implement custom authorization handlers enables tailored solutions to meet complex authorization needs. In the following chapters, we will delve deeper into integrating these authorization strategies with various authentication flows, ensuring a comprehensive security framework for ASP.NET Core applications.

Securing APIs with JWT and Bearer Tokens

In today's web applications, especially with the rise of single-page applications (SPAs) and mobile clients, securing APIs is paramount. JSON Web Tokens (JWT) and bearer tokens provide a powerful and flexible way to authenticate and authorize users accessing APIs. In this section, we will explore what JWTs and bearer tokens are, how to implement them in an ASP.NET Core application, and best practices for securing your APIs.

1. Understanding JWT and Bearer Tokens
What is a JSON Web Token (JWT)?

A JSON Web Token (JWT) is an open standard (RFC 7519) that defines a compact and self-contained way for securely transmitting information between parties as a JSON object. This information can be verified and trusted because it is digitally signed. JWTs can be signed using a secret (with the HMAC algorithm) or a public/private key pair using RSA or ECDSA.

A typical JWT consists of three parts, separated by dots (.):

Header: Contains metadata about the token, including the type (JWT) and the signing algorithm (e.g., HMAC SHA256).

```json
Copy code
{
    "alg": "HS256",
    "typ": "JWT"
}
```

Payload: Contains the claims, which are the statements about an entity (typically, the user) and additional data. Claims can be standard (like sub, iss, exp) or custom claims defined by the developer.

```json
Copy code
{
    "sub": "1234567890",
    "name": "John Doe",
    "admin": true,
    "exp": 1516239022
}
```

Signature: To create the signature part, you take the encoded header, the encoded payload, a secret, and the algorithm specified in the header, and you sign it. This signature ensures that the sender of the JWT is who it says it is and that the message wasn't changed along the way.

A complete JWT looks like this:

```
Copy code
eyJhbGci0iJIUzI1NiIs
InR5cCI6IkpXVCJ9.
eyJzdWIi0iIxMjM0NTY3
ODkwIiwibmFtZSI6Ikp
vaG4gRG9lIiwibmFtZSI6
```

ADVANCED AUTHENTICATION AND AUTHORIZATION TECHNIQUES

```
IkpvaG4gRG9lIiw
iaWF0IjoxNTE2MjM
5MDIyfQ.SflKxwRJSMeKKF2QT
4fwpMeJf36POk6yJV_adQssw5c
```

What are Bearer Tokens?

Bearer tokens are a type of access token that is used in OAuth 2.0. When a user successfully logs in, the server issues a bearer token, which is sent along with each API request to authorize access. The server verifies the token before granting access to protected resources.

JWTs can be used as bearer tokens, allowing the client to include the JWT in the HTTP Authorization header as follows:

```makefile
Copy code
Authorization: Bearer <token>
```

2. Implementing JWT Authentication in ASP.NET Core

To secure your APIs using JWT and bearer tokens, you need to follow several steps to configure your ASP.NET Core application properly.

Step 1: Install Required NuGet Packages

First, ensure you have the necessary NuGet packages installed. Use the following command to add the JWT authentication package:

```bash
Copy code
dotnet add package Microsoft.AspNetCore.Authentication.JwtBearer
```

Step 2: Configure JWT Authentication in Startup.cs

In the Startup.cs file, configure the JWT authentication service in the ConfigureServices method:

```csharp
public void ConfigureServices(IServiceCollection services)
{
    services.AddAuthentication(options =>
    {
        options.DefaultAuthenticateScheme =
        JwtBearerDefaults.AuthenticationScheme;
        options.DefaultChallengeScheme =
        JwtBearerDefaults.AuthenticationScheme;
    })
    .AddJwtBearer(options =>
    {
        options.TokenValidationParameters = new
        TokenValidationParameters
        {
            ValidateIssuer = true,
            ValidateAudience = true,
            ValidateLifetime = true,
            ValidateIssuerSigningKey = true,
            ValidIssuer = Configuration["Jwt:Issuer"],
            ValidAudience = Configuration["Jwt:Audience"],
            IssuerSigningKey = new
            SymmetricSecurityKey(Encoding.UTF8.GetBytes(Configuration["Jwt:Key"]))
        };
    });

    services.AddControllers();
}
```

In this configuration:

- **ValidateIssuer**: Ensures the token was issued by a trusted issuer.
- **ValidateAudience**: Ensures the token is intended for the correct audience.
- **ValidateLifetime**: Validates that the token has not expired.
- **ValidateIssuerSigningKey**: Validates that the token is signed with a

ADVANCED AUTHENTICATION AND AUTHORIZATION TECHNIQUES

valid key.

Step 3: Generate JWTs

You need to create a method to generate JWTs upon user login. Here is an example of how to create a token:

```csharp
Copy code
public string GenerateJWT(User user)
{
    var claims = new[]
    {
        new Claim(JwtRegisteredClaimNames.Sub, user.Email),
        new Claim(JwtRegisteredClaimNames.Jti,
        Guid.NewGuid().ToString()),
        new Claim("Role", user.Role) // Custom claim
    };

    var key = new SymmetricSecurityKey(Encoding.UTF8.GetBytes(Configuration["Jwt:Key"]));
    var creds = new SigningCredentials(key,
    SecurityAlgorithms.HmacSha256);

    var token = new JwtSecurityToken(
        issuer: Configuration["Jwt:Issuer"],
        audience: Configuration["Jwt:Audience"],
        claims: claims,
        expires: DateTime.Now.AddMinutes(30),
        signingCredentials: creds);

    return new JwtSecurityTokenHandler().WriteToken(token);
}
```

In this method:

- Claims are created to store user information.
- A symmetric security key is created using a secret key from the

configuration.
- A JwtSecurityToken is created with an expiration time, issuer, audience, and signing credentials.

Step 4: Protecting Your API Endpoints

Once JWT authentication is set up, you can protect your API endpoints by using the [Authorize] attribute:

```csharp
Copy code
[Authorize]
[HttpGet("protected")]
public IActionResult ProtectedEndpoint()
{
    return Ok("You are authorized to access this endpoint.");
}
```

This action will only be accessible to users with a valid JWT.

3. Best Practices for Using JWTs and Bearer Tokens

To ensure the security and efficiency of your API when using JWTs and bearer tokens, consider the following best practices:

- **Use HTTPS**: Always use HTTPS to prevent token interception during transmission.
- **Keep Tokens Short-Lived**: Limit the lifespan of your tokens to reduce the impact of stolen tokens. Use refresh tokens if necessary to allow users to obtain new tokens without re-authentication.
- **Implement Token Revocation**: While JWTs are stateless, implement a mechanism to revoke tokens, such as a token blacklist or changing user passwords.
- **Use Strong Secrets**: Ensure that your signing keys are complex and kept secure. Consider using a secure key management solution.
- **Validate Tokens Properly**: Always validate the token on each request and check claims to enforce authorization.

ADVANCED AUTHENTICATION AND AUTHORIZATION TECHNIQUES

- **Limit Token Scope:** Use claims to limit the scope of what actions the bearer token can perform, especially in sensitive operations.
- **Implement Logging and Monitoring**: Log authentication attempts and monitor for unusual activity, such as multiple failed login attempts or token misuse.

4. Handling Token Expiration and Refreshing Tokens

Token expiration is an important aspect of security. Once a token has expired, it should no longer be accepted for authentication. To maintain user sessions without requiring frequent re-login, implement a refresh token mechanism.

Step 1: Generate Refresh Tokens

Alongside your JWT, generate a refresh token that can be used to obtain new access tokens without re-authenticating the user. Store this refresh token securely, typically in a database.

```csharp
Copy code
public string GenerateRefreshToken()
{
    var randomNumber = new byte[32];
    using (var rng = RandomNumberGenerator.Create())
    {
        rng.GetBytes(randomNumber);
        return Convert.ToBase64String(randomNumber);
    }
}
```

Step 2: Refreshing Access Tokens

Create an endpoint for refreshing tokens:

```csharp
Copy code
[HttpPost("refresh-token")]
public IActionResult RefreshToken
```

```
([FromBody] RefreshTokenRequest request)
{
    var user = ValidateRefreshToken(request.RefreshToken);
    if (user == null)
    {
        return Unauthorized();
    }

    var newJwt = GenerateJWT(user);
    var newRefreshToken = GenerateRefreshToken();

    // Store new refresh token in the database...

    return Ok(new { Token = newJwt,
RefreshToken = newRefreshToken });
}
```

In this endpoint, validate the provided refresh token and, if valid, generate a new JWT and a new refresh token.

Securing APIs with JWT and bearer tokens is a powerful strategy that enhances the security and flexibility of your application. By implementing JWT authentication, you can provide secure access to your APIs while maintaining a seamless user experience. Following best practices and implementing token management strategies, such as token expiration and refresh tokens, will further protect your application from unauthorized access. In the subsequent sections, we will explore additional strategies for enhancing security, such as integrating OAuth and OpenID Connect for comprehensive authentication solutions.

Integrating External Login Providers (e.g., Google, Facebook, Microsoft)

Integrating external login providers into your ASP.NET Core application allows users to authenticate using their existing accounts from

ADVANCED AUTHENTICATION AND AUTHORIZATION TECHNIQUES

popular services such as Google, Facebook, and Microsoft. This not only enhances user convenience by reducing the need to create new accounts but also improves security through established authentication mechanisms. In this section, we will explore how to set up and configure external login providers in an ASP.NET Core application, ensuring a smooth integration process.

1. Understanding External Authentication

External authentication enables users to log in using their credentials from trusted third-party providers. This process typically involves redirecting users to the provider's login page, where they authenticate. Upon successful authentication, the provider redirects users back to your application with a token or code that can be exchanged for user information.

Advantages of External Authentication:
- **User Convenience**: Users can log in quickly using accounts they already have.
- **Security**: Relying on established providers can reduce the risk associated with storing user credentials.
- **Reduced Friction**: Fewer account creation barriers can lead to higher user conversion rates.

2. Setting Up Google Authentication

To set up Google authentication, you need to register your application with the Google Developer Console and configure your ASP.NET Core application.

Step 1: Register Your Application with Google

1. Go to the Google Developer Console.
2. Create a new project.
3. Navigate to "Credentials" and click on "Create credentials."
4. Select "OAuth client ID."
5. Configure the consent screen by providing the necessary details.

6. Choose "Web application" as the application type.
7. Add your redirect URI (e.g., https://localhost:5001/signin-google).
8. Note the **Client ID** and **Client Secret** generated for your application.

Step 2: Configure Google Authentication in ASP.NET Core

In your Startup.cs file, add the Google authentication services:

```csharp
Copy code
public void ConfigureServices(IServiceCollection services)
{
    services.AddAuthentication(options =>
    {
        options.DefaultScheme =
        CookieAuthenticationDefaults.AuthenticationScheme;
        options.DefaultChallengeScheme =
        GoogleDefaults.AuthenticationScheme;
    })
    .AddCookie()
    .AddGoogle(options =>
    {
        options.ClientId =
        Configuration["Authentication:Google:ClientId"];
        options.ClientSecret =
        Configuration["Authentication:Google:ClientSecret"];
    });

    services.AddControllersWithViews();
}
```

In this code, we configure authentication to use cookies for local sessions and Google for external logins. The Client ID and Client Secret should be stored in the appsettings.json file:

```json
Copy code
```

ADVANCED AUTHENTICATION AND AUTHORIZATION TECHNIQUES

```
{
  "Authentication": {
    "Google": {
      "ClientId": "your-client-id",
      "ClientSecret": "your-client-secret"
    }
  }
}
```

Step 3: Create a Login Action

Create a controller action to initiate the Google login process:

```csharp
Copy code
public class AccountController : Controller
{
    [HttpGet("login")]
    public IActionResult Login(string returnUrl = null)
    {
        ViewData["ReturnUrl"] = returnUrl;
        return View();
    }

    [HttpPost("login")]
    public IActionResult Login(LoginViewModel model, string returnUrl = null)
    {
        // Perform local login or redirect to external login
        return LocalRedirect(returnUrl ?? "/");
    }

    [HttpGet("signin-google")]
    public IActionResult GoogleLogin(string returnUrl = null)
    {
        var redirectUrl = Url.Action("GoogleResponse", "Account", new { returnUrl });
        var properties = new AuthenticationProperties { RedirectUri = redirectUrl };
```

```csharp
        return Challenge(properties,
        GoogleDefaults.AuthenticationScheme);
    }

    [HttpGet("google-response")]
    public async Task<IActionResult>
GoogleResponse(string returnUrl = null)
    {
        var result = await HttpContext.AuthenticateAsync
(CookieAuthenticationDefaults.AuthenticationScheme);
        if (!result.Succeeded)
        {
            return RedirectToAction(nameof(Login));
        }

        var claims = result.Principal.Claims.ToList();
        // Retrieve user information and create or update user
        record...

        return LocalRedirect(returnUrl ?? "/");
    }
}
```

In this code:

- The GoogleLogin action initiates the login process.
- The GoogleResponse action processes the authentication response from Google, retrieves user claims, and handles user creation or updating.

3. Setting Up Facebook Authentication

Integrating Facebook authentication involves similar steps to Google but requires registration with Facebook.

Step 1: Register Your Application with Facebook

1. Go to the Facebook for Developers page.
2. Create a new app and set it up for Facebook Login.

ADVANCED AUTHENTICATION AND AUTHORIZATION TECHNIQUES

3. Configure the app settings and add the redirect URI (e.g., https://localhost:5001/signin-facebook).
4. Note the **App ID** and **App Secret**.

Step 2: Configure Facebook Authentication in ASP.NET Core
Add Facebook authentication in your Startup.cs file:

```csharp
Copy code
public void ConfigureServices(IServiceCollection services)
{
    services.AddAuthentication(options =>
    {
        options.DefaultScheme = CookieAuthenticationDefaults.AuthenticationScheme;
        options.DefaultChallengeScheme = FacebookDefaults.AuthenticationScheme;
    })
    .AddCookie()
    .AddFacebook(options =>
    {
        options.AppId = Configuration["Authentication:Facebook:AppId"];
        options.AppSecret = Configuration["Authentication:Facebook:AppSecret"];
    });

    services.AddControllersWithViews();
}
```

In the appsettings.json file, include:

```json
Copy code
{
  "Authentication": {
    "Facebook": {
```

```
      "AppId": "your-app-id",
      "AppSecret": "your-app-secret"
    }
  }
}
```

Step 3: Create the Facebook Login Action

You can create similar controller actions for Facebook as you did for Google:

```csharp
[HttpGet("signin-facebook")]
public IActionResult FacebookLogin(string returnUrl = null)
{
    var redirectUrl = Url.Action("FacebookResponse", "Account",
    new { returnUrl });
    var properties = new AuthenticationProperties
{ RedirectUri = redirectUrl };
    return Challenge(properties,
    FacebookDefaults.AuthenticationScheme);
}

[HttpGet("facebook-response")]
public async Task<IActionResult>
 FacebookResponse(string returnUrl = null)
{
    var result = await HttpContext.AuthenticateAsync
(CookieAuthenticationDefaults.AuthenticationScheme);
    if (!result.Succeeded)
    {
        return RedirectToAction(nameof(Login));
    }

    var claims = result.Principal.Claims.ToList();
    // Retrieve user information and create
or update user record...
```

ADVANCED AUTHENTICATION AND AUTHORIZATION TECHNIQUES

```
    return LocalRedirect(returnUrl ?? "/");
}
```

4. Setting Up Microsoft Authentication

Integrating Microsoft account authentication requires similar registration with the Microsoft Azure portal.

Step 1: Register Your Application with Microsoft

1. Go to the Azure Portal and register a new application.
2. Set up the application for Microsoft identity platform, enabling the appropriate permissions.
3. Add the redirect URI (e.g., https://localhost:5001/signin-microsoft).
4. Note the **Application (client) ID** and **Directory (tenant) ID**.

Step 2: Configure Microsoft Authentication in ASP.NET Core

Add Microsoft authentication in your Startup.cs file:

```csharp
Copy code
public void ConfigureServices(IServiceCollection services)
{
    services.AddAuthentication(options =>
    {
        options.DefaultScheme =
        CookieAuthenticationDefaults.AuthenticationScheme;
        options.DefaultChallengeScheme =
        MicrosoftAccountDefaults.AuthenticationScheme;
    })
    .AddCookie()
    .AddMicrosoftAccount(options =>
    {
        options.ClientId =
        Configuration["Authentication:Microsoft:ClientId"];
        options.ClientSecret =
        Configuration["Authentication:Microsoft:ClientSecret"];
    });
```

```
    services.AddControllersWithViews();
}
```

Update your appsettings.json:

```json
Copy code
{
  "Authentication": {
    "Microsoft": {
      "ClientId": "your-client-id",
      "ClientSecret": "your-client-secret"
    }
  }
}
```

Step 3: Create the Microsoft Login Action

Similar to the previous providers, create actions for Microsoft authentication:

```csharp
Copy code
[HttpGet("signin-microsoft")]
public IActionResult MicrosoftLogin(string returnUrl = null)
{
    var redirectUrl = Url.Action
("MicrosoftResponse", "Account", new { returnUrl });
    var properties = new AuthenticationProperties { RedirectUri
    = redirectUrl };
    return Challenge(properties,
    MicrosoftAccountDefaults.AuthenticationScheme);
}

[HttpGet("microsoft-response")]
public async Task<IActionResult>
 MicrosoftResponse(string returnUrl = null)
```

ADVANCED AUTHENTICATION AND AUTHORIZATION TECHNIQUES

```csharp
{
    var result = await HttpContext.AuthenticateAsync(CookieAuthenticationDefaults.AuthenticationScheme);
    if (!result.Succeeded)
    {
        return RedirectToAction(nameof(Login));
    }

    var claims = result.Principal.Claims.ToList();
    // Retrieve user information and create or update user record...

    return LocalRedirect(returnUrl ?? "/");
}
```

5. Handling User Information and Claims

When users authenticate via external providers, you will typically want to retrieve additional user information, such as their email address and name. This information is available through claims.

You can access claims in the response action, as shown in the examples above. Typically, you will create or update a user in your application's database based on the external authentication result.

```csharp
Copy code
var email = claims.FirstOrDefault(c => c.Type == ClaimTypes.Email)?.Value;
var name = claims.FirstOrDefault(c => c.Type == ClaimTypes.Name)?.Value;

// Check if the user already exists
var user = await _userManager.FindByEmailAsync(email);
if (user == null)
{
    user = new ApplicationUser { UserName = email, Email = email, FullName = name };
    await _userManager.CreateAsync(user);
```

```
}

// Sign in the user
await _signInManager.SignInAsync(user,
 isPersistent: false);
```

Integrating external login providers such as Google, Facebook, and Microsoft into your ASP.NET Core application enhances user experience by providing convenient and secure authentication options. By following the outlined steps, you can easily configure your application to utilize these external authentication mechanisms. This not only streamlines the login process for users but also leverages the security features of established identity providers, significantly reducing the risks associated with user credential management. In subsequent sections, we will explore advanced features in ASP.NET Core Identity and how to customize authentication flows further.

Advanced Topics: Two-Factor Authentication and Social Logins

As web applications continue to evolve, the need for robust security measures becomes increasingly important. Two-factor authentication (2FA) and social logins are two advanced techniques that enhance the security and user experience of your ASP.NET Core applications. This section will explore how to implement these features effectively.

1. Understanding Two-Factor Authentication (2FA)

Two-factor authentication adds an extra layer of security to the authentication process by requiring users to provide two different types of information to verify their identity. This typically includes something the user knows (like a password) and something the user has (like a mobile device for receiving a one-time code).

Benefits of 2FA:

ADVANCED AUTHENTICATION AND AUTHORIZATION TECHNIQUES

- **Enhanced Security**: Even if a password is compromised, the second factor protects against unauthorized access.
- **User Trust**: Users feel more secure knowing that additional verification is required.
- **Compliance**: Many regulatory frameworks require multi-factor authentication for sensitive applications.

2. Implementing Two-Factor Authentication in ASP.NET Core

ASP.NET Core Identity provides built-in support for 2FA, allowing developers to easily enable it in their applications. The most common methods for 2FA include SMS, email, and authenticator apps like Google Authenticator.

Step 1: Configure 2FA in Startup.cs

First, ensure that your application is set up to support 2FA. In your Startup.cs, you need to configure Identity services:

```csharp
Copy code
public void ConfigureServices(IServiceCollection services)
{
    services.AddIdentity<ApplicationUser, IdentityRole>(options =>
    {
        // Password settings
        options.Password.RequireDigit = true;
        options.Password.RequireLowercase = true;
        options.Password.RequireNonAlphanumeric = true;
        options.Password.RequireUppercase = true;
        options.Password.RequiredLength = 6;

        // Lockout settings
        options.Lockout.AllowedForNewUsers = true;
        options.Lockout.MaxFailedAccessAttempts = 5;
        options.Lockout.DefaultLockoutTimeSpan =
        TimeSpan.FromMinutes(5);
    })
```

```
    .AddEntityFrameworkStores<ApplicationDbContext>()
    .AddDefaultTokenProviders();

    services.AddControllersWithViews();
}
```

Step 2: Enable 2FA for Users

Users must opt into 2FA. You can provide an interface for users to enable this feature in their account settings.

Example: Account Controller Method to Enable 2FA

```csharp
Copy code
[HttpPost]
[ValidateAntiForgeryToken]
public async Task<IActionResult> Enable2FA()
{
    var user = await _userManager.GetUserAsync(User);
    var enable2FAResult = await
    _userManager.SetTwoFactorEnabledAsync(user, true);

    if (enable2FAResult.Succeeded)
    {
        // Notify user and redirect
        return RedirectToAction("Index");
    }

    return View("Error");
}
```

Step 3: Sending Two-Factor Codes

To send a 2FA code, you can use email or SMS. The following example uses an authenticator app (such as Google Authenticator) to generate a code.

Example: Generate and Display 2FA Code

```csharp
Copy code
public async Task<IActionResult> Generate2FACode()
{
    var user = await _userManager.GetUserAsync(User);
    var authenticatorKey = await _userManager.GetTwoFactorAuthenticatorKeyAsync(user);

    var model = new TwoFactorAuthenticationViewModel
    {
        AuthenticatorKey = authenticatorKey,
        // Display the QR code here for the authenticator app
    };

    return View(model);
}
```

Step 4: Validating the 2FA Code

When the user attempts to log in, you need to validate the provided 2FA code:

```csharp
Copy code
public async Task<IActionResult> Validate2FACode(string code)
{
    var user = await _userManager.GetUserAsync(User);
    var result = await _userManager.VerifyTwoFactorTokenAsync(user, _userManager.Options.Tokens.AuthenticatorTokenProvider, code);

    if (result)
    {
        // Log the user in
        await _signInManager.SignInAsync(user, isPersistent: false);
        return RedirectToAction("Index", "Home");
    }
```

```
        ModelState.AddModelError(string.Empty, "Invalid two-factor
        code.");
        return View();
}
```

3. Understanding Social Logins

Social logins allow users to authenticate using their accounts from social media platforms, such as Google, Facebook, or Twitter. This method simplifies the registration and login processes, allowing users to bypass traditional account creation forms.

Benefits of Social Logins:

- **User Convenience**: Users can log in quickly without needing to remember multiple passwords.
- **Access to Rich User Profiles**: Social logins can provide additional profile information, enhancing the user experience.
- **Increased Sign-Ups:** Reduces barriers to entry, leading to higher conversion rates.

4. Implementing Social Logins

Incorporating social logins into your ASP.NET Core application is straightforward, as discussed in the previous sections. Ensure you have registered your application with the respective social media provider to obtain the necessary credentials.

Step 1: Configure Social Logins in Startup.cs

You must add the authentication services for each social login provider in your Startup.cs:

```csharp
Copy code
services.AddAuthentication()
    .AddGoogle(options =>
```

ADVANCED AUTHENTICATION AND AUTHORIZATION TECHNIQUES

```
{
    options.ClientId =
    Configuration["Authentication:Google:ClientId"];
    options.ClientSecret =
    Configuration["Authentication:Google:ClientSecret"];
})
.AddFacebook(options =>
{
    options.AppId =
    Configuration["Authentication:Facebook:AppId"];
    options.AppSecret =
    Configuration["Authentication:Facebook:AppSecret"];
});
```

Step 2: Create Login Actions for Social Logins

You will need to create specific actions in your account controller to handle logins via these providers:

```csharp
Copy code
[HttpGet("signin-google")]
public IActionResult GoogleLogin(string returnUrl = null)
{
    var redirectUrl = Url.Action
("GoogleResponse", "Account", new { returnUrl });
    var properties =
new AuthenticationProperties
{ RedirectUri = redirectUrl };
    return Challenge(properties,
    GoogleDefaults.AuthenticationScheme);
}
```

This action will initiate the authentication flow for Google, as shown in previous examples.

5. Best Practices for 2FA and Social Logins

- **User Education**: Educate users on the importance of enabling 2FA and the benefits of social logins.

- **Security Checks**: Regularly review and audit your authentication mechanisms to identify vulnerabilities.
- **Fallback Options**: Provide fallback options for users who may not have access to their second factor (e.g., backup codes).
- **Monitor Login Activity**: Implement logging and monitoring for unusual login patterns or failed login attempts.

Implementing two-factor authentication and social logins in your ASP.NET Core application significantly enhances security and user experience. By leveraging these advanced authentication techniques, you can protect user accounts more effectively while making the login process more convenient. As you continue to develop your application, consider these strategies to improve both security and usability, ensuring a more secure environment for your users. In the following sections, we will explore additional advanced topics in ASP.NET Core, focusing on optimizing application performance and enhancing user experience.

Building RESTful APIs and Integrating Web APIs

Introduction to RESTful Services in ASP.NET Core 3

In today's web-driven world, the demand for robust, scalable, and maintainable APIs is at an all-time high. RESTful services have emerged as a preferred architectural style for building web APIs due to their simplicity, scalability, and statelessness. ASP.NET Core 3 provides a powerful framework for creating RESTful services that can handle a wide array of applications, from web apps to mobile applications. In this chapter, we will explore the principles of REST, the advantages of using ASP.NET Core for building RESTful APIs, and how to implement these services effectively.

1. Understanding REST Architecture

REST, which stands for Representational State Transfer, is an architectural style designed for networked applications. It leverages HTTP methods, URIs, and stateless communication, promoting a clear separation between the client and server. RESTful services are based on a few key principles:

- **Statelessness**: Each request from a client contains all the information needed to process that request. The server does not store any session state related to the client, leading to a simpler and more scalable architecture.

- **Resource Identification**: Resources are identified through URIs (Uniform Resource Identifiers). Each resource is represented by a unique URL, making it easy for clients to interact with specific resources.
- **Use of Standard HTTP Methods**: RESTful APIs utilize standard HTTP methods to perform operations on resources:
- **GET**: Retrieve data from the server.
- **POST**: Create a new resource.
- **PUT**: Update an existing resource.
- **DELETE**: Remove a resource.
- **Representation of Resources**: Resources can be represented in multiple formats, including JSON, XML, or HTML. JSON has become the most popular format for APIs due to its lightweight nature and ease of use with JavaScript.
- **HATEOAS (Hypermedia as the Engine of Application State)**: Clients interact with the application entirely through hypermedia provided dynamically by the server, allowing the server to guide the client through the available actions and state transitions.

2. Advantages of Building RESTful Services with ASP.NET Core

ASP.NET Core is a cross-platform, high-performance framework for building modern, cloud-based, internet-connected applications. When it comes to creating RESTful services, ASP.NET Core offers several advantages:

- **Performance**: ASP.NET Core is designed to be fast and efficient, supporting high throughput and low latency. It utilizes the Kestrel web server, which is optimized for performance.
- **Cross-Platform**: ASP.NET Core can run on Windows, macOS, and Linux, making it a flexible choice for deploying RESTful services in various environments.
- **Modular and Lightweight**: The framework allows developers to include only the necessary libraries and dependencies, reducing the

application's footprint and enhancing performance.
- **Built-In Support for Dependency Injection**: ASP.NET Core has a built-in dependency injection (DI) system, promoting a cleaner architecture and easier testing.
- **Integration with Entity Framework Core**: For data access, ASP.NET Core seamlessly integrates with Entity Framework Core, providing a powerful ORM for managing database interactions.
- **Comprehensive Middleware Pipeline**: The middleware pipeline in ASP.NET Core allows for easy configuration of cross-cutting concerns such as logging, authentication, and error handling.

3. Designing a RESTful API

When designing a RESTful API, it is essential to follow best practices to ensure that the API is intuitive, consistent, and easy to use. Here are some key considerations:

1. Resource Naming Conventions

- Use nouns to represent resources (e.g., /products, /customers).
- Use plural nouns to represent collections (e.g., /products for a collection of products).
- Avoid verbs in URLs; instead, use HTTP methods to define actions.

2. Versioning

Version your API to manage changes and ensure backward compatibility. Common versioning strategies include:

- **URI Versioning**: Include the version number in the URI (e.g., /api/v1/products).
- **Query Parameter Versioning**: Use a query parameter to specify the version (e.g., /api/products?v=1).
- **Header Versioning**: Include the version in the request header (e.g., Accept: application/vnd.myapi.v1+json).

3. HTTP Status Codes

Use standard HTTP status codes to indicate the outcome of API requests:

- **200 OK**: Successful request.
- **201 Created**: Resource successfully created.
- **204 No Content**: Successful request with no content (e.g., deletion).
- **400 Bad Request**: Invalid request format or parameters.
- **404 Not Found**: Resource not found.
- **500 Internal Server Error**: Unexpected server error.

4. Pagination and Filtering

For endpoints that return large collections of resources, implement pagination and filtering to enhance performance and user experience. Common strategies include:

- **Pagination**: Use query parameters to control the page size and number (e.g., /products?page=2&pageSize=10).
- **Filtering**: Allow users to filter results based on specific criteria (e.g., /products?category=electronics).

4. Implementing a Simple RESTful API in ASP.NET Core 3

Now that we have a solid understanding of RESTful services and their advantages in ASP.NET Core, let's walk through the implementation of a simple RESTful API.

Step 1: Creating the ASP.NET Core Project

1. Open a terminal or command prompt.
2. Create a new ASP.NET Core Web API project:

```bash
Copy code
```

BUILDING RESTFUL APIS AND INTEGRATING WEB APIS

```
dotnet new webapi -n MyRestfulApi
cd MyRestfulApi
```

1. Open the project in your preferred IDE.

Step 2: Defining the Model

Define a simple model class to represent a resource. For example, let's create a Product class:

```csharp
Copy code
public class Product
{
    public int Id { get; set; }
    public string Name { get; set; }
    public decimal Price { get; set; }
}
```

Step 3: Creating the Repository

Create a simple repository to manage products. For the sake of this example, we'll use an in-memory list:

```csharp
Copy code
public interface IProductRepository
{
    IEnumerable<Product> GetAllProducts();
    Product GetProductById(int id);
    void AddProduct(Product product);
    void UpdateProduct(Product product);
    void DeleteProduct(int id);
}

public class InMemoryProductRepository : IProductRepository
{
```

```csharp
    private readonly List<Product> _products = new 
    List<Product>();

    public IEnumerable<Product> GetAllProducts() => _products;

    public Product GetProductById(int id) =>
    _products.FirstOrDefault(p => p.Id == id);

    public void AddProduct(Product product)
    {
        product.Id = _products.Count + 1;
        _products.Add(product);
    }

    public void UpdateProduct(Product product)
    {
        var existingProduct = GetProductById(product.Id);
        if (existingProduct != null)
        {
            existingProduct.Name = product.Name;
            existingProduct.Price = product.Price;
        }
    }

    public void DeleteProduct(int id)
    {
        var product = GetProductById(id);
        if (product != null)
        {
            _products.Remove(product);
        }
    }
}
```

Step 4: Setting Up the Controller

Create a controller to handle HTTP requests related to products:

BUILDING RESTFUL APIS AND INTEGRATING WEB APIS

```csharp
Copy code
[ApiController]
[Route("api/[controller]")]
public class ProductsController : ControllerBase
{
    private readonly IProductRepository _repository;

    public ProductsController(IProductRepository repository)
    {
        _repository = repository;
    }

    [HttpGet]
    public IActionResult GetProducts()
    {
        var products = _repository.GetAllProducts();
        return Ok(products);
    }

    [HttpGet("{id}")]
    public IActionResult GetProduct(int id)
    {
        var product = _repository.GetProductById(id);
        if (product == null) return NotFound();
        return Ok(product);
    }

    [HttpPost]
    public IActionResult CreateProduct([FromBody] Product product)
    {
        _repository.AddProduct(product);
        return CreatedAtAction(nameof(GetProduct), new { id = product.Id }, product);
    }

    [HttpPut("{id}")]
    public IActionResult UpdateProduct(int id, [FromBody] Product product)
```

```csharp
    {
        product.Id = id;
        _repository.UpdateProduct(product);
        return NoContent();
    }

    [HttpDelete("{id}")]
    public IActionResult DeleteProduct(int id)
    {
        _repository.DeleteProduct(id);
        return NoContent();
    }
}
```

Step 5: Registering the Repository in Startup.cs

To enable dependency injection for the repository, register it in the Startup.cs file:

```csharp
Copy code
public void ConfigureServices(IServiceCollection services)
{
    services.AddControllers();
    services.AddSingleton<IProductRepository,
    InMemoryProductRepository>();
}
```

Step 6: Running the API

Run the application:

```bash
Copy code
dotnet run
```

Use a tool like Postman or a web browser to test the API endpoints (e.g., http://localhost:5000/api/products).

Building RESTful services with ASP.NET Core 3 provides a flexible and powerful approach to developing APIs that are scalable, maintainable, and easy to use. By adhering to REST principles and leveraging the features of ASP.NET Core, developers can create robust APIs that serve a wide variety of applications. As you continue to develop your APIs, consider best practices in design, security, and performance to ensure a great experience for your users. In the next sections, we will delve deeper into integrating third-party APIs and securing your RESTful services.

Creating Controllers for API Endpoints

In ASP.NET Core, controllers are pivotal in managing the flow of data between the client and the server for your web applications and APIs. They handle incoming requests, interact with the data model, and return the appropriate responses. This section will guide you through creating controllers for API endpoints, including the principles of routing, handling various HTTP methods, and managing responses effectively.

1. Understanding Controllers in ASP.NET Core

In ASP.NET Core MVC, a controller is a class that handles HTTP requests and returns HTTP responses. Each controller typically corresponds to a specific resource or set of related resources. The core responsibilities of a controller include:

- **Routing Requests**: Identifying which requests should be handled by the controller.
- **Processing Input**: Handling incoming data from requests.
- **Interacting with Models**: Using services and repositories to manipulate data.
- **Returning Responses**: Formatting and sending back responses to the client.

Controllers in ASP.NET Core derive from the ControllerBase class, which provides essential functionalities for API development.

2. Setting Up a New Controller

To create a controller in an ASP.NET Core application, follow these steps:

Step 1: Create a New Controller Class

In your project, create a new folder called Controllers if it doesn't already exist. Inside this folder, create a new class file named ProductsController.cs.

```csharp
Copy code
using Microsoft.AspNetCore.Mvc;
using System.Collections.Generic;

namespace MyRestfulApi.Controllers
{
    [ApiController]
    [Route("api/[controller]")]
    public class ProductsController : ControllerBase
    {
        // Dependency injection of a product service or
        repository will go here
    }
}
```

Step 2: Define the Constructor and Dependencies

In the constructor, you will inject any services or repositories needed to handle data operations. For this example, let's assume we have an IProductRepository:

```csharp
Copy code
private readonly IProductRepository _repository;

public ProductsController(IProductRepository repository)
```

```
{
    _repository = repository;
}
```

3. Creating API Endpoints

Now that we have a basic structure for our controller, let's implement the actual API endpoints. Each method in the controller corresponds to a specific HTTP method and operation.

1. GET: Retrieve All Products

To retrieve a list of all products, implement the following endpoint:

```csharp
Copy code
[HttpGet]
public IActionResult GetAllProducts()
{
    var products = _repository.GetAllProducts();
    return Ok(products);
}
```

In this method:

- HttpGet indicates that this method responds to GET requests.
- Ok(products) returns an HTTP 200 status code along with the list of products.

2. GET: Retrieve a Product by ID

To get a specific product, use the following method:

```csharp
Copy code
[HttpGet("{id}")]
public IActionResult GetProductById(int id)
{
```

```csharp
    var product = _repository.GetProductById(id);
    if (product == null)
    {
        return NotFound(); // Returns 404 if the product is not
        found
    }
    return Ok(product); // Returns the product with a 200 status
}
```

Here:

- {id} in the route specifies that this method takes a parameter.
- NotFound() returns a 404 status if the product is not found.

3. POST: Create a New Product

For adding a new product, implement the following:

```csharp
Copy code
[HttpPost]
public IActionResult CreateProduct([FromBody] Product product)
{
    if (product == null)
    {
        return BadRequest(); // Returns 400 if the request body
        is null
    }

    _repository.AddProduct(product);
    return CreatedAtAction(nameof(GetProductById), new { id =
    product.Id }, product);
}
```

In this method:

- FromBody indicates that the product object will be deserialized from the request body.

BUILDING RESTFUL APIS AND INTEGRATING WEB APIS

- CreatedAtAction returns a 201 status code and includes a link to the newly created resource.

4. PUT: Update an Existing Product

To update an existing product, use the following:

```csharp
Copy code
[HttpPut("{id}")]
public IActionResult UpdateProduct(int id, [FromBody] Product product)
{
    if (product == null || product.Id != id)
    {
        return BadRequest(); // Returns 400 if the product is
        null or IDs do not match
    }

    _repository.UpdateProduct(product);
    return NoContent(); // Returns 204 if the update is
    successful
}
```

In this method:

- NoContent() returns a 204 status code, indicating the update was successful but no content is returned.

5. DELETE: Remove a Product

To delete a product, implement the following method:

```csharp
Copy code
[HttpDelete("{id}")]
public IActionResult DeleteProduct(int id)
{
```

```
    _repository.DeleteProduct(id);
    return NoContent(); // Returns 204 if deletion is successful
}
```

This method returns a 204 status code after successfully deleting the specified product.

4. Handling Errors and Validation
Error Handling

Proper error handling is crucial for any API. You can enhance your controller by implementing global error handling and validating input data.

- **Global Error Handling**: Use middleware to catch unhandled exceptions and return appropriate HTTP responses.
- **Model Validation**: Use data annotations on your model classes to enforce validation rules, and check ModelState.IsValid in your action methods.

Example of Model Validation:

```csharp
Copy code
public class Product
{
    public int Id { get; set; }

    [Required]
    [StringLength(100, MinimumLength = 3)]
    public string Name { get; set; }

    [Range(0.01, double.MaxValue, ErrorMessage = "Price must be greater than zero.")]
    public decimal Price { get; set; }
}
```

In your controller method, check if the model state is valid:

```csharp
Copy code
if (!ModelState.IsValid)
{
    return BadRequest(ModelState); // Returns 400 with
    validation errors
}
```

5. Testing Your API Endpoints

After implementing your controller, you should thoroughly test the API endpoints to ensure they function correctly. Here are some popular methods for testing:

- **Postman**: A powerful API testing tool that allows you to send requests and view responses easily.
- **cURL**: A command-line tool for making HTTP requests.
- **Unit Tests**: Write unit tests using a testing framework (e.g., xUnit, NUnit) to ensure each endpoint behaves as expected.

Example of Testing a GET Endpoint Using Postman:

1. Open Postman and create a new GET request.
2. Enter the URL for your API (e.g., http://localhost:5000/api/products).
3. Click "Send" to see the response.

Creating controllers for API endpoints in ASP.NET Core is a straightforward process that empowers developers to build robust and maintainable RESTful services. By defining clear routes, handling various HTTP methods, and managing responses appropriately, you can create an intuitive API for your clients. Remember to incorporate error handling, validation, and thorough testing to ensure your API is reliable and user-friendly. In the next sections, we will explore advanced topics such as securing your API and integrating third-party services.

Using Attributes to Structure and Secure API Endpoints

In ASP.NET Core, attributes play a crucial role in defining the behavior of controllers and their actions, providing a clean and declarative way to configure API endpoints. Attributes enable developers to specify routing, apply filters, enforce authorization, and define response formats directly at the method level. In this section, we will explore various attributes used in ASP.NET Core for structuring and securing API endpoints, ensuring that your application remains well-organized and secure.

1. Understanding Routing Attributes

ASP.NET Core allows developers to define routes directly in the controller using routing attributes. This approach leads to more intuitive and readable code. The main routing attributes include:

- **[Route]**: Specifies the base route for a controller or action method.
- **[HttpGet]**, **[HttpPost]**, **[HttpPut]**, **[HttpDelete]**: Specifies the HTTP method for the action.

Example of Using Routing Attributes:

```csharp
Copy code
[ApiController]
[Route("api/[controller]")]
public class ProductsController : ControllerBase
{
    [HttpGet]
    public IActionResult GetAllProducts() { /* Implementation */ }

    [HttpGet("{id}")]
```

```
    public IActionResult GetProductById(int id) { /*
    Implementation */ }

    [HttpPost]
    public IActionResult CreateProduct([FromBody] Product
    product) { /* Implementation */ }

    [HttpPut("{id}")]
    public IActionResult UpdateProduct(int id, [FromBody]
    Product product) { /* Implementation */ }

    [HttpDelete("{id}")]
    public IActionResult DeleteProduct(int id) { /*
    Implementation */ }
}
```

In this example, the [Route] attribute defines a base path for all actions in the ProductsController, and specific methods define the HTTP verbs they respond to.

2. Route Constraints

Route constraints can be used to restrict the types of values accepted in route parameters. This can enhance the clarity and reliability of your API. You can apply constraints directly in the route template.

Example of Using Route Constraints:

```csharp
Copy code
[HttpGet("{id:int}")]
public IActionResult GetProductById(int id) { /* Implementation
*/ }
```

In this example, the route will only match if the id parameter is an integer. If a non-integer is provided, a 404 Not Found response will be returned automatically.

Common Route Constraints:

- int: Matches an integer.
- double: Matches a double.
- bool: Matches a boolean.
- string: Matches a string (default).
- minlength, maxlength: Specifies minimum and maximum lengths for strings.

3. Applying Filters with Attributes

Filters in ASP.NET Core provide a way to run code before or after certain stages in the request processing pipeline. ASP.NET Core offers several built-in filter attributes that can be applied at both the controller and action level:

- **[ServiceFilter]**: Applies a service filter, allowing you to inject dependencies into your filters.
- **[TypeFilter]**: Similar to ServiceFilter, but allows for more complex instantiation of the filter.
- **[Authorize]**: Enforces authorization policies, ensuring only authorized users can access certain actions.
- **[AllowAnonymous]**: Overrides the Authorize attribute, allowing access without authentication.

Example of Using Filters:

```csharp
csharp
Copy code
[Authorize]
[Route("api/[controller]")]
public class ProductsController : ControllerBase
{
    [HttpGet]
    public IActionResult GetAllProducts() { /* Implementation */ }
```

```
[HttpGet("{id}")]
[AllowAnonymous]
public IActionResult GetProductById(int id) { /*
Implementation */ }
}
```

In this example, the Authorize attribute requires authentication for all actions in the ProductsController, except for GetProductById, which allows anonymous access.

4. Securing API Endpoints with Authorization Attributes

Security is a critical aspect of any API, and ASP.NET Core provides powerful built-in mechanisms for securing endpoints. Using the [Authorize] attribute, you can enforce security policies at the controller or action level.

1. Role-Based Authorization

You can restrict access to specific roles using the Roles parameter:

```csharp
Copy code
[Authorize(Roles = "Admin")]
public IActionResult CreateProduct([FromBody] Product product)
{ /* Implementation */ }
```

This endpoint will only be accessible to users with the "Admin" role.

2. Policy-Based Authorization

ASP.NET Core supports more complex authorization scenarios through policies. You can define a policy in the Startup.cs file and apply it using the [Authorize] attribute:

Defining a Policy:

```csharp
Copy code
```

```csharp
public void ConfigureServices(IServiceCollection services)
{
    services.AddAuthorization(options =>
    {
        options.AddPolicy("RequireAdministratorRole", policy =>
        policy.RequireRole("Admin"));
    });
    // Other services
}
```

Applying a Policy:

```csharp
Copy code
[Authorize(Policy = "RequireAdministratorRole")]
public IActionResult CreateProduct([FromBody] Product product)
{ /* Implementation */ }
```

5. Customizing Responses with Response Attributes

ASP.NET Core allows you to customize the responses returned from your API methods using various response attributes.

- **[Produces]**: Specifies the types of responses the action can produce. You can set content types like application/json or application/xml.
- **[ProducesResponseType]**: Documents the possible HTTP response types, enhancing API documentation generated by tools like Swagger.

Example of Customizing Responses:

```csharp
Copy code
[HttpGet("{id}")]
[Produces("application/json")]
[ProducesResponseType(typeof(Product), StatusCodes.Status200OK)]
[ProducesResponseType(StatusCodes.Status404NotFound)]
```

BUILDING RESTFUL APIS AND INTEGRATING WEB APIS

```csharp
public IActionResult GetProductById(int id)
{
    var product = _repository.GetProductById(id);
    if (product == null) return NotFound();
    return Ok(product);
}
```

In this example, the method specifies that it produces JSON and documents the potential response types.

6. Combining Attributes for Clean API Design

One of the key strengths of using attributes in ASP.NET Core is the ability to combine them for a clean and concise API design. You can mix routing, authorization, and response attributes on your action methods for maximum clarity.

Example of a Well-Structured Action Method:

```csharp
Copy code
[HttpPost]
[Authorize(Roles = "Admin")]
[ProducesResponseType(typeof(Product), StatusCodes.Status201Created)]
[ProducesResponseType(StatusCodes.Status400BadRequest)]
public IActionResult CreateProduct([FromBody] Product product)
{
    if (!ModelState.IsValid)
    {
        return BadRequest(ModelState);
    }

    _repository.AddProduct(product);
    return CreatedAtAction(nameof(GetProductById), new { id = product.Id }, product);
}
```

This method clearly states that it requires admin authorization, produces a specific response type, and includes validation checks, all while maintaining a clean and understandable structure.

Using attributes to structure and secure API endpoints in ASP.NET Core enhances the readability, maintainability, and security of your API. Attributes enable you to clearly define routing, enforce authorization policies, and customize responses in a declarative manner. By following best practices and leveraging these attributes effectively, you can build robust APIs that are easy to navigate and secure. In the next sections, we will explore how to integrate authentication methods and manage user roles effectively within your APIs.

Versioning APIs and Working with OpenAPI/Swagger

As your web application evolves, you will likely need to make changes to your APIs. This could involve adding new features, modifying existing endpoints, or even breaking changes that require careful consideration of how consumers interact with your API. API versioning is a strategy that enables you to manage changes in your API while maintaining backward compatibility for existing clients. Additionally, utilizing OpenAPI (formerly known as Swagger) helps document your API, making it easier for consumers to understand how to interact with it. In this section, we will explore API versioning techniques and how to integrate OpenAPI/Swagger for documentation.

1. Understanding API Versioning

API versioning allows you to introduce changes to your API without disrupting existing clients. There are several strategies for versioning APIs in ASP.NET Core, including:
- **URI Versioning**: Including the version number in the URI.
- **Query String Versioning**: Specifying the version in the query string of the request.
- **Header Versioning**: Using custom headers to specify the API version.
- **Media Type Versioning**: Including the version in the Accept header.

Example of URI Versioning:

```csharp
Copy code
[ApiController]
[Route("api/v{version:apiVersion}/[controller]")]
public class ProductsController : ControllerBase
{
    // Version 1
    [HttpGet]
    [MapToApiVersion("1.0")]
    public IActionResult GetAllProductsV1() { /* Implementation */ }

    // Version 2
    [HttpGet]
    [MapToApiVersion("2.0")]
    public IActionResult GetAllProductsV2() { /* Implementation */ }
}
```

In this example, the URI structure clearly indicates the version of the API being accessed, allowing clients to specify which version they want to interact with.

2. Implementing API Versioning in ASP.NET Core

To implement API versioning in ASP.NET Core, you need to install the Microsoft.AspNetCore.Mvc.Versioning NuGet package. This package provides the necessary functionality to manage API versions.

Step 1: Install the Package

You can install the package using the NuGet Package Manager or by running the following command in the Package Manager Console:

```bash
Copy code
dotnet add package Microsoft.AspNetCore.Mvc.Versioning
```

Step 2: Configure API Versioning in Startup.cs

In the ConfigureServices method of your Startup.cs file, add API versioning services:

```csharp
Copy code
public void ConfigureServices(IServiceCollection services)
{
    services.AddApiVersioning(options =>
    {
        options.ReportApiVersions = true; // Include version information in response headers
        options.AssumeDefaultVersionWhenUnspecified = true; // Set default version
        options.DefaultApiVersion = new ApiVersion(1, 0); // Default version
    });
}
```

Step 3: Using the Versioning Attributes in Controllers

You can now use the [ApiVersion] and [MapToApiVersion] attributes in your controllers to specify versions for each action.

3. Documenting Your API with OpenAPI/Swagger

OpenAPI is a specification that allows you to describe your API's endpoints, request/response types, and other important details. Swagger is a set of tools that implement the OpenAPI specification, providing a user-friendly interface for developers to explore your API.

1. Integrating Swagger in Your ASP.NET Core Application

To integrate Swagger into your ASP.NET Core application, you need to install the Swashbuckle.AspNetCore NuGet package.

Step 1: Install the Package

Use the following command to install the Swagger package:

BUILDING RESTFUL APIS AND INTEGRATING WEB APIS

```bash
Copy code
dotnet add package Swashbuckle.AspNetCore
```

Step 2: Configure Swagger in Startup.cs

In the ConfigureServices method, add Swagger services:

```csharp
Copy code
public void ConfigureServices(IServiceCollection services)
{
    services.AddSwaggerGen(c =>
    {
        c.SwaggerDoc("v1", new OpenApiInfo { Title = "My API",
        Version = "v1" });
        c.SwaggerDoc("v2", new OpenApiInfo { Title = "My API",
        Version = "v2" });
    });
}
```

In the Configure method, enable middleware for serving generated Swagger as a JSON endpoint and the Swagger UI:

```csharp
Copy code
public void Configure(IApplicationBuilder app,
IWebHostEnvironment env)
{
    if (env.IsDevelopment())
    {
        app.UseDeveloperExceptionPage();
    }

    app.UseRouting();

    // Enable middleware to serve generated Swagger as a JSON
    endpoint
```

```
    app.UseSwagger();

    // Enable middleware to serve swagger-ui (HTML, JS, CSS,
    etc.)
    app.UseSwaggerUI(c =>
    {
        c.SwaggerEndpoint("/swagger/v1/swagger.json", "My API
        V1");
        c.SwaggerEndpoint("/swagger/v2/swagger.json", "My API
        V2");
        c.RoutePrefix = string.Empty; // Set Swagger UI at the
        app's root
    });

    app.UseEndpoints(endpoints =>
    {
        endpoints.MapControllers();
    });
}
```

This configuration enables Swagger and Swagger UI, allowing you to view and interact with your API documentation at http://localhost:5000/swagger.

4. Customizing Swagger Documentation

You can enhance the generated Swagger documentation by adding XML comments for your controllers and action methods. To do this, follow these steps:

Step 1: Enable XML Documentation in the Project File

In your .csproj file, add the following property to enable XML documentation generation:

```xml
Copy code
<PropertyGroup>
    <GenerateDocumentationFile>true</GenerateDocumentationFile>
```

BUILDING RESTFUL APIS AND INTEGRATING WEB APIS

```
</PropertyGroup>
```

Step 2: Specify the XML Documentation File in Swagger Configuration

Modify the Swagger configuration in Startup.cs to include the XML documentation file:

```csharp
Copy code
public void ConfigureServices(IServiceCollection services)
{
    services.AddSwaggerGen(c =>
    {
        c.SwaggerDoc("v1", new OpenApiInfo { Title = "My API", Version = "v1" });
        c.SwaggerDoc("v2", new OpenApiInfo { Title = "My API", Version = "v2" });

        // Set the comments path for the Swagger JSON and UI
        var xmlFile = $"{Assembly.GetExecutingAssembly().GetName().Name}.xml";
        var xmlPath = Path.Combine(AppContext.BaseDirectory, xmlFile);
        c.IncludeXmlComments(xmlPath);
    });
}
```

Step 3: Add Comments to Your Controller and Action Methods

Add XML comments above your controllers and action methods to describe their functionality. For example:

```csharp
Copy code
/// <summary>
/// Retrieves all products.
/// </summary>
/// <returns>A list of products.</returns>
```

```
[HttpGet]
public IActionResult GetAllProducts() { /* Implementation */ }
```

This documentation will appear in the Swagger UI, helping users understand how to use your API effectively.

5. Testing and Exploring Your API with Swagger UI

Once you have integrated Swagger and added XML documentation, you can test your API directly from the Swagger UI. This is a great way to verify that your API endpoints work as expected and provide users with an interactive experience.

Using Swagger UI:

- Navigate to http://localhost:5000/swagger in your web browser.
- You will see a list of your API endpoints organized by version.
- Click on an endpoint to expand its details, including request parameters and response types.
- Use the "Try it out" feature to send requests directly from the interface, providing a seamless way to test your API.

Versioning APIs and leveraging OpenAPI/Swagger are essential practices for maintaining and documenting your web services effectively. By implementing a clear versioning strategy, you can ensure that clients can continue to use older versions of your API while adopting new features. Integrating OpenAPI and Swagger provides valuable documentation that enhances the developer experience, making your API easier to understand and use. In the next sections, we will delve into advanced topics like integrating authentication and authorization, ensuring your API is both secure and robust.

Best Practices for Designing and Documenting APIs

BUILDING RESTFUL APIS AND INTEGRATING WEB APIS

Creating an effective API goes beyond just making it functional; it involves designing it in a way that is intuitive, consistent, and well-documented. By following best practices for API design and documentation, you ensure that your APIs are easy to use, maintain, and evolve over time. This section will cover essential principles and practices to help you create robust APIs that developers will appreciate.

1. RESTful Principles

When designing APIs, adhering to RESTful principles is crucial for creating a predictable and user-friendly interface. Here are key REST principles to consider:

- **Statelessness**: Each API request should contain all the information needed for the server to fulfill it. No client context is stored on the server between requests.
- **Resource-Based URIs**: Use nouns to represent resources in your URIs. This makes it clear what the API deals with.
- **HTTP Methods**: Utilize the correct HTTP methods to indicate the desired action:
- GET: Retrieve data.
- POST: Create a new resource.
- PUT: Update an existing resource.
- DELETE: Remove a resource.
- **Use of Status Codes**: Return appropriate HTTP status codes to indicate the outcome of a request (e.g., 200 OK, 201 Created, 404 Not Found, 500 Internal Server Error).

Example of a RESTful URI Design:

```arduino
Copy code
GET /api/products           // Retrieve all products
POST /api/products          // Create a new product
GET /api/products/{id}      // Retrieve a product by ID
PUT /api/products/{id}      // Update a product by ID
```

```
DELETE /api/products/{id}    // Delete a product by ID
```

2. Versioning Strategy

Versioning is crucial for maintaining backward compatibility as you enhance your API. Choose a versioning strategy that fits your application needs, such as URI versioning or header versioning, and be consistent in its implementation. Include the version number in the URI or as part of the HTTP headers to help clients easily identify the version they are interacting with.

Example of Header Versioning:

Clients can specify the version in the request header:

```bash
Copy code
GET /api/products
Headers:
   Accept: application/vnd.myapi.v1+json
```

3. Consistent Naming Conventions

Maintain consistency in naming conventions for resources, endpoints, and parameters. Use plural nouns for resource names (e.g., /products instead of /product) and camelCase for JSON properties. This improves readability and helps developers quickly grasp the structure of your API.

Example of Consistent Naming:

```json
Copy code
{
   "productId": 1,
   "productName": "Widget",
   "price": 19.99
}
```

4. Pagination and Filtering

APIs that return large datasets should implement pagination and filtering to enhance performance and usability. This allows clients to retrieve manageable chunks of data and helps minimize server load.

- **Pagination**: Implement query parameters to control pagination, such as page and pageSize.
- **Filtering**: Allow clients to filter results based on specific criteria, using query parameters.

Example of Pagination and Filtering:

```bash
Copy code
GET /api/products?page=1&pageSize=10&category=tools
```

5. Error Handling

A well-defined error handling strategy is critical for guiding clients in troubleshooting issues. Use standardized error responses that provide meaningful information, such as error codes and messages. Include details like:

- **Error Code**: A unique identifier for the error type.
- **Message**: A user-friendly message explaining the error.
- **Details**: Additional information that can help diagnose the problem.

Example of an Error Response:

```json
Copy code
{
  "errorCode": "PRODUCT_NOT_FOUND",
  "message": "The product with the specified ID was not found.",
  "details": {
    "requestedId": 10
```

        }
    }

6. Documentation with OpenAPI/Swagger

Good documentation is essential for helping users understand how to interact with your API. Utilize OpenAPI specifications to create clear, interactive documentation with Swagger UI. Document each endpoint, including:

- **Summary**: A brief description of the endpoint's purpose.
- **Parameters**: Details about query parameters, path parameters, and request bodies.
- **Response Types**: Document the expected response formats and status codes.

Example of OpenAPI Documentation:

```yaml
Copy code
paths:
  /api/products:
    get:
      summary: Retrieve all products
      parameters:
        - name: page
          in: query
          description: Page number for pagination
          required: false
          schema:
            type: integer
        - name: pageSize
          in: query
          description: Number of products per page
          required: false
          schema:
            type: integer
```

```
responses:
  '200':
    description: A list of products
  '500':
    description: Internal server error
```

7. Security Considerations

Security is a paramount concern for any API. Implement security measures to protect your data and services:

- **Authentication and Authorization**: Use OAuth2, JWT, or API keys to secure endpoints and ensure that users have the necessary permissions to access resources.
- **Input Validation**: Always validate and sanitize user input to prevent injection attacks.
- **HTTPS**: Enforce the use of HTTPS to secure data in transit.

Example of Securing an Endpoint with Authorization:

```csharp
Copy code
[Authorize]
[HttpGet]
public IActionResult GetAllProducts() { /* Implementation */ }
```

8. Testing Your API

Regular testing is vital to ensure your API remains functional as changes are made. Implement automated tests to verify:

- **Unit Tests**: Test individual components of your API.
- **Integration Tests**: Ensure that different components of your API work together as expected.
- **Performance Tests**: Assess how your API performs under load.

Use tools like Postman or Swagger UI to manually test endpoints and validate responses.

9. Feedback and Iteration

After launching your API, gather feedback from users and stakeholders. Use this input to make improvements and iterate on your design. Regularly update your documentation to reflect changes in your API.

Designing and documenting APIs is a complex but rewarding process. By adhering to best practices, you create APIs that are not only functional but also user-friendly, secure, and maintainable. A well-designed API enhances the developer experience, encouraging adoption and ensuring that your services can evolve gracefully over time. In the next sections, we will explore advanced topics, such as caching strategies and performance optimization techniques, to further enhance your API's capabilities.

Integrating Front-End Frameworks (React, Angular, and Vue)

Choosing the Right Front-End Framework for Your Project
As the web development landscape continues to evolve, the choice of front-end frameworks has become increasingly crucial. For developers working with ASP.NET Core 3, the integration of robust front-end technologies can significantly enhance the user experience and streamline development processes. This chapter will provide a comprehensive analysis of popular front-end frameworks—React, Angular, and Vue—highlighting their strengths, weaknesses, and ideal use cases to help you make an informed decision for your project.

1. Understanding the Front-End Landscape
Before diving into specific frameworks, it is important to understand the role of front-end technologies in modern web applications. Front-end frameworks provide a structured way to build user interfaces, manage application state, and interact with back-end services. They enable developers to create dynamic, responsive applications that can run across various devices and platforms.

The key considerations when choosing a front-end framework include:

- **Project requirements**: The specific needs of the application, including performance, scalability, and functionality.
- **Team expertise**: The skill set and familiarity of your development

team with particular frameworks.
- **Ecosystem and community**: The availability of resources, libraries, and community support for the framework.
- **Long-term maintainability**: The framework's longevity and how well it is supported over time.

2. Overview of Front-End Frameworks

React

Overview: Developed by Facebook, React is a JavaScript library for building user interfaces. It emphasizes component-based architecture, allowing developers to create reusable UI components.

Strengths:

- **Component Reusability**: React promotes a modular approach to UI development, making it easy to create reusable components.
- **Virtual DOM**: The use of a virtual DOM enhances performance by minimizing direct manipulation of the actual DOM, resulting in faster rendering.
- **Rich Ecosystem**: A vast array of libraries and tools, such as Redux for state management and React Router for routing, enhances functionality and flexibility.

Weaknesses:

- **Steeper Learning Curve**: The JSX syntax and component lifecycle can be challenging for beginners.
- **Frequent Updates**: React's fast-paced development means that new features and updates can require ongoing adjustments in code.

Ideal Use Cases:

- Applications requiring a highly interactive user interface.
- Projects with a need for reusable components.

- Single Page Applications (SPAs) that require dynamic content updates.

Angular

Overview: Angular, developed by Google, is a comprehensive framework for building web applications. It offers a complete solution with integrated tools and libraries for building, testing, and deploying applications.

Strengths:

- **Full-Featured Framework**: Angular includes built-in solutions for routing, state management, and form handling, reducing the need for third-party libraries.
- **Dependency Injection**: The framework's dependency injection system enhances code modularity and testability.
- **TypeScript Support**: Angular is built with TypeScript, which provides static typing and improved tooling.

Weaknesses:

- **Complexity**: Angular's extensive features and concepts can be overwhelming for newcomers.
- **Performance Overhead**: Due to its comprehensive nature, Angular applications may experience performance overhead if not optimized properly.

Ideal Use Cases:

- Large-scale enterprise applications where a robust framework is beneficial.
- Applications requiring a structured approach to development.
- Projects that can leverage TypeScript's features for improved code quality.

Vue.js

Overview: Vue.js is a progressive JavaScript framework for building user interfaces. It can be adopted incrementally, allowing developers to integrate it into existing projects.

Strengths:

- **Simplicity**: Vue.js is easy to learn and integrate, making it an attractive option for new developers.
- **Flexibility**: Vue allows developers to structure applications in various ways, from simple HTML applications to complex SPAs.
- **Reactive Data Binding**: Vue's two-way data binding simplifies the synchronization between the model and the view.

Weaknesses:

- **Ecosystem**: While growing, Vue's ecosystem is not as extensive as React or Angular, which may limit available libraries and tools.
- **Community Size**: Although supportive, the Vue community is smaller compared to React and Angular, which can impact the availability of resources.

Ideal Use Cases:

- Smaller projects or prototypes that require quick setup and development.
- Applications where simplicity and ease of integration are priorities.
- Projects that benefit from reactive data updates without excessive overhead.

3. Comparing Frameworks: Key Factors

When evaluating which framework to choose, consider the following factors:

Performance

- **React**: Offers superior performance with its virtual DOM, particularly for applications with frequent updates.
- **Angular**: Can be optimized for performance, but the complexity may introduce overhead.
- **Vue.js**: Generally offers good performance, especially for smaller applications, with reactive data binding contributing to efficiency.

Learning Curve

- **React**: Moderate learning curve due to JSX and the need to understand component life cycles.
- **Angular**: Steeper learning curve due to its comprehensive feature set and reliance on TypeScript.
- **Vue.js**: Easiest for beginners, with a gentle learning curve and clear documentation.

Development Speed

- **React**: Fast development with reusable components, but may require additional libraries for routing and state management.
- **Angular**: Slower initial setup due to its complexity, but offers a complete solution that can speed up later stages of development.
- **Vue.js**: Quick to set up and iterate upon, making it ideal for rapid prototyping.

Community and Ecosystem

- **React**: Large community and extensive ecosystem, with a wealth of resources, tutorials, and third-party libraries.
- **Angular**: Strong backing from Google and a well-established ecosystem, although it can be more opinionated.
- **Vue.js**: A growing community, but fewer resources compared to React and Angular, which may impact long-term support.

4. Making Your Decision

To make an informed decision, follow these steps:

1. **Assess Project Requirements**: Identify the specific needs of your application, including expected load, user interactions, and data handling requirements.
2. **Evaluate Team Skills**: Consider your team's existing knowledge and proficiency with each framework. Opt for a framework that aligns with their expertise to facilitate a smoother development process.
3. **Prototype**: If possible, create small prototypes using the frameworks you are considering. This hands-on experience can reveal insights into usability, performance, and how well the framework fits your project.
4. **Long-Term Considerations**: Think about future maintenance and scalability. Will the framework continue to be supported? Is there a risk of the community dwindling?
5. **Consult the Community**: Engage with developer communities or forums to gather insights and feedback from other developers who have experience with the frameworks.

Choosing the right front-end framework is a crucial step in building a successful web application. React, Angular, and Vue each have their strengths and weaknesses, making them suitable for different project requirements and team expertise. By thoroughly evaluating your project needs, team skills, and long-term goals, you can select the framework that best aligns with your vision. The right choice will empower your development process, improve user experience, and ultimately contribute to the success of your application. In the following sections, we will explore how to integrate these front-end frameworks with ASP.NET Core 3 to create seamless and dynamic web applications.

INTEGRATING FRONT-END FRAMEWORKS (REACT, ANGULAR, AND VUE)

Setting Up JavaScript Frameworks with ASP.NET Core

Integrating a JavaScript framework with ASP.NET Core allows you to leverage the strengths of both environments, enhancing your web application's functionality and user experience. This section will guide you through the process of setting up popular front-end frameworks—React, Angular, and Vue—with ASP.NET Core, providing a seamless development experience.

1. Prerequisites

Before starting, ensure that you have the following installed on your development machine:
- **.NET Core SDK**: Download and install the latest version of the .NET Core SDK from the official .NET website.
- **Node.js and npm**: Install Node.js, which includes npm (Node Package Manager), from the Node.js website. This will allow you to manage JavaScript packages.
- **A code editor**: Use an IDE or code editor such as Visual Studio, Visual Studio Code, or JetBrains Rider for your ASP.NET Core development.

2. Creating an ASP.NET Core Project

To set up your ASP.NET Core project, follow these steps:

1. **Open a Command Prompt or Terminal**: Navigate to the directory where you want to create your new project.
2. **Create a New Project**:

```bash
Copy code
dotnet new webapp -n MyWebApp
cd MyWebApp
```

1. This command creates a new ASP.NET Core web application using

Razor Pages.

2. **Run the Application**: To ensure everything is set up correctly, run:

```bash
Copy code
dotnet run
```

You should see your application running at http://localhost:5000.

3. Setting Up React with ASP.NET Core

To integrate React into your ASP.NET Core application, follow these steps:

Step 1: Install Create React App

You can set up a React application using the Create React App tool. In your terminal, run:

```bash
Copy code
npx create-react-app clientapp
```

This command creates a new directory named clientapp containing a React application.

Step 2: Configure ASP.NET Core to Serve React

To serve the React application from your ASP.NET Core backend, modify your Startup.cs file:

1. **Add Static Files Middleware**: In the Configure method, add the following code to enable serving static files:

INTEGRATING FRONT-END FRAMEWORKS (REACT, ANGULAR, AND VUE)

```csharp
Copy code
app.UseStaticFiles();
```

1. **Set Up Routing**: Ensure that all routes are handled by the React app. You can add this configuration before the call to app.UseEndpoints():

```csharp
Copy code
app.UseEndpoints(endpoints =>
{
    endpoints.MapControllers();
    endpoints.MapFallbackToFile("index.html"); // serve React's
    index.html for any unknown paths
});
```

Step 3: Build the React Application

To build the React app for production, navigate to the clientapp directory and run:

```bash
Copy code
npm run build
```

This command generates a build folder containing optimized static files. Make sure the ASP.NET Core application can serve files from this folder.

Step 4: Run Your Application

Go back to the root of your ASP.NET Core project and run it again:

```
bash
Copy code
dotnet run
```

Visit http://localhost:5000, and you should see your React app integrated with your ASP.NET Core backend.

4. Setting Up Angular with ASP.NET Core

Integrating Angular with ASP.NET Core is similarly straightforward. Follow these steps:

Step 1: Install Angular CLI

To create an Angular application, install the Angular CLI globally:

```bash
Copy code
npm install -g @angular/cli
```

Step 2: Create a New Angular Project

Navigate to your project directory and create a new Angular application:

```bash
Copy code
ng new clientapp --routing --style=scss
```

This command creates an Angular application in the clientapp folder with routing and SCSS support.

Step 3: Configure ASP.NET Core to Serve Angular

Modify your Startup.cs file to serve Angular files:

Add Static Files Middleware: Similar to React, ensure static files are served:

INTEGRATING FRONT-END FRAMEWORKS (REACT, ANGULAR, AND VUE)

```csharp
Copy code
app.UseStaticFiles();
```

Set Up Routing: Modify the routing configuration in the Configure method:

```csharp
Copy code
app.UseEndpoints(endpoints =>
{
    endpoints.MapControllers();
    endpoints.MapFallbackToFile("index.html"); // serve Angular's index.html for any unknown paths
});
```

Step 4: Build the Angular Application

To build your Angular application for production, navigate to the clientapp directory and run:

```bash
Copy code
ng build --prod
```

This command compiles the Angular application and creates an output in the dist/clientapp directory.

Step 5: Run Your Application

Return to the root of your ASP.NET Core project and run:

```bash
Copy code
dotnet run
```

Visit http://localhost:5000 to see your Angular application running with

ASP.NET Core.

5. Setting Up Vue.js with ASP.NET Core

Setting up Vue.js in an ASP.NET Core application involves a few similar steps:

Step 1: Install Vue CLI

Install Vue CLI globally using npm:

```bash
Copy code
npm install -g @vue/cli
```

Step 2: Create a New Vue Project

Create a new Vue application in your project directory:

```bash
Copy code
vue create clientapp
```

You'll be prompted to select features for your Vue application. Choose the options that suit your project.

Step 3: Configure ASP.NET Core to Serve Vue

Modify your Startup.cs file to serve Vue files:

Add Static Files Middleware:

```csharp
Copy code
app.UseStaticFiles();
```

Set Up Routing: In the Configure method:

```csharp
Copy code
```

INTEGRATING FRONT-END FRAMEWORKS (REACT, ANGULAR, AND VUE)

```
app.UseEndpoints(endpoints =>
{
    endpoints.MapControllers();
    endpoints.MapFallbackToFile("index.html"); // serve Vue's
    index.html for any unknown paths
});
```

Step 4: Build the Vue Application

To build your Vue application, navigate to the clientapp directory and run:

```bash
Copy code
npm run build
```

This will generate a dist folder containing the production-ready files.

Step 5: Run Your Application

Return to the root of your ASP.NET Core project and execute:

```bash
Copy code
dotnet run
```

Access your application at http://localhost:5000, and you should see your Vue.js app integrated into the ASP.NET Core backend.

6. Handling API Requests

Regardless of the front-end framework you choose, you will likely need to interact with your ASP.NET Core back-end API. Here are general practices for making API requests:

- **Use Axios or Fetch**: For React and Vue, Axios is a popular library for making HTTP requests, while the Fetch API is available natively in modern browsers.

- **Configure Base URL**: In your front-end app, configure the base URL for your API endpoints to point to your ASP.NET Core server. This can be done in environment configuration files.
- **Handle CORS**: If your front-end and back-end are served from different origins during development, configure Cross-Origin Resource Sharing (CORS) in ASP.NET Core by adding the CORS middleware in Startup.cs:

```csharp
Copy code
services.AddCors(options =>
{
    options.AddPolicy("AllowAll",
        builder =>
        {
            builder.AllowAnyOrigin()
                .AllowAnyMethod()
                .AllowAnyHeader();
        });
});

app.UseCors("AllowAll");
```

Integrating a JavaScript framework with ASP.NET Core enhances your application's interactivity and responsiveness. By following the steps outlined above, you can successfully set up React, Angular, or Vue in your ASP.NET Core project. Each framework offers unique features and strengths, allowing you to choose one that aligns best with your project requirements. As you proceed, ensure to implement best practices for API interactions, security, and performance optimization to create a well-rounded web application. In the next sections, we will explore how to enhance your applications further by implementing state management and routing techniques specific to each framework.

Building a Single-Page Application (SPA) with ASP.NET Core and React

Single-Page Applications (SPAs) have become the norm for modern web development, providing users with seamless interactions without the need for full-page reloads. Combining ASP.NET Core with React allows developers to create efficient and interactive web applications that enhance user experiences. This section will guide you through the process of building a simple SPA using ASP.NET Core and React, covering the necessary configurations, key components, and best practices.

1. Project Setup

To build a SPA with ASP.NET Core and React, you'll start by setting up your development environment and creating the initial project structure.

Step 1: Create a New ASP.NET Core Project

1. Open a terminal or command prompt.
2. Navigate to the desired directory and create a new ASP.NET Core project using the following command:

```bash
Copy code
dotnet new webapp -n MyReactSPA
cd MyReactSPA
```

This command creates a new web application using the Razor Pages template. We will later integrate React into this project.

Step 2: Create the React Application

In your project directory, set up a new React application using Create React App:

```
bash
Copy code
npx create-react-app ClientApp
```

This command creates a new directory called ClientApp containing a fully functional React application.

2. Configure ASP.NET Core to Serve the React Application

To ensure that your ASP.NET Core application can serve the React application, you'll need to adjust the Startup.cs file and configure your application to handle the routing appropriately.

Step 1: Modify Startup.cs

Open the Startup.cs file and make the following changes:

Add Static File Middleware: Ensure your application can serve static files:

```csharp
Copy code
public void Configure(IApplicationBuilder app, IWebHostEnvironment env)
{
    if (env.IsDevelopment())
    {
        app.UseDeveloperExceptionPage();
    }
    else
    {
        app.UseExceptionHandler("/Home/Error");
        app.UseHsts();
    }

    app.UseHttpsRedirection();
    app.UseStaticFiles();

    app.UseRouting();
```

INTEGRATING FRONT-END FRAMEWORKS (REACT, ANGULAR, AND VUE)

```
    app.UseAuthorization();

    app.UseEndpoints(endpoints =>
    {
        endpoints.MapControllers();
        endpoints.MapFallbackToFile("index.html"); // This
        serves the React app for all unknown paths
    });
}
```

Enable CORS (if necessary): If you're testing your React app separately, you may need to configure CORS:

```csharp
Copy code
services.AddCors(options =>
{
    options.AddPolicy("AllowAll",
        builder =>
            builder.AllowAnyOrigin().AllowAnyMethod().AllowAnyHeader());
});
```

3. Building the React Application

Once your ASP.NET Core project is configured, it's time to focus on developing your React SPA.

Step 1: Create Components

In your ClientApp/src directory, you can start building your components. For instance, create a simple Home component:

Create a new file called Home.js in the src directory:

```javascript
Copy code
import React from 'react';

const Home = () => {
```

```
    return (
        <div>
            <h1>Welcome to My React SPA!</h1>
            <p>This is a simple single-page application built
            with ASP.NET Core and React.</p>
        </div>
    );
};

export default Home;
```

Create an App.js file to set up your routing:

```javascript
Copy code
import React from 'react';
import { BrowserRouter as Router, Route, Switch } from
'react-router-dom';
import Home from './Home';

const App = () => {
    return (
        <Router>
            <Switch>
                <Route path="/" exact component={Home} />
                {/* Additional routes can be added here */}
            </Switch>
        </Router>
    );
};

export default App;
```

Update your index.js file to render the App component:

```
javascript
Copy code
```

INTEGRATING FRONT-END FRAMEWORKS (REACT, ANGULAR, AND VUE)

```
import React from 'react';
import ReactDOM from 'react-dom';
import App from './App';

ReactDOM.render(<App />, document.getElementById('root'));
```

Step 2: Adding Routing

Using React Router, you can easily manage different routes in your SPA. Install React Router in the ClientApp directory:

```bash
Copy code
npm install react-router-dom
```

Now, you can create additional components and set up routes in your App.js as shown above. Simply create new component files (e.g., About.js) and add routes accordingly.

4. Setting Up API Endpoints

To make your SPA more interactive, you'll need to communicate with your ASP.NET Core backend through API calls. Here's how you can set this up:

Step 1: Create a Simple API Controller

In the ASP.NET Core project, create a new controller to handle API requests. Create a folder called Controllers, and inside, create a new file called ApiController.cs:

```csharp
Copy code
using Microsoft.AspNetCore.Mvc;

namespace MyReactSPA.Controllers
{
```

```csharp
[Route("api/[controller]")]
[ApiController]
public class ApiController : ControllerBase
{
    [HttpGet("data")]
    public IActionResult GetData()
    {
        var data = new { message = "Hello from the ASP.NET 
        Core API!" };
        return Ok(data);
    }
}
```

This simple API controller provides a single endpoint that returns a message.

Step 2: Fetch Data in React

In your Home.js component, fetch data from the ASP.NET Core API using the Fetch API or Axios. For example, modify the Home.js component to include a data fetch:

```javascript
Copy code
import React, { useEffect, useState } from 'react';

const Home = () => {
    const [data, setData] = useState(null);

    useEffect(() => {
        fetch('/api/api/data')
            .then(response => response.json())
            .then(data => setData(data));
    }, []);

    return (
        <div>
            <h1>Welcome to My React SPA!</h1>
```

INTEGRATING FRONT-END FRAMEWORKS (REACT, ANGULAR, AND VUE)

```
            {data && <p>{data.message}</p>}
        </div>
    );
};

export default Home;
```

5. Building and Running Your Application

Now that your application is set up, you can build and run it:

Build the React Application: Navigate to the ClientApp directory and build your React app:

```bash
Copy code
npm run build
```

Run the ASP.NET Core Application: Go back to your ASP.NET Core project root and run:

```bash
Copy code
dotnet run
```

Access Your Application: Open a web browser and navigate to http://localhost:5000. You should see your React SPA, and the API message should be displayed as part of the home page.

6. Best Practices for SPA Development

When building a SPA with ASP.NET Core and React, consider the following best practices:

- **State Management**: Use a state management library like Redux or Context API for managing application state, especially in larger applications.

- **Code Splitting**: Implement code splitting using React's lazy and Suspense to load components only when needed, improving initial load times.
- **Error Handling**: Implement robust error handling for API calls to provide a better user experience.
- **Performance Optimization**: Optimize the React application by minimizing bundle size and leveraging memoization techniques to prevent unnecessary re-renders.
- **Security**: Ensure proper authentication and authorization measures are in place when dealing with sensitive data or user-specific actions.

Building a Single-Page Application with ASP.NET Core and React offers a powerful combination for creating dynamic and responsive web applications. By following the steps outlined in this section, you can successfully set up your development environment, create components, configure routing, and implement API interactions. As you progress, continue to explore advanced features and best practices to enhance your SPA further, ensuring a smooth user experience and maintainability for your application. In the following sections, we will delve into advanced topics, including state management and performance optimization strategies for SPAs.

Using Angular with ASP.NET Core for Client-Side Interactivity

Angular, a powerful front-end framework by Google, is highly popular for creating complex, interactive, and scalable Single-Page Applications (SPAs). Integrating Angular with ASP.NET Core provides a robust solution for building dynamic web applications, allowing for full control over both client and server-side development in a unified environment. This section will walk you through setting up Angular with ASP.NET Core, building core features, and leveraging Angular's two-way data binding

INTEGRATING FRONT-END FRAMEWORKS (REACT, ANGULAR, AND VUE)

and reactive capabilities to achieve seamless client-side interactivity.

1. Setting Up an ASP.NET Core Project with Angular

ASP.NET Core provides a project template specifically for Angular that streamlines the setup process. Here's how to get started:

Step 1: Create a New ASP.NET Core Angular Project

To generate a new ASP.NET Core project with Angular, run the following command in the terminal:

```bash
Copy code
dotnet new angular -n MyAngularApp
cd MyAngularApp
```

The dotnet new angular command creates an ASP.NET Core project pre-configured with Angular, setting up both server and client code within a single solution. You'll find an AngularApp folder, which contains the Angular client app, and the Controllers folder for the ASP.NET Core API.

Step 2: Project Structure Overview

- **ClientApp**: Contains the Angular app, including all components, services, and modules.
- **Controllers**: Contains the API controllers used by ASP.NET Core to provide data and handle requests from the Angular client.

This setup enables both projects to be developed and deployed together, with Angular serving as the front end and ASP.NET Core handling backend operations.

2. Configuring the Development Environment

To build and run your Angular and ASP.NET Core project effectively, set up the environment for seamless development.

Install Angular CLI: To work efficiently with Angular, make sure you have the Angular CLI installed globally:

```bash
Copy code
npm install -g @angular/cli
```

Set up Proxy Configuration (optional): If you're running the Angular client separately (for example, during local development), set up a proxy to redirect API calls from the Angular app to the ASP.NET Core API. Add a proxy.conf.json file in the ClientApp directory with the following content:

```json
Copy code
{
    "/api": {
        "target": "http://localhost:5000",
        "secure": false
    }
}
```

Run the Application: You can run both Angular and ASP.NET Core together with the dotnet run command, or if you're debugging Angular independently, navigate to the ClientApp directory and run:

```bash
Copy code
ng serve --proxy-config proxy.conf.json
```

3. Building Components and Services in Angular

With Angular's component-based architecture, you can create modular, reusable pieces of functionality that work seamlessly with ASP.NET Core APIs.

Step 1: Create a Component

INTEGRATING FRONT-END FRAMEWORKS (REACT, ANGULAR, AND VUE)

Use Angular CLI to generate a new component in your Angular project. For example, to create a Dashboard component:

```bash
Copy code
ng generate component Dashboard
```

This command creates a new component in the src/app directory, which includes the template, stylesheet, and TypeScript file.

Step 2: Create a Service for API Communication

Services in Angular are ideal for handling HTTP requests. Use Angular's HttpClient module to communicate with the ASP.NET Core API:

Create a service:

```bash
Copy code
ng generate service data
```

In the newly created data.service.ts file, add a method to fetch data from the ASP.NET Core API:

```typescript
Copy code
import { Injectable } from '@angular/core';
import { HttpClient } from '@angular/common/http';
import { Observable } from 'rxjs';

@Injectable({
    providedIn: 'root'
})
export class DataService {

    private apiUrl = '/api/data';
```

```typescript
    constructor(private http: HttpClient) {}

    getData(): Observable<any> {
        return this.http.get<any>(this.apiUrl);
    }
}
```

Inject the DataService in the component and call the API:

```typescript
import { Component, OnInit } from '@angular/core';
import { DataService } from '../data.service';

@Component({
    selector: 'app-dashboard',
    templateUrl: './dashboard.component.html'
})
export class DashboardComponent implements OnInit {
    data: any;

    constructor(private dataService: DataService) {}

    ngOnInit(): void {
        this.dataService.getData().subscribe(response => {
            this.data = response;
        });
    }
}
```

4. Two-Way Data Binding and Interactivity

Angular's two-way data binding allows for dynamic data updating between the HTML template and the component TypeScript file, making it easier to manage interactive elements.

In the component's template (dashboard.component.html), you can bind the data variable to display the data retrieved from the ASP.NET Core API:

INTEGRATING FRONT-END FRAMEWORKS (REACT, ANGULAR, AND VUE)

```html
html
Copy code
<div *ngIf="data">
    <h2>{{ data.title }}</h2>
    <p>{{ data.message }}</p>
</div>
```

With this setup, Angular automatically reflects any changes made to data in the view, enhancing client-side interactivity.

5. Using Angular Modules for Structuring and Scaling

As the application grows, organizing components and services into Angular modules makes it easier to maintain and scale. Modules allow you to group related components, services, and pipes.

Create a feature module:

```bash
bash
Copy code
ng generate module dashboard
```

Add the DashboardComponent and any related components to this module, importing it in the AppModule for a well-structured, modular approach.

Setting Up Routing

Angular Router enables SPA routing, allowing users to navigate between views without refreshing the page.

Define routes in app-routing.module.ts:

```typescript
typescript
Copy code
import { NgModule } from '@angular/core';
import { RouterModule, Routes } from '@angular/router';
import { DashboardComponent } from
```

```
'./dashboard/dashboard.component';

const routes: Routes = [
    { path: '', component: DashboardComponent },
    // Additional routes can be added here
];

@NgModule({
    imports: [RouterModule.forRoot(routes)],
    exports: [RouterModule]
})
export class AppRoutingModule { }
```

Use Angular's RouterLink directive in the template to create navigable links.

7. Best Practices for Angular Integration

To ensure a smooth, scalable development experience, follow these best practices:

- **Lazy Loading Modules**: Load feature modules only when needed to reduce the initial bundle size.
- **Caching API Responses**: Use RxJS operators like shareReplay to cache API responses where appropriate, reducing load on your ASP.NET Core server.
- **Error Handling**: Handle API errors gracefully in your services and components.
- **Component-Based Architecture**: Break down complex UIs into smaller, reusable components for better maintainability and testability.

INTEGRATING FRONT-END FRAMEWORKS (REACT, ANGULAR, AND VUE)

Using Angular with ASP.NET Core allows for a seamless and highly interactive web application experience. With Angular's dynamic front-end capabilities and ASP.NET Core's powerful backend, this combination provides everything needed to build a full-featured SPA. From configuring the project to implementing data services and ensuring scalability, this setup facilitates building sophisticated web applications that provide a responsive and engaging user experience. In the next section, we'll explore advanced topics such as state management and server-side rendering, further enhancing your application's performance and interactivity.

Vue.js Integration: Lightweight SPA with ASP.NET Core

Vue.js is a progressive JavaScript framework known for its simplicity, reactivity, and versatility, making it ideal for building lightweight Single-Page Applications (SPAs). Integrating Vue.js with ASP.NET Core creates a powerful, efficient framework for developing dynamic, responsive web applications. In this section, we'll walk through setting up a Vue.js SPA with ASP.NET Core, covering configuration, core features, and techniques for achieving a smooth integration that maximizes interactivity and performance.

1. Setting Up an ASP.NET Core Project with Vue.js

Although ASP.NET Core doesn't have a built-in Vue.js template, setting up the framework manually is straightforward and allows full control over both client and server environments.

Step 1: Create a New ASP.NET Core Web API Project

First, create an ASP.NET Core project to serve as the backend for the Vue.js frontend.

```bash
Copy code
dotnet new webapi -n MyVueApp
cd MyVueApp
```

This creates a new Web API project named MyVueApp with a structure suitable for a RESTful API that Vue.js can consume.

Step 2: Add the Vue.js Application

Inside the project directory, use the Vue CLI to create a Vue.js app. Ensure you've installed the Vue CLI globally if you haven't already:

```bash
Copy code
npm install -g @vue/cli
```

Then, create the Vue project inside a ClientApp folder within your ASP.NET Core project:

```bash
Copy code
vue create ClientApp
```

Select the desired configuration (e.g., with Vue Router and Vuex for state management) and wait for the CLI to install the dependencies and set up the project.

2. Configuring ASP.NET Core to Serve the Vue.js Application

To enable ASP.NET Core to serve the Vue.js app, you'll configure the Startup.cs file.

Step 1: Enable Static Files

In Startup.cs, make sure the application can serve static files:

```csharp
Copy code
public void Configure(IApplicationBuilder app, IWebHostEnvironment env)
{
    if (env.IsDevelopment())
    {
        app.UseDeveloperExceptionPage();
    }
    else
    {
        app.UseExceptionHandler("/Home/Error");
        app.UseHsts();
    }

    app.UseHttpsRedirection();
    app.UseStaticFiles();

    app.UseRouting();

    app.UseEndpoints(endpoints =>
    {
        endpoints.MapControllers();
        endpoints.MapFallbackToFile("index.html"); // This serves the Vue.js app for all unknown routes
    });
}
```

Step 2: Configure CORS (Optional)

If you're testing the Vue.js app separately, configure CORS in Startup.cs to allow cross-origin requests:

```csharp
Copy code
services.AddCors(options =>
{
    options.AddPolicy("AllowAll", builder =>
```

```
    {
        builder.AllowAnyOrigin().AllowAnyMethod().AllowAnyHeader();
    });
});
```

With CORS set up, you can run the Vue.js app independently for development, but keep it within the ASP.NET Core pipeline for production.

3. Building Vue.js Components and API Integration

Vue.js uses components to create modular, reusable parts of the user interface. Here's how to set up components and integrate them with the ASP.NET Core API.

Step 1: Create a Component

In the src/components directory of your Vue app, create a simple Home.vue component:

```vue
Copy code
<template>
  <div>
    <h1>Welcome to My Vue SPA!</h1>
    <p>{{ message }}</p>
  </div>
</template>

<script>
export default {
  data() {
    return {
      message: ''
    }
  },
  created() {
    this.fetchMessage();
  },
```

INTEGRATING FRONT-END FRAMEWORKS (REACT, ANGULAR, AND VUE)

```
  methods: {
    fetchMessage() {
      fetch('/api/data')
        .then(response => response.json())
        .then(data => {
          this.message = data.message;
        });
    }
  }
}
</script>

<style scoped>
/* Add any component-specific styles here */
</style>
```

This component fetches data from the ASP.NET Core API and displays it upon creation.

Step 2: Create an ASP.NET Core API Endpoint

In the ASP.NET Core project, create a controller to serve data to the Vue component:

Inside the Controllers folder, create a new file ApiController.cs:

```
csharp
Copy code
using Microsoft.AspNetCore.Mvc;

namespace MyVueApp.Controllers
{
    [Route("api/[controller]")]
    [ApiController]
    public class ApiController : ControllerBase
    {
        [HttpGet("data")]
        public IActionResult GetData()
        {
            var data = new { message = "Hello from the ASP.NET
```

```
        Core API!" };
        return Ok(data);
    }
  }
}
```

This controller has a GetData endpoint, which returns a JSON object with a message.

Step 3: Fetch Data in Vue

Within the Vue component's fetchMessage method, the API endpoint is called to retrieve and display data. This demonstrates how Vue and ASP.NET Core can seamlessly interact via HTTP requests.

4. Configuring Routing in Vue

Vue Router enables SPA navigation, allowing users to switch between pages without reloading.

Install Vue Router (if not installed):

```bash
Copy code
npm install vue-router
```

Define Routes: Create a new router.js file in src to define your routes:

```javascript
Copy code
import Vue from 'vue';
import Router from 'vue-router';
import Home from './components/Home.vue';

Vue.use(Router);

export default new Router({
```

```
    mode: 'history',
    routes: [
        {
            path: '/',
            name: 'Home',
            component: Home
        },
        // Additional routes can be added here
    ]
});
```

Initialize Router in main.js:

```javascript
Copy code
import Vue from 'vue';
import App from './App.vue';
import router from './router';

Vue.config.productionTip = false;

new Vue({
    router,
    render: h => h(App),
}).$mount('#app');
```

5. State Management with Vuex

For larger SPAs, Vuex provides a centralized state management solution, allowing components to share state and making it easier to manage application data.

Install Vuex:

```bash
Copy code
npm install vuex
```

C# WEB DEVELOPMENT WITH ASP.NET CORE 3

Set Up a Vuex Store: Create a new file store.js in src:

```javascript
import Vue from 'vue';
import Vuex from 'vuex';

Vue.use(Vuex);

export default new Vuex.Store({
    state: {
        message: ''
    },
    mutations: {
        setMessage(state, payload) {
            state.message = payload;
        }
    },
    actions: {
        fetchMessage({ commit }) {
            fetch('/api/data')
                .then(response => response.json())
                .then(data => {
                    commit('setMessage', data.message);
                });
        }
    }
});
```

Use the Store in Components:

In a component, use Vuex actions and state to fetch and display data:

```javascript
created() {
    this.$store.dispatch('fetchMessage');
}
computed: {
```

INTEGRATING FRONT-END FRAMEWORKS (REACT, ANGULAR, AND VUE)

```
    message() {
        return this.$store.state.message;
    }
}
```

6. Running the Application

To run both the Vue app and ASP.NET Core API:

Build the Vue Application:

```bash
Copy code
npm run build
```

Run the ASP.NET Core Application:

```bash
Copy code
dotnet run
```

With this setup, the Vue app and ASP.NET Core API will work together seamlessly, with Vue managing the client-side interactivity and ASP.NET Core handling data and backend operations.

7. Best Practices for Vue and ASP.NET Core Integration

Consider the following best practices for building scalable applications:

- **Use Environment Variables**: Set API URLs and other environment-dependent variables in a .env file.
- **Optimize Vue Components**: Break down large components and avoid re-rendering by leveraging computed properties and watchers.
- **Lazy Loading and Code Splitting**: Use Vue's import() syntax for lazy loading components, reducing initial load time for larger applications.
- **Implement Error Handling**: Use centralized error handling in Vue

for a smoother user experience.
- **Authentication and Authorization**: Secure your API endpoints and manage access in Vue components, especially for sensitive data.

Integrating Vue.js with ASP.NET Core is a powerful way to develop lightweight, interactive SPAs. Vue's reactivity and ease of use combined with ASP.NET Core's backend capabilities create a robust development environment for web applications. By following the setup, configuration, and best practices outlined here, you can efficiently build and deploy a modern, performant SPA that leverages the strengths of both Vue.js and ASP.NET Core. The next sections will explore more advanced topics, including performance optimization and deployment strategies, for a production-ready Vue and ASP.NET Core application.

Handling API Calls and Asynchronous Data with JavaScript Frameworks

Modern web applications rely heavily on asynchronous data interactions with backend APIs. When integrating JavaScript frameworks like Vue.js, React, or Angular with ASP.NET Core, managing asynchronous API calls effectively is essential for creating responsive and performant applications. In this section, we'll explore best practices and techniques for handling API requests, managing asynchronous data, error handling, and optimizing performance within JavaScript frameworks.

1. Understanding Asynchronous JavaScript and Promises

Before diving into API integration, it's crucial to understand how JavaScript handles asynchronous operations. JavaScript frameworks utilize promises and async/await syntax to execute tasks without blocking the main thread, enhancing app responsiveness.
- **Promises**: Objects that represent the eventual completion or failure of an asynchronous operation.

```javascript
Copy code
fetch('/api/data')
  .then(response => response.json())
  .then(data => console.log(data))
  .catch(error => console.error('Error fetching data:', error));
```

- **Async/Await**: Provides a cleaner, more readable syntax for handling promises.

```javascript
Copy code
async function fetchData() {
  try {
    const response = await fetch('/api/data');
    const data = await response.json();
    console.log(data);
  } catch (error) {
    console.error('Error fetching data:', error);
  }
}
```

Most frameworks support async functions, making async/await an efficient choice for handling API calls.

2. Setting Up API Services in JavaScript Frameworks

For maintainability and separation of concerns, it's best practice to centralize API calls in a service layer. This layer encapsulates all API requests, making it easier to handle retries, errors, and data transformations.

Example: Setting Up an API Service in Vue.js

In Vue, create a dedicated service file (apiService.js) that handles API requests.

```
javascript
Copy code
// src/services/apiService.js
export default {
  async fetchData() {
    try {
      const response = await fetch('/api/data');
      if (!response.ok) throw new Error('Network response was
      not ok');
      return await response.json();
    } catch (error) {
      console.error('API fetch error:', error);
      throw error;
    }
  }
};
```

Example: Using Axios in React and Angular

For HTTP requests, libraries like Axios provide a more flexible, promise-based API and improved error handling.

```
javascript
Copy code
import axios from 'axios';

const fetchData = async () => {
  try {
    const response = await axios.get('/api/data');
    return response.data;
  } catch (error) {
    console.error('Error fetching data:', error);
    throw error;
  }
};
```

This service can be injected into components or modules in frameworks like Angular, allowing reusable API interactions across the application.

3. Making API Calls and Displaying Data in Components

INTEGRATING FRONT-END FRAMEWORKS (REACT, ANGULAR, AND VUE)

After setting up an API service, data can be retrieved and displayed within UI components. Each framework has its approach for managing component state and rendering asynchronous data.

Fetching Data in Vue.js

In Vue, the created or mounted lifecycle hooks are commonly used for initiating API calls as they fire after component setup.

```javascript
Copy code
// src/components/DataDisplay.vue
<template>
  <div>
    <p v-if="loading">Loading...</p>
    <p v-else-if="error">{{ error.message }}</p>
    <div v-else>{{ data }}</div>
  </div>
</template>

<script>
import apiService from '../services/apiService.js';

export default {
  data() {
    return {
      data: null,
      loading: true,
      error: null
    };
  },
  async created() {
    try {
      this.data = await apiService.fetchData();
    } catch (err) {
      this.error = err;
    } finally {
      this.loading = false;
    }
```

```
    }
  };
</script>
```

This setup uses reactive properties to manage loading, error, and data states. As a result, the UI automatically updates as the data is retrieved or if an error occurs.

Fetching Data in React

React recommends using hooks like useEffect to handle data fetching in functional components.

```javascript
Copy code
import React, { useEffect, useState } from 'react';
import axios from 'axios';

const DataDisplay = () => {
  const [data, setData] = useState(null);
  const [loading, setLoading] = useState(true);
  const [error, setError] = useState(null);

  useEffect(() => {
    const fetchData = async () => {
      try {
        const result = await axios.get('/api/data');
        setData(result.data);
      } catch (err) {
        setError(err);
      } finally {
        setLoading(false);
      }
    };

    fetchData();
  }, []);

  if (loading) return <p>Loading...</p>;
```

INTEGRATING FRONT-END FRAMEWORKS (REACT, ANGULAR, AND VUE)

```
    if (error) return <p>{error.message}</p>;
    return <div>{data}</div>;
};

export default DataDisplay;
```

With useEffect, data is fetched on component mount, and state updates trigger a re-render, displaying data or errors as needed.

4. Handling API Errors and Retries

Error handling is a vital part of asynchronous API management. All frameworks support centralized error handling and can log errors or retry failed requests when necessary.

Example: Implementing Error Handling and Retry Logic

In the API service, use try-catch blocks and introduce retry logic for failed API calls:

```javascript
Copy code
async function fetchDataWithRetry(url, retries = 3) {
  for (let i = 0; i < retries; i++) {
    try {
      const response = await fetch(url);
      if (!response.ok) throw new Error('Request failed');
      return await response.json();
    } catch (error) {
      if (i === retries - 1) throw error;
    }
  }
}
```

This function retries a request up to three times before throwing an error, improving robustness for network-related failures.

5. Optimizing API Requests for Performance

Efficient handling of API requests is essential, especially for data-intensive applications. Consider the following optimization techniques:

- **Debouncing and Throttling**: Prevent excessive API calls by limiting how often functions are executed. Debouncing is particularly useful for search inputs or other rapid-fire interactions.
- **Batching Requests**: Combine multiple requests into a single payload to reduce the number of API calls.
- **Caching Responses**: Cache frequently requested data to reduce server load and improve client performance. Libraries like React Query (for React) or vue-query (for Vue) handle caching and background data refreshing efficiently.

6. Using Context and State Management for Asynchronous Data

For larger applications, asynchronous data can be stored in centralized state management tools like Vuex (Vue), Redux (React), or NgRx (Angular). This approach avoids prop drilling and provides a single source of truth for data.

Vuex Example

Vuex allows asynchronous actions to be dispatched and results stored in the global state.

```javascript
Copy code
// store.js
export default new Vuex.Store({
  state: {
    data: null
  },
  mutations: {
    setData(state, payload) {
      state.data = payload;
    }
  },
  actions: {
    async fetchData({ commit }) {
```

INTEGRATING FRONT-END FRAMEWORKS (REACT, ANGULAR, AND VUE)

```
      try {
        const data = await apiService.fetchData();
        commit('setData', data);
      } catch (error) {
        console.error('Error fetching data:', error);
      }
    }
  }
});
```

Components can then access this data from Vuex rather than fetching it individually, improving data consistency across the application.

Asynchronous API handling is central to developing responsive, efficient, and robust SPAs. By leveraging centralized services, managing API calls with error handling and retry logic, optimizing performance, and implementing state management, you can build scalable applications that deliver a smooth user experience. Each JavaScript framework provides tools and patterns to handle API interactions effectively, allowing you to select the best approach for your application's needs. In the next sections, we will explore real-time data handling and WebSocket integration to further enhance interactivity in modern web applications.

Middleware and Dependency Injection in ASP.NET Core

Understanding the Middleware Pipeline and Its Role in Request Handling

In ASP.NET Core, middleware plays a central role in handling HTTP requests and responses, forming the core processing pipeline for every incoming request. The middleware pipeline processes each request sequentially, applying various components to handle aspects like authentication, logging, error handling, and response formatting. This modular approach allows developers to control how requests are handled and responses are generated, enhancing application flexibility and performance.

This section delves into the structure and function of the middleware pipeline, illustrating how to configure, customize, and effectively utilize middleware to streamline request handling in ASP.NET Core applications.

1. What is Middleware in ASP.NET Core?

Middleware in ASP.NET Core refers to components that are executed as part of the HTTP request pipeline, either acting on the request and passing it forward or acting on the response after subsequent middleware has completed. Each middleware component in the pipeline has a specific role—whether security, routing, or error handling—and can either stop the pipeline (thus ending the request) or call the next middleware component to continue processing.

MIDDLEWARE AND DEPENDENCY INJECTION IN ASP.NET CORE

In simple terms, middleware is responsible for processing requests, altering them as needed, and returning responses based on application-specific needs.

Example: Basic Middleware Component

```csharp
Copy code
public class SimpleMiddleware
{
    private readonly RequestDelegate _next;

    public SimpleMiddleware(RequestDelegate next)
    {
        _next = next;
    }

    public async Task InvokeAsync(HttpContext context)
    {
        // Process request here
        Console.WriteLine("Handling request...");

        await _next(context); // Call the next middleware

        // Process response here
        Console.WriteLine("Handling response...");
    }
}
```

In this example, SimpleMiddleware logs messages before and after the request proceeds to the next middleware in the pipeline.

2. The Structure of the Middleware Pipeline

The middleware pipeline is configured in the Startup class, specifically within the Configure method. Each middleware component added to this pipeline executes in the order it's registered, making the sequence critical for defining how requests are processed.

Example: Configuring Middleware in Startup.cs

```csharp
Copy code
public class Startup
{
    public void Configure(IApplicationBuilder app)
    {
        app.UseRouting();
        app.UseAuthentication();
        app.UseAuthorization();
        app.UseEndpoints(endpoints =>
        {
            endpoints.MapControllers();
        });
    }
}
```

In this example:

- **UseRouting** sets up the routing middleware to map requests to controllers.
- **UseAuthentication** checks for valid authentication tokens or cookies before allowing access to secure routes.
- **UseAuthorization** applies role or policy-based permissions based on authenticated user roles.

Key Components of Middleware:

- **Request Handling**: Intercepts, modifies, or stops requests.
- **Response Handling**: Alters response data before sending it back to the client.
- **Short-Circuiting**: Ends request processing early if certain conditions are met (e.g., an unauthorized access).
- **Order Dependency**: The order of middleware components determines how and when each component processes the request and

response.

3. Commonly Used Built-In Middleware

ASP.NET Core includes various built-in middleware components for handling common concerns:

- **Static File Middleware** (UseStaticFiles): Serves static files (e.g., images, CSS, JavaScript) directly without further processing.
- **Routing Middleware** (UseRouting): Determines the appropriate endpoint based on request URLs.
- **Authentication and Authorization Middleware** (UseAuthentication, UseAuthorization): Ensures requests are authenticated and authorized based on policies.
- **CORS Middleware** (UseCors): Handles Cross-Origin Resource Sharing (CORS) rules, allowing or restricting resource access from different origins.
- **Exception Handling Middleware** (UseExceptionHandler): Manages application errors by capturing and returning error information.

Each of these components serves a specific purpose within the pipeline, making the middleware ecosystem modular, flexible, and easily extensible.

4. Creating Custom Middleware

In addition to built-in middleware, ASP.NET Core allows developers to create custom middleware to address application-specific requirements, such as logging or custom request headers.

Example: Custom Middleware for Logging

```csharp
Copy code
public class LoggingMiddleware
{
    private readonly RequestDelegate _next;
```

```
    public LoggingMiddleware(RequestDelegate next)
    {
        _next = next;
    }

    public async Task InvokeAsync(HttpContext context)
    {
        Console.WriteLine($"Request: {context.Request.Method} 
        {context.Request.Path}");

        await _next(context);

        Console.WriteLine($"Response Status: 
        {context.Response.StatusCode}");
    }
}
```

To register custom middleware in the pipeline, use the UseMiddleware extension method in the Configure method of Startup.

```
csharp
Copy code
public void Configure(IApplicationBuilder app)
{
    app.UseMiddleware<LoggingMiddleware>();
    // Other middleware registrations
}
```

This middleware logs the HTTP method and path of the incoming request, as well as the status code of the response, allowing developers to monitor request flow.

5. Middleware Ordering and Request Short-Circuiting

Order is critical in the middleware pipeline. Some middleware components, such as authentication, must be positioned before others, like authorization, to ensure they function correctly. Middleware can also short-circuit the pipeline if certain conditions are met. For instance, if a request fails an authorization check, the UseAuthorization middleware can end the request early by returning an error, skipping any subsequent middleware.

Example: Short-Circuiting Middleware for Authorization

```csharp
Copy code
public class AuthorizationMiddleware
{
    private readonly RequestDelegate _next;

    public AuthorizationMiddleware(RequestDelegate next)
    {
        _next = next;
    }

    public async Task InvokeAsync(HttpContext context)
    {
        if (!context.User.Identity.IsAuthenticated)
        {
            context.Response.StatusCode = StatusCodes.Status401Unauthorized;
            return; // Short-circuits the pipeline, ending request here
        }

        await _next(context); // Proceed to the next middleware
    }
}
```

Here, unauthorized requests are blocked, and the pipeline is short-circuited by not calling _next.

6. Exception Handling in Middleware

Handling exceptions in the middleware pipeline allows for consistent error responses and centralized error logging. ASP.NET Core provides the UseExceptionHandler middleware for this purpose, which catches exceptions in the pipeline and returns a custom error response.

Example: Global Exception Handler

```csharp
Copy code
public void Configure(IApplicationBuilder app)
{
    app.UseExceptionHandler("/error"); // Redirects to error handling endpoint
}
```

Example: Custom Exception Middleware

You can also create custom middleware for more granular exception handling:

```csharp
Copy code
public class ExceptionHandlingMiddleware
{
    private readonly RequestDelegate _next;

    public ExceptionHandlingMiddleware(RequestDelegate next)
    {
        _next = next;
    }

    public async Task InvokeAsync(HttpContext context)
    {
        try
        {
            await _next(context);
        }
        catch (Exception ex)
        {
            Console.WriteLine($"Exception: {ex.Message}");
            context.Response.StatusCode = StatusCodes.Status500InternalServerError;
            await context.Response.WriteAsync
```

MIDDLEWARE AND DEPENDENCY INJECTION IN ASP.NET CORE

```
("An error occurred.");
        }
    }
}
```

This middleware intercepts any unhandled exceptions and responds with a 500 Internal Server Error status code.

7. Performance Optimization with Middleware

The middleware pipeline can impact application performance, particularly when the request volume is high. Optimizing middleware placement and design helps minimize latency.

- **Minimize Processing in Custom Middleware**: Avoid long-running or computationally intensive tasks in custom middleware. Offload such tasks to background services when possible.
- **Use Conditional Logic**: Use conditional logic to bypass unnecessary middleware processing for certain request types.
- **Reduce I/O Operations**: Limit disk and network I/O operations within the middleware to prevent bottlenecks.
- **Leverage Caching**: Use caching middleware to reduce redundant processing for frequently requested resources.

Example: Adding Caching to Improve Middleware Performance

```csharp
csharp
Copy code
public void Configure(IApplicationBuilder app)
{
    app.UseResponseCaching(); // Enables caching for responses
    app.UseStaticFiles();
  // Serves static files efficiently
}
```

UseResponseCaching middleware allows frequently requested content to be cached, improving load times and reducing processing requirements.

Middleware forms the backbone of request handling in ASP.NET Core, providing a modular, extensible pipeline for request and response processing. By understanding and controlling middleware components, developers can tailor the request handling flow to meet specific application requirements, enhance performance, and ensure a secure, reliable user experience. The next sections will explore dependency injection, another core ASP.NET Core feature that complements middleware by managing service dependencies efficiently. Together, these components enable the creation of scalable, maintainable web applications.

Building Custom Middleware for Logging, Error Handling, and Security

In the ASP.NET Core framework, custom middleware serves as a powerful tool that allows developers to implement application-specific functionalities such as logging, error handling, and security measures. This section outlines the design and implementation of custom middleware components tailored for these common concerns, enabling you to enhance the overall behavior and resilience of your ASP.NET Core applications.

1. Custom Middleware for Logging

Logging is essential for monitoring application behavior, troubleshooting issues, and maintaining operational visibility. A custom logging middleware can capture and log details about incoming requests, outgoing responses, and any exceptions that occur during processing. This data is invaluable for diagnosing issues and understanding usage patterns.

Implementing a Custom Logging Middleware

To create a logging middleware, follow these steps:

MIDDLEWARE AND DEPENDENCY INJECTION IN ASP.NET CORE

1. **Create the Middleware Class**: Define a class that implements a constructor accepting a RequestDelegate and an InvokeAsync method to process requests.
2. **Capture Request and Response Data**: Within the InvokeAsync method, log the details of the request before passing it to the next middleware. After the response is generated, log the response details as well.

Example: Logging Middleware Implementation

```csharp
Copy code
public class LoggingMiddleware
{
    private readonly RequestDelegate _next;

    public LoggingMiddleware(RequestDelegate next)
    {
        _next = next;
    }

    public async Task InvokeAsync(HttpContext context)
    {
        // Log request information
        Console.WriteLine($"Incoming Request: {context.Request.Method} {context.Request.Path}");

        // Call the next middleware in the pipeline
        await _next(context);

        // Log response information
        Console.WriteLine($"Outgoing Response: {context.Response.StatusCode}");
    }
}
```

Registering the Middleware

In the Startup class, register the logging middleware within the Configure method to ensure it runs during the request pipeline:

```csharp
Copy code
public void Configure(IApplicationBuilder app)
{
    app.UseMiddleware<LoggingMiddleware>();
    // Other middleware registrations...
}
```

With this middleware in place, every request and response will be logged to the console, providing insights into the flow of data through the application.

2. Custom Middleware for Error Handling

Error handling middleware is crucial for gracefully managing exceptions that may occur during request processing. By centralizing error handling, you can ensure consistent responses and log errors effectively.

Implementing Error Handling Middleware

To create a custom error handling middleware:

1. **Create the Middleware Class**: Define a class similar to the logging middleware but focus on catching exceptions.
2. **Catch Exceptions**: Use a try-catch block within the InvokeAsync method to catch exceptions and log them while returning a user-friendly error response.

Example: Error Handling Middleware Implementation

```csharp
Copy code
public class ErrorHandlingMiddleware
{
```

MIDDLEWARE AND DEPENDENCY INJECTION IN ASP.NET CORE

```csharp
    private readonly RequestDelegate _next;

    public ErrorHandlingMiddleware(RequestDelegate next)
    {
        _next = next;
    }

    public async Task InvokeAsync(HttpContext context)
    {
        try
        {
            await _next(context); // Call the next middleware
        }
        catch (Exception ex)
        {
            // Log the exception (you can use a logging framework here)
            Console.WriteLine($"An error occurred: {ex.Message}");

            // Set the response status code and content
            context.Response.StatusCode = StatusCodes.Status500InternalServerError;
            await context.Response.WriteAsync("An unexpected error occurred. Please try again later.");
        }
    }
}
```

Registering the Error Handling Middleware

Register the error handling middleware early in the pipeline to catch exceptions from subsequent middleware:

```csharp
Copy code
public void Configure(IApplicationBuilder app)
{
```

```
    app.UseMiddleware<ErrorHandlingMiddleware>();
    // Other middleware registrations...
}
```

By placing this middleware at the top of the pipeline, it ensures that all unhandled exceptions are caught and processed, preventing them from propagating and causing application crashes.

3. Custom Middleware for Security

Security middleware can help enforce application security policies, such as preventing unauthorized access, protecting sensitive data, and enforcing content security policies. Custom middleware for security can check user authentication status, inspect headers, and apply rate limiting.

Implementing Security Middleware

A security middleware might focus on validating authentication tokens and enforcing user authorization before allowing requests to proceed.

Example: Security Middleware Implementation

```csharp
Copy code
public class SecurityMiddleware
{
    private readonly RequestDelegate _next;

    public SecurityMiddleware(RequestDelegate next)
    {
        _next = next;
    }

    public async Task InvokeAsync(HttpContext context)
    {
        // Check for a valid authentication token (this is a simple example)
        if (!context.Request.Headers.ContainsKey
```

```
("Authorization"))
        {
            context.Response.StatusCode =
            StatusCodes.Status401Unauthorized;
            await context.Response.
WriteAsync("Authorization header is missing.");
            return; // Short-circuit the pipeline
        }

        // Proceed to the next middleware
        await _next(context);
    }
}
```

Registering the Security Middleware

Register the security middleware in the Configure method, ideally before any middleware that requires authenticated access:

```csharp
Copy code
public void Configure(IApplicationBuilder app)
{
    app.UseMiddleware<SecurityMiddleware>();
    // Other middleware registrations...
}
```

This middleware checks for the presence of an Authorization header. If it's missing, it returns a 401 Unauthorized response, effectively preventing further processing.

Building custom middleware for logging, error handling, and security enhances the robustness of ASP.NET Core applications. By modularizing these concerns, developers can easily maintain and extend application functionality while ensuring a consistent user experience. As applications grow in complexity, these middleware components play a crucial role in monitoring, securing, and managing the flow of requests and responses, thereby improving overall performance and reliability.

In the next section, we will explore the essential concepts of dependency injection, which further complement middleware by efficiently managing service lifetimes and dependencies in your ASP.NET Core applications.

Advanced Dependency Injection Patterns and Service Lifetimes

Dependency Injection (DI) is a fundamental design pattern used in ASP.NET Core to achieve Inversion of Control (IoC). By injecting dependencies into classes rather than creating them internally, applications become more modular, testable, and maintainable. This section explores advanced dependency injection patterns, the different service lifetimes in ASP.NET Core, and how to leverage these concepts to build scalable applications.

1. Understanding Dependency Injection in ASP.NET Core

ASP.NET Core has a built-in dependency injection container that manages the creation and lifetimes of services. Services are typically registered in the ConfigureServices method of the Startup class, where developers can define how dependencies are resolved throughout the application.

Example: Registering Services in Startup.cs

```csharp
Copy code
public void ConfigureServices
(IServiceCollection services)
{
    services.AddTransient<IMyService, MyService>();
    services.AddScoped<IUserRepository, UserRepository>();
    services.AddSingleton
<ILoggingService, LoggingService>();
}
```

MIDDLEWARE AND DEPENDENCY INJECTION IN ASP.NET CORE

In this example:

- **AddTransient** creates a new instance of the service each time it is requested.
- **AddScoped** creates a new instance for each client request (scope).
- **AddSingleton** creates a single instance that is shared throughout the application's lifetime.

Understanding these service lifetimes is critical for building efficient applications and avoiding common pitfalls such as memory leaks and unwanted shared states.

2. Service Lifetimes Explained

ASP.NET Core supports three primary service lifetimes: Transient, Scoped, and Singleton. Each lifetime has its use cases and implications for memory management and state persistence.

- **Transient**: Services registered as transient are created each time they are requested. This is useful for lightweight, stateless services. However, using transient services excessively can lead to increased overhead due to the frequent instantiation of objects.
- **Use Case**: Use transient services for stateless services, such as utility classes that perform calculations or formatting.
- **Scoped**: Services registered as scoped are created once per request within the scope. In web applications, this means a new instance is created for each HTTP request. Scoped services can maintain state throughout the request but are disposed of when the request completes.
- **Use Case**: Use scoped services for services that interact with a database, where you want to ensure a consistent context per request.
- **Singleton**: Services registered as singleton are created the first time they are requested and reused throughout the application. Singleton services are ideal for shared data or services that maintain global state.

- **Use Case**: Use singleton services for caching mechanisms or configuration services that do not require instance-specific data.

Example: Registering Different Service Lifetimes

```csharp
Copy code
public void ConfigureServices(IServiceCollection services)
{
    services.AddTransient<ITransientService, TransientService>();
    services.AddScoped<IScopedService, ScopedService>();
    services.AddSingleton<ISingletonService, SingletonService>();
}
```

3. Advanced Dependency Injection Patterns

In addition to the basic patterns, there are several advanced techniques that can enhance the effectiveness of dependency injection in your ASP.NET Core applications:

- **Factory Pattern**: Implement a factory for creating instances of services, which can be particularly useful when the construction logic is complex or varies based on parameters.
- **Example: Factory Pattern Implementation**

```csharp
Copy code
public interface IServiceFactory
{
    IMyService CreateService();
}
```

```csharp
public class ServiceFactory : IServiceFactory
{
    private readonly IServiceProvider _serviceProvider;

    public ServiceFactory(IServiceProvider serviceProvider)
    {
        _serviceProvider = serviceProvider;
    }

    public IMyService CreateService()
    {
        return _serviceProvider.GetService<IMyService>();
    }
}
```

- Register the factory:

```csharp
Copy code
services.AddSingleton<IServiceFactory, ServiceFactory>();
```

- **Decorator Pattern**: Use the decorator pattern to extend the functionality of existing services without modifying their code. This is useful for cross-cutting concerns like logging, caching, or adding additional processing.
- **Example: Logging Decorator**

```csharp
Copy code
public class LoggingServiceDecorator : IMyService
{
```

```csharp
    private readonly IMyService _innerService;
    private readonly ILogger<LoggingServiceDecorator> _logger;

    public LoggingServiceDecorator(IMyService innerService,
    ILogger<LoggingServiceDecorator> logger)
    {
        _innerService = innerService;
        _logger = logger;
    }

    public void DoWork()
    {
        _logger.LogInformation("Starting work.");
        _innerService.DoWork();
        _logger.LogInformation("Work completed.");
    }
}
```

- Register the decorator:

```csharp
Copy code
services.AddTransient<IMyService, MyService>();
services.Decorate<IMyService, LoggingServiceDecorator>();
```

- **Service Locator Pattern**: Although generally discouraged in favor of constructor injection, the service locator pattern can be used when you need to resolve dependencies at runtime dynamically. However, it can make testing more challenging.
- **Example: Service Locator Implementation**

```csharp
Copy code
public class ServiceLocator
{
    private readonly IServiceProvider _serviceProvider;

    public ServiceLocator(IServiceProvider serviceProvider)
    {
        _serviceProvider = serviceProvider;
    }

    public T GetService<T>() =>
_serviceProvider.GetService<T>();
}
```

4. Scoped Services and Lifetimes in a Web Context

Understanding how scoped services work in a web application is crucial for correctly managing dependencies and data. In ASP.NET Core, scoped services are created per request, allowing developers to maintain a consistent state across multiple components involved in handling the same request.

Example: Using Scoped Services in Controllers

```csharp
Copy code
public class MyController : ControllerBase
{
    private readonly IMyService _myService;

    public MyController(IMyService myService)
    {
        _myService = myService;
    }

    public IActionResult Get()
    {
        var data = _myService.GetData();
```

```
        return Ok(data);
    }
}
```

Here, IMyService is resolved as a scoped service, ensuring that all data processed within this controller method belongs to the same request scope.

Best Practices:

- Avoid injecting scoped services into singleton services to prevent potential issues with scoped service lifetimes.
- Consider the implications of sharing state across requests when using singleton services.

5. Managing Dependencies with Configuration and Options Pattern

ASP.NET Core also provides support for managing application settings and configurations through the Options pattern. This allows you to bind configuration settings to classes and inject them as services.

Implementing the Options Pattern
Define a Configuration Class:

```
csharp
Copy code
public class MyOptions
{
    public string Setting1 { get; set; }
    public int Setting2 { get; set; }
}
```

Configure the Options: In the ConfigureServices method, bind your configuration section to the options class.

```csharp
Copy code
public void ConfigureServices(IServiceCollection services)
{
    services.Configure<MyOptions>(Configuration.GetSection("MyOptions"));
}
```

Injecting Options: Inject IOptions<MyOptions> into your services or controllers to access the configuration values.

```csharp
Copy code
public class MyService
{
    private readonly MyOptions _options;

    public MyService(IOptions<MyOptions> options)
    {
        _options = options.Value;
    }

    public void DoSomething()
    {
        Console.WriteLine($"Setting1: {_options.Setting1}");
    }
}
```

Advanced dependency injection patterns and a thorough understanding of service lifetimes are crucial for building maintainable and scalable ASP.NET Core applications. By leveraging the built-in DI container, utilizing advanced patterns like factories and decorators, and managing configurations effectively, developers can ensure that their applications are robust, testable, and adaptable to change.

In the next section, we will explore the best practices for configuring services, optimizing performance, and ensuring that your application architecture remains clean and effective throughout its lifecycle.

Real-World Examples: Caching, Security, and Custom Filters

In ASP.NET Core, the ability to effectively manage services and dependencies through dependency injection (DI) allows developers to build flexible and maintainable applications. This section provides practical, real-world examples of how to implement caching, security, and custom filters within the context of DI, showcasing the powerful capabilities of the framework in addressing common application requirements.

1. Caching in ASP.NET Core

Caching is a critical performance optimization technique used to store frequently accessed data in memory, thereby reducing the number of requests made to databases or external services. ASP.NET Core provides several caching mechanisms, including in-memory caching, distributed caching, and response caching. The use of DI makes it easy to manage caching dependencies.

Implementing In-Memory Caching

To use in-memory caching in an ASP.NET Core application, follow these steps:

Register the Caching Services: In the ConfigureServices method of your Startup class, add the in-memory caching service.

```csharp
Copy code
public void ConfigureServices(IServiceCollection services)
{
    services.AddControllers();
    services.AddMemoryCache(); // Register in-memory caching
}
```

MIDDLEWARE AND DEPENDENCY INJECTION IN ASP.NET CORE

Inject and Use the IMemoryCache Service: You can now inject IMemoryCache into your controllers or services to cache data.

Example: Caching Data in a Service

```csharp
Copy code
public class ProductService
{
    private readonly IMemoryCache _cache;

    public ProductService(IMemoryCache cache)
    {
        _cache = cache;
    }

    public Product GetProduct(int id)
    {
        // Try to get the product from cache
        if (!_cache.TryGetValue(id, out Product product))
        {
            // If not found in cache, fetch from database
            product = FetchProductFromDatabase(id);

            // Store in cache for future requests
            _cache.Set(id, product, TimeSpan.FromMinutes(5)); // Set cache with expiration
        }
        return product;
    }

    private Product FetchProductFromDatabase(int id)
    {
        // Simulate database access
        return new Product { Id = id, Name = "Product " + id };
    }
}
```

Using the Caching Service: In your controller, inject ProductService to access cached products.

Example: Controller Utilizing Caching

```csharp
Copy code
[ApiController]
[Route("api/[controller]")]
public class ProductsController : ControllerBase
{
    private readonly ProductService _productService;

    public ProductsController(ProductService productService)
    {
        _productService = productService;
    }

    [HttpGet("{id}")]
    public IActionResult GetProduct(int id)
    {
        var product = _productService.GetProduct(id);
        return Ok(product);
    }
}
```

This implementation allows for fast retrieval of products by caching them in memory, significantly reducing database calls and improving response times.

2. Implementing Security in ASP.NET Core

Security is paramount in web applications. ASP.NET Core provides several features for implementing security, including authentication and authorization mechanisms. Utilizing DI allows for a flexible and manageable security architecture.

Implementing Role-Based Security

Configure Identity Services: First, set up ASP.NET Core Identity in your application.

MIDDLEWARE AND DEPENDENCY INJECTION IN ASP.NET CORE

```csharp
Copy code
public void ConfigureServices(IServiceCollection services)
{
    services.AddDbContext<ApplicationDbContext>(options =>
        options.UseSqlServer(Configuration.GetConnectionString("DefaultConnection")));

    services.AddIdentity<IdentityUser, IdentityRole>()
        .AddEntityFrameworkStores<ApplicationDbContext>()
        .AddDefaultTokenProviders();
}
```

Create a Role-Based Authorization Policy: Define a policy for role-based access in the ConfigureServices method.

```csharp
Copy code
services.AddAuthorization(options =>
{
    options.AddPolicy("RequireAdministratorRole",
        policy => policy.RequireRole("Administrator"));
});
```

Using Authorize Attributes: Apply the [Authorize] attribute to controllers or actions to enforce role-based security.

Example: Securing a Controller Action

```csharp
Copy code
[Authorize(Policy = "RequireAdministratorRole")]
[ApiController]
[Route("api/[controller]")]
public class AdminController : ControllerBase
```

```csharp
{
    [HttpGet]
    public IActionResult GetSensitiveData()
    {
        return Ok("This is protected data accessible only to
        administrators.");
    }
}
```

User Registration and Role Assignment: Implement user registration and assign roles programmatically.

Example: User Registration with Role Assignment

```csharp
Copy code
public async Task RegisterUser(string email, string password)
{
    var user = new IdentityUser
{ UserName = email, Email = email };
    var result = await _userManager.CreateAsync(user, password);

    if (result.Succeeded)
    {
        await _userManager.AddToRoleAsync
(user, "Administrator"); // Assign role
    }
}
```

This example demonstrates how to use ASP.NET Core's built-in identity and authorization features to create a secure API with role-based access control.

3. Custom Filters in ASP.NET Core

Filters in ASP.NET Core provide a way to execute code before or after an action method is called. Custom filters can be used for cross-cutting

MIDDLEWARE AND DEPENDENCY INJECTION IN ASP.NET CORE

concerns such as logging, authorization, caching, and exception handling. Utilizing DI in filters allows you to inject dependencies seamlessly.

Creating a Custom Action Filter

Implement the IAsyncActionFilter Interface: Create a custom action filter by implementing the IAsyncActionFilter interface.

Example: Logging Action Filter

```csharp
Copy code
public class LoggingActionFilter : IAsyncActionFilter
{
    private readonly ILogger<LoggingActionFilter> _logger;

    public LoggingActionFilter
(ILogger<LoggingActionFilter> logger)
    {
        _logger = logger;
    }

    public async Task OnActionExecutionAsync
(ActionExecutingContext context,
ActionExecutionDelegate next)
    {
        _logger.LogInformation
("Executing action: {ActionName}",
context.ActionDescriptor.DisplayName);
        await next();
// Call the next filter or action
        _logger.LogInformation
("Executed action: {ActionName}",
context.ActionDescriptor.DisplayName);
    }
}
```

Register the Filter Globally or Per-Controller: You can register your custom filter globally in the Startup class or apply it to specific controllers.

Global Registration Example

```csharp
Copy code
public void ConfigureServices(IServiceCollection services)
{
    services.AddControllers(options =>
    {
        options.Filters.Add<LoggingActionFilter>(); // Register
        globally
    });
}
```

Per-Controller Registration Example

```csharp
Copy code
[ServiceFilter(typeof(LoggingActionFilter))]
[ApiController]
[Route("api/[controller]")]
public class ProductsController : ControllerBase
{
    [HttpGet]
    public IActionResult GetProducts()
    {
        return Ok(new List<string>
{ "Product1", "Product2" });
    }
}
```

Customizing Filters for Specific Scenarios: You can create various filters for different scenarios, such as caching responses or handling exceptions.

Example: Caching Action Results

```csharp
Copy code
```

```csharp
public class CacheActionFilter : IAsyncActionFilter
{
    private readonly IMemoryCache _cache;

    public CacheActionFilter(IMemoryCache cache)
    {
        _cache = cache;
    }

    public async Task OnActionExecutionAsync
(ActionExecutingContext context,
ActionExecutionDelegate next)
    {
        var cacheKey = context.HttpContext.Request.Path.ToString();
        if (_cache.TryGetValue(cacheKey, out var cachedResult))
        {
            context.Result = (IActionResult)cachedResult; // Return cached result
            return;
        }

        var result = await next(); // Call the action
        _cache.Set(cacheKey, result); // Cache the result
    }
}
```

This caching filter example can be registered similarly to the logging filter, providing a straightforward mechanism for optimizing response times for frequently accessed endpoints.

Real-world applications often face challenges related to caching, security, and cross-cutting concerns such as logging and error handling. By leveraging ASP.NET Core's powerful dependency injection framework, developers can create modular, maintainable solutions that effectively address these challenges. Implementing caching improves performance, while robust security mechanisms protect sensitive data. Custom filters further enhance the architecture by promoting code reuse and separation of concerns.

Security Essentials for Modern Web Applications

Best Practices for Securing ASP.NET Core Applications

In today's digital landscape, securing web applications is paramount. With the increasing number of cyber threats, ensuring that ASP.NET Core applications are secure requires a comprehensive approach that encompasses various aspects of security. This chapter outlines the best practices for securing ASP.NET Core applications, focusing on fundamental security principles, authentication and authorization mechanisms, data protection, and secure coding practices.

1. Adopting Security Principles

Defense in Depth

Implementing a defense-in-depth strategy means layering multiple security measures to protect the application. If one layer fails, additional layers still provide protection. This strategy includes securing the application itself, the infrastructure it runs on, and the data it manages.

Least Privilege Principle

Ensure that users and services have only the permissions necessary to perform their tasks. This limits the potential damage from compromised accounts and reduces the attack surface. In ASP.NET Core, implement role-based access control (RBAC) to enforce least privilege.

Fail Securely

When errors occur, design the application to fail securely, avoiding the exposure of sensitive data. For example, when catching exceptions, log the error without revealing stack traces or detailed error messages to end users. Use generic error pages for production environments.

2. Authentication and Authorization Best Practices
Use ASP.NET Core Identity

ASP.NET Core Identity provides a robust framework for managing user authentication and authorization. It supports various authentication methods, including cookies, tokens, and external providers. Ensure you use Identity for user management and authentication.

Enable Two-Factor Authentication (2FA): Add an extra layer of security by enabling 2FA for user accounts. This can be done via SMS, email, or authenticator apps. ASP.NET Core Identity supports 2FA out of the box.

```csharp
Copy code
services.Configure<IdentityOptions>(options =>
{
    options.Tokens.AuthenticatorTokenProvider =
    TokenOptions.DefaultAuthenticatorProvider;
    options.SignIn.RequireConfirmedAccount =
 true; // Require email confirmation
});
```

Implement OAuth and OpenID Connect: For applications requiring third-party authentication, utilize OAuth and OpenID Connect for secure authentication flows. ASP.NET Core provides middleware to easily integrate with providers like Google, Facebook, and Microsoft.

```csharp
Copy code
services.AddAuthentication()
    .AddGoogle(options =>
    {
        options.ClientId = Configuration["Google:ClientId"];
        options.ClientSecret = Configuration["Google:ClientSecret"];
    });
```

Use Policies for Fine-Grained Authorization

Define authorization policies to manage access controls effectively. Policies can incorporate role requirements, claims, or custom criteria. This ensures that different users have access to appropriate resources based on their roles or attributes.

```csharp
Copy code
services.AddAuthorization(options =>
{
    options.AddPolicy("AdminOnly", policy =>
    policy.RequireRole("Administrator"));
});
```

Avoid Hardcoding Secrets

Do not hardcode secrets (like API keys or connection strings) in your application code. Instead, use secure mechanisms for storing sensitive information, such as:

- **Environment Variables**: Store secrets in environment variables.
- **User Secrets**: For development, use the Secret Manager tool to store sensitive information.
- **Azure Key Vault or AWS Secrets Manager**: For production, utilize a dedicated secret management service.

3. Data Protection Strategies
Use HTTPS Everywhere

Always use HTTPS to encrypt data in transit. In ASP.NET Core, enforce HTTPS by using middleware that redirects HTTP requests to HTTPS.

```csharp
Copy code
public void Configure(IApplicationBuilder app, IHostingEnvironment env)
{
    app.UseHttpsRedirection(); // Redirect HTTP to HTTPS
}
```

Implement Data Protection for Sensitive Data

ASP.NET Core provides a data protection API for encrypting and protecting sensitive data, such as user information and configuration settings. Use the built-in data protection services to encrypt data at rest.

```csharp
Copy code
public void ConfigureServices(IServiceCollection services)
{
    services.AddDataProtection()
        .PersistKeysToFileSystem(new
        DirectoryInfo(@"\\server\share\keys"));
 // Store keys securely
}
```

Use Entity Framework Core to Prevent SQL Injection

Always use parameterized queries or Entity Framework Core's LINQ queries to prevent SQL injection attacks. Do not concatenate user input directly into SQL queries.

```csharp
Copy code
```

```
var products = await _context.Products
    .Where(p => p.Name.Contains(searchTerm)) // Safe from SQL
    injection
    .ToListAsync();
```

4. Secure Coding Practices
Input Validation and Sanitization

Always validate and sanitize user input to prevent attacks such as cross-site scripting (XSS) and SQL injection. Use model validation attributes and libraries like FluentValidation to enforce input validation rules.

```csharp
Copy code
public class ProductModel
{
    [Required]
    [StringLength(100, MinimumLength = 1)]
    public string Name { get; set; }
}
```

Prevent Cross-Site Scripting (XSS)

When displaying user-generated content, always encode output to prevent XSS attacks. Use built-in HTML encoding features provided by Razor views.

```html
Copy code
<p>@Html.DisplayFor(model => model.UserInput)</p> // Automatically encodes HTML
```

Cross-Site Request Forgery (CSRF) Protection

ASP.NET Core includes built-in CSRF protection using AntiForgery tokens. Ensure that forms include the necessary tokens, and use the [ValidateAntiForgeryToken] attribute on actions that handle form submissions.

```csharp
Copy code
[HttpPost]
[ValidateAntiForgeryToken]
public IActionResult SubmitForm(FormModel model)
{
    // Handle form submission
}
```

Limit Request Size and Rate Limiting

Protect against denial-of-service attacks by limiting the request size and implementing rate limiting. ASP.NET Core allows you to configure these limits easily.

```csharp
Copy code
services.Configure<IISServerOptions>(options =>
{
    options.MaxRequestBodySize = 10 * 1024; // Limit to 10 KB
});
```

5. Logging and Monitoring for Security

Implement Structured Logging

Use structured logging to capture security-related events, such as failed login attempts and access to sensitive data. Libraries like Serilog and NLog support structured logging in ASP.NET Core applications.

```csharp
Copy code
_log.LogWarning("Failed login attempt for user: {UserName}", username);
```

Monitor Application Health and Security Events

Set up monitoring for application health and security events. Use

Application Insights or similar services to track application performance and security-related metrics, such as response times and error rates.

6. Regular Security Audits and Updates
Conduct Regular Security Audits

Periodically review your code and configuration for security vulnerabilities. Conduct penetration testing and use automated tools to identify potential weaknesses.

Keep Dependencies Up-to-Date

Regularly update ASP.NET Core and third-party libraries to the latest versions to benefit from security patches and enhancements. Use tools like NuGet Package Manager to manage and update dependencies efficiently.

Securing an ASP.NET Core application involves a comprehensive approach that integrates best practices in authentication, authorization, data protection, secure coding, and ongoing monitoring. By implementing these strategies, developers can significantly reduce the risk of security breaches and ensure that their applications are resilient against common threats. The security landscape is constantly evolving, so maintaining awareness of the latest security trends and adapting accordingly is essential for safeguarding web applications in an increasingly complex environment.

Configuring HTTPS and Handling Sensitive Data

As web applications become more prevalent in our everyday lives, ensuring the security and integrity of data transmitted between clients and servers is critical. In this section, we will explore how to configure HTTPS in ASP.NET Core applications and manage sensitive data effectively. By implementing these practices, developers can significantly enhance the security posture of their applications.

1. Understanding HTTPS
What is HTTPS?

Hypertext Transfer Protocol Secure (HTTPS) is an extension of HTTP that uses Transport Layer Security (TLS) to encrypt data transmitted between a web server and a client (such as a web browser). HTTPS ensures that communications remain private and secure, protecting against eavesdropping and man-in-the-middle attacks.

Why Use HTTPS?
- **Data Encryption**: HTTPS encrypts the data exchanged between the client and server, ensuring that sensitive information, such as login credentials and personal data, is not easily intercepted.
- **Data Integrity**: HTTPS protects data from being altered or corrupted during transmission.
- **Authentication**: HTTPS verifies the identity of the website, assuring users that they are communicating with the legitimate site and not an imposter.

2. Configuring HTTPS in ASP.NET Core
1. Obtain an SSL Certificate

To enable HTTPS, you need an SSL/TLS certificate issued by a trusted Certificate Authority (CA). You can obtain certificates from various providers, including Let's Encrypt (free), Comodo, and DigiCert. For development purposes, ASP.NET Core provides a self-signed certificate option.

2. Configure HTTPS in ASP.NET Core

After obtaining a certificate, configure your ASP.NET Core application to use HTTPS. This can be accomplished through the Kestrel web server configuration in the Program.cs file or the appsettings.json file.

Using Program.cs:

SECURITY ESSENTIALS FOR MODERN WEB APPLICATIONS

```csharp
Copy code
public class Program
{
    public static void Main(string[] args)
    {
        CreateHostBuilder(args).Build().Run();
    }

    public static IHostBuilder CreateHostBuilder(string[] args) =>
        Host.CreateDefaultBuilder(args)
.ConfigureWebHostDefaults(webBuilder =>
            {
webBuilder.UseStartup<Startup>()
.UseKestrel(options =>
                {
options.ListenAnyIP(5000); // HTTP
options.ListenAnyIP(5001, listenOptions =>
                    {
listenOptions.UseHttps
("path/to/certificate.pfx", "yourpassword");
                    });
                });
            });
}
```

Using appsettings.json:

You can also specify HTTPS settings in appsettings.json:

```json
Copy code
{
  "Kestrel": {
    "Endpoints": {
      "Https": {
        "Url": "https://localhost:5001",
        "Certificate": {
          "Path": "path/to/certificate.pfx",
```

```
            "Password": "yourpassword"
        }
      }
    }
  }
}
```

3. Redirect HTTP to HTTPS

To ensure that all traffic is encrypted, redirect HTTP requests to HTTPS. This can be achieved using middleware in the Startup.cs file.

```csharp
Copy code
public void Configure(IApplicationBuilder app, IWebHostEnvironment env)
{
    if (env.IsDevelopment())
    {
        app.UseDeveloperExceptionPage();
    }
    else
    {
        app.UseExceptionHandler("/Home/Error");
        app.UseHsts(); // Adds the Strict-Transport-Security header
    }

    app.UseHttpsRedirection(); // Redirects HTTP to HTTPS
    app.UseStaticFiles();
    app.UseRouting();
    app.UseAuthorization();
    app.UseEndpoints(endpoints =>
    {
        endpoints.MapControllerRoute(
            name: "default",
            pattern: "{controller=Home}/{action=Index}/{id?}");
    });
}
```

4. Testing HTTPS Configuration

After configuring HTTPS, test the application to ensure that it correctly redirects HTTP requests to HTTPS and that SSL certificates are valid. You can use tools like SSL Labs' SSL Test to analyze your configuration and ensure that best practices are followed.

3. Handling Sensitive Data
1. Protecting Sensitive Information

When dealing with sensitive data such as passwords, credit card information, and personal details, it's essential to implement measures that protect this information both at rest and in transit.

2. Use Data Protection APIs

ASP.NET Core provides a Data Protection API (DPAPI) that offers a simple way to protect sensitive data. The API can be used to encrypt and decrypt data, ensuring that sensitive information remains confidential.

```csharp
csharp
Copy code
public class SensitiveDataService
{
    private readonly IDataProtector _protector;

    public SensitiveDataService(IDataProtectionProvider provider)
    {
        _protector = provider.CreateProtector("SensitiveData");
    }

    public string Protect(string data)
    {
        return _protector.Protect(data);
    }

    public string Unprotect(string protectedData)
```

```
    {
        return _protector.Unprotect(protectedData);
    }
}
```

3. Secure Storage for Sensitive Information

When storing sensitive data, ensure that you utilize secure methods. Avoid using plain text storage for sensitive information. Instead, consider the following:

- **Database Encryption**: Use encryption at the database level to protect sensitive fields. Many databases support built-in encryption features (e.g., SQL Server Transparent Data Encryption).
- **Environment Variables**: Store sensitive configuration settings, such as connection strings and API keys, in environment variables rather than hardcoding them in your application code.
- **User Secrets**: For development, use ASP.NET Core's User Secrets feature to manage sensitive information securely without checking it into source control.

```bash
Copy code
dotnet user-secrets set "ConnectionStrings:DefaultConnection" "YourConnectionString"
```

4. Input Validation and Sanitization

Implement input validation and sanitization to protect sensitive data from common attacks, such as SQL injection and XSS. Always validate and sanitize user inputs before processing them.

```csharp
Copy code
```

```csharp
public IActionResult Submit(UserInputModel model)
{
    if (ModelState.IsValid)
    {
        // Process input
    }
    return View(model);
}
```

5. Logging Sensitive Information Carefully

Be cautious when logging data that may include sensitive information. Always sanitize logs to remove sensitive data, and avoid logging passwords, personal identification numbers (PINs), or sensitive user data.

```
csharp
Copy code
_log.LogInformation("User {UserName}
 has logged in.", userName);
```

Configuring HTTPS and handling sensitive data are critical components of securing ASP.NET Core applications. By ensuring that data is transmitted securely via HTTPS and that sensitive information is protected both at rest and in transit, developers can create robust applications that safeguard user information and maintain trust. Incorporating these practices into your development lifecycle will enhance the overall security posture of your web applications, allowing you to focus on delivering value to your users without compromising their safety.

Protection Against Common Web Vulnerabilities (e.g., XSS, CSRF, SQL Injection)

In today's web landscape, security vulnerabilities pose significant threats to applications and their users. Understanding common vulnerabilities and implementing strategies to mitigate them is crucial for developers working with ASP.NET Core applications. This section will focus on three prevalent vulnerabilities—Cross-Site Scripting (XSS), Cross-Site Request Forgery (CSRF), and SQL Injection—and provide practical techniques for defending against them.

1. Cross-Site Scripting (XSS)
What is XSS?

Cross-Site Scripting (XSS) is a security vulnerability that allows attackers to inject malicious scripts into web pages viewed by other users. This can lead to unauthorized access to sensitive information, session hijacking, and more. XSS attacks typically occur when user input is not properly sanitized and is then rendered in the browser.

Types of XSS:

- **Stored XSS**: The injected script is stored on the server (e.g., in a database) and served to users when they access the affected page.
- **Reflected XSS**: The script is reflected off a web server, often via a URL parameter, and executed immediately in the user's browser.
- **DOM-based XSS**: The vulnerability exists in the client-side scripts rather than server-side processing, allowing attackers to manipulate the Document Object Model (DOM) to execute malicious code.

Mitigation Strategies for XSS:

Input Validation and Sanitization: Always validate and sanitize user inputs. Use libraries like HtmlSanitizer to clean HTML content by removing potentially dangerous tags and attributes.

```csharp
Copy code
var sanitizedInput = HtmlSanitizer.Sanitize(userInput);
```

Output Encoding: Encode output to prevent untrusted data from being interpreted as executable code. ASP.NET Core's Razor views automatically HTML-encode output by using the @ symbol.

```html
html
Copy code
<p>@Model.UserInput</p> // Automatically HTML-encoded
```

Content Security Policy (CSP): Implement a CSP to restrict the sources of scripts and other content that browsers are allowed to load. This helps mitigate the risk of XSS by blocking unauthorized script execution.

```csharp
csharp
Copy code
public void Configure(IApplicationBuilder app)
{
    app.Use(async (context, next) =>
    {
        context.Response.Headers.Add
("Content-Security-Policy", "script-src 'self'");
        await next();
    });
}
```

2. Cross-Site Request Forgery (CSRF)
What is CSRF?

Cross-Site Request Forgery (CSRF) is an attack that tricks a user's browser into making unauthorized requests to a different site where the user is authenticated. If the user is logged in, the malicious request can perform actions on behalf of the user without their consent.

Mitigation Strategies for CSRF:

Anti-Forgery Tokens: ASP.NET Core provides built-in support for CSRF protection using anti-forgery tokens. Include the [ValidateAntiF orgeryToken] attribute on actions that process form submissions, and ensure that your forms contain the anti-forgery token.

```csharp
Copy code
[HttpPost]
[ValidateAntiForgeryToken]
public IActionResult SubmitForm(FormModel model)
{
    // Process form submission
}
```

In your Razor views, include the token in forms using the @Html.AntiForgeryToken() helper:

```html
Copy code
<form asp-action="SubmitForm" method="post">
    @Html.AntiForgeryToken()
    <!-- Other form fields -->
</form>
```

SameSite Cookie Attribute: Set the SameSite attribute for cookies to prevent them from being sent with cross-origin requests. This helps mitigate CSRF attacks by restricting how cookies are sent in requests.

```csharp
Copy code
services.ConfigureApplicationCookie(options =>
{
    options.Cookie.SameSite = SameSiteMode.Strict;
});
```

Use HTTP Referrer Header: Validate the HTTP Referrer header to ensure that requests are coming from your application's pages. However, this is not a foolproof solution, as some browsers may not send the header.

3. SQL Injection
   What is SQL Injection?

SECURITY ESSENTIALS FOR MODERN WEB APPLICATIONS

SQL Injection is a vulnerability that allows attackers to execute arbitrary SQL code against your database by manipulating input data. This can lead to unauthorized access, data breaches, and loss of data integrity.

Mitigation Strategies for SQL Injection:

Parameterized Queries: Always use parameterized queries or prepared statements when interacting with databases. This prevents attackers from injecting malicious SQL code by separating data from commands.

```csharp
Copy code
var products = await _context.Products
    .FromSqlRaw("SELECT * FROM Products WHERE Name = {0}",
    productName)
    .ToListAsync();
```

Entity Framework Core: When using Entity Framework Core, take advantage of its LINQ queries, which automatically parameterize queries and help prevent SQL injection.

```csharp
Copy code
var products = await _context.Products
    .Where(p => p.Name.Contains(searchTerm))
    .ToListAsync();
```

Input Validation: Validate and sanitize user inputs to ensure they conform to expected formats before processing them. For example, restrict input lengths and types based on the expected data.

```csharp
Copy code
public class ProductModel
{
    [Required]
```

```
    [StringLength(100, MinimumLength = 1)]
    public string Name { get; set; }
}
```

Use ORM Tools: Utilize Object-Relational Mapping (ORM) tools like Entity Framework Core, which abstract database access and reduce the risk of SQL injection through proper parameterization and query generation.

Protecting ASP.NET Core applications from common web vulnerabilities like XSS, CSRF, and SQL injection requires a proactive and layered approach. By implementing best practices such as input validation, output encoding, anti-forgery tokens, and parameterized queries, developers can significantly reduce the risk of these vulnerabilities.

Incorporating these strategies into the development lifecycle not only secures the application but also builds trust with users, ensuring that their sensitive data remains protected against malicious attacks. Continuous education and vigilance in security practices are essential in adapting to evolving threats and maintaining a secure web application environment.

Configuring Authentication Policies and Authorization Schemes

Effective security in web applications hinges on robust authentication and authorization mechanisms. ASP.NET Core provides a flexible and comprehensive framework for configuring authentication policies and authorization schemes. This section will guide you through the process of establishing authentication policies, defining authorization schemes, and integrating them into your ASP.NET Core applications.

1. Understanding Authentication and Authorization

Authentication is the process of verifying the identity of a user or service, while **authorization** determines what resources or actions an authenticated user is allowed to access. In ASP.NET Core, authentication and authorization are separate concerns, which allows for flexible security

SECURITY ESSENTIALS FOR MODERN WEB APPLICATIONS

configurations.

- **Authentication** verifies who the user is.
- **Authorization** determines what an authenticated user can do.

2. Configuring Authentication Policies

Authentication policies in ASP.NET Core allow you to define rules that dictate how users can authenticate with your application. The most common authentication types are cookie authentication and token-based authentication (JWT).

1. Setting Up Cookie Authentication

To implement cookie authentication, you need to configure the authentication middleware in the Startup.cs file.

```csharp
Copy code
public void ConfigureServices(IServiceCollection services)
{
    services.AddAuthentication(options =>
    {
        options.DefaultAuthenticateScheme = 
        CookieAuthenticationDefaults.AuthenticationScheme;
        options.DefaultSignInScheme = 
        CookieAuthenticationDefaults.AuthenticationScheme;
        options.DefaultChallengeScheme = 
        CookieAuthenticationDefaults.AuthenticationScheme;
    })
    .AddCookie(options =>
    {
        options.LoginPath = "/Account/Login";
        options.LogoutPath = "/Account/Logout";
        options.AccessDeniedPath = "/Account/AccessDenied";
    });

    services.AddControllersWithViews();
```

}

2. Setting Up JWT Bearer Authentication

If you're building an API or SPA that requires token-based authentication, configure JWT Bearer authentication as follows:

```csharp
Copy code
public void ConfigureServices(IServiceCollection services)
{
    services.AddAuthentication(JwtBearerDefaults.AuthenticationScheme)
        .AddJwtBearer(options =>
        {
            options.TokenValidationParameters = new TokenValidationParameters
            {
                ValidateIssuer = true,
                ValidateAudience = true,
                ValidateLifetime = true,
                ValidateIssuerSigningKey = true,
                ValidIssuer = "YourIssuer",
                ValidAudience = "YourAudience",
                IssuerSigningKey = new SymmetricSecurityKey(Encoding.UTF8.GetBytes("YourSecretKey"))
            };
        });

    services.AddControllers();
}
```

In both cases, ensure that you add the authentication middleware in the Configure method:

```csharp
Copy code
public void Configure(IApplicationBuilder app, IWebHostEnvironment env)
{
    app.UseRouting();
    app.UseAuthentication();
    app.UseAuthorization();

    app.UseEndpoints(endpoints =>
    {
        endpoints.MapControllers();
    });
}
```

3. Creating Authorization Policies

Authorization policies define the rules that determine whether a user has access to specific resources or actions. You can create custom authorization policies based on user claims, roles, or other criteria.

1. Defining a Custom Authorization Policy

You can define a custom authorization policy in the ConfigureServices method. For example, let's create a policy that requires users to have a specific claim:

```csharp
Copy code
public void ConfigureServices(IServiceCollection services)
{
    services.AddAuthorization(options =>
    {
        options.AddPolicy("RequireAdminRole", policy =>
            policy.RequireRole("Admin"));

        options.AddPolicy("RequireCustomClaim", policy =>
            policy.RequireClaim
```

```
    ("CustomClaim", "ClaimValue"));
        });
}
```

2. Applying Policies to Controllers or Actions

Once you have defined a policy, you can apply it to controllers or specific actions using the [Authorize] attribute:

```csharp
Copy code
[Authorize(Policy = "RequireAdminRole")]
public class AdminController : Controller
{
    public IActionResult Index()
    {
        return View();
    }
}

[Authorize(Policy = "RequireCustomClaim")]
public class CustomClaimController : Controller
{
    public IActionResult Index()
    {
        return View();
    }
}
```

4. Integrating Authorization Schemes

ASP.NET Core supports multiple authorization schemes, allowing you to use different authentication methods within the same application. You can specify which authentication scheme to use when applying authorization.

1. Specifying an Authentication Scheme in Authorization Attributes

To apply a specific authentication scheme, you can use the AuthenticationSchemes property in the [Authorize] attribute:

```csharp
Copy code
[Authorize(AuthenticationSchemes = 
JwtBearerDefaults.AuthenticationScheme)]
public class ApiController : ControllerBase
{
    public IActionResult Get()
    {
        return Ok("This is a secured API response.");
    }
}
```

2. Combining Multiple Policies

You can also combine multiple policies to ensure that users meet multiple criteria for authorization. For example:

```csharp
Copy code
[Authorize(Policy = "RequireAdminRole,RequireCustomClaim")]
public class CombinedPolicyController : Controller
{
    public IActionResult Index()
    {
        return View();
    }
}
```

5. Testing and Troubleshooting Authentication and Authorization

Testing authentication and authorization can help identify configuration issues and ensure that security measures are effective.

1. Logging and Monitoring

Enable logging for authentication and authorization events to track access attempts and troubleshoot issues. You can configure logging in the appsettings.json file:

```json
Copy code
{
  "Logging": {
    "LogLevel": {
      "Default": "Information",
      "Microsoft.AspNetCore.Authentication": "Debug",
      "Microsoft.AspNetCore.Authorization": "Debug"
    }
  }
}
```

2. Testing with Postman or cURL

When testing APIs, tools like Postman or cURL can be invaluable. For instance, you can send a request to your API with a Bearer token to test if authorization is correctly enforced:

```bash
Copy code
curl -H "Authorization: Bearer your_jwt_token" https://localhost:5001/api/values
```

3. Handling Authorization Failures

When an authorization failure occurs, ensure that your application gracefully handles the response. You can customize the behavior for unauthorized requests by implementing middleware that captures such events.

```csharp
Copy code
app.Use(async (context, next) =>
{
    await next();
    if (context.Response.StatusCode == 403) // Forbidden
```

```
    {
        context.Response.Redirect
("/Account/AccessDenied");
    }
});
```

Configuring authentication policies and authorization schemes in ASP.NET Core allows developers to create secure applications that protect resources and enforce access control based on user roles and claims. By implementing cookie authentication, JWT Bearer tokens, and custom authorization policies, you can ensure that your application is secure and that only authorized users have access to sensitive actions and resources.

Continuously reviewing and testing your authentication and authorization configurations will enhance your application's security and provide a better user experience. By employing best practices in authentication and authorization, you can build robust ASP.NET Core applications that meet modern security requirements.

Working with Environment-Based Security Settings

In modern web development, configuring security settings based on the application's environment (development, staging, production) is critical for ensuring both flexibility and security. ASP.NET Core provides a straightforward way to manage environment-specific configurations, allowing developers to tailor security settings to fit each deployment scenario. This section will explore how to implement environment-based security settings effectively, including using the built-in configuration system and applying different security measures for various environments.

1. Understanding ASP.NET Core Environments

ASP.NET Core supports multiple environments, which you can define and use to differentiate configurations during development, testing, and production. The common environments are:

- **Development**: The environment where developers actively work on features and bug fixes.
- **Staging**: A pre-production environment used for testing before deployment to production.
- **Production**: The live environment where the application is accessible to end users.

The environment can be set through the ASPNETCORE_ENVIRONMENT environment variable or through launch settings in development tools.

Setting the Environment:

You can set the environment in several ways:

- Via the command line:

```bash
Copy code
set ASPNETCORE_ENVIRONMENT=Development
```

- In Visual Studio, by modifying the launchSettings.json file:

```json
Copy code
"profiles": {
    "IIS Express": {
        "commandName": "IISExpress",
        "launchBrowser": true,
        "environmentVariables": {
```

```
        "ASPNETCORE_ENVIRONMENT": "Development"
      }
    }
}
```

- Through the hosting environment in Azure or other cloud services.

2. Configuring Environment-Based Settings

ASP.NET Core uses the configuration system to read settings from various sources, including JSON files, environment variables, and command-line arguments. You can create environment-specific configuration files, allowing you to override default settings based on the environment.

1. Using appsettings.json and Environment-Specific Files

You can define a default appsettings.json file and then create additional files for specific environments, such as appsettings.Development.json or appsettings.Production.json. ASP.NET Core automatically loads the appropriate settings based on the current environment.

Example of appsettings.json:

```json
Copy code
{
  "Logging": {
    "LogLevel": {
      "Default": "Information",
      "Microsoft": "Warning"
    }
  },
  "AllowedHosts": "*",
  "ConnectionStrings": {
    "DefaultConnection": "Server=localhost;Database=MyDb;Trusted_Connection=True;"
  }
```

}

Example of appsettings.Development.json:

```json
Copy code
{
  "Logging": {
    "LogLevel": {
      "Default": "Debug",
      "Microsoft": "Information"
    }
  },
  "ConnectionStrings": {
    "DefaultConnection": "Server=localhost;Database=MyDevDb;Trusted_Connection=True;"
  }
}
```

In this configuration, when running in the Development environment, the application will use the connection string defined in appsettings.Development.json, while in Production, it will use the connection string defined in appsettings.json.

2. Accessing Configuration Values

You can access these configuration values in your application using dependency injection. For example, to access the connection string:

```csharp
Copy code
public class MyService
{
    private readonly string _connectionString;

    public MyService(IConfiguration configuration)
```

```
    {
        _connectionString = 
        configuration.GetConnectionString("DefaultConnection");
    }
}
```

3. Applying Security Settings Based on Environment

Different environments may require different security settings. For instance, development environments may use relaxed security measures to facilitate testing, while production environments must enforce strict security practices.

1. Configuring CORS Policies

You might want to enable more relaxed CORS policies in a development environment to allow for easier API testing. For example:

```csharp
Copy code
public void ConfigureServices(IServiceCollection services)
{
    if (Environment.IsDevelopment())
    {
        services.AddCors(options =>
        {
            options.AddPolicy("AllowAll",
                builder =>
                {
                    builder.AllowAnyOrigin()
                        .AllowAnyHeader()
                        .AllowAnyMethod();
                });
        });
    }
    else
    {
        services.AddCors(options =>
        {
```

```
            options.AddPolicy("AllowSpecific",
                builder =>
                {
    builder.WithOrigins("https://www.yoursite.com")
                        .AllowAnyHeader()
                        .AllowAnyMethod();
                });
        });
    }
}
```

2. Enabling HTTPS Redirection

In production environments, HTTPS redirection is essential for securing communication. You can conditionally enable HTTPS redirection based on the environment:

```csharp
Copy code
public void Configure(IApplicationBuilder
 app, IWebHostEnvironment env)
{
    if (env.IsProduction())
    {
        app.UseHttpsRedirection();
    }

    app.UseRouting();
    app.UseAuthentication();
    app.UseAuthorization();

    app.UseEndpoints(endpoints =>
    {
        endpoints.MapControllers();
    });
}
```

3. Customizing Error Handling

Custom error handling is also vital. In development, you might want

SECURITY ESSENTIALS FOR MODERN WEB APPLICATIONS

detailed error messages, while in production, you should provide generic error responses to avoid exposing sensitive information.

```csharp
Copy code
public void Configure(IApplicationBuilder app, IWebHostEnvironment env)
{
    if (env.IsDevelopment())
    {
        app.UseDeveloperExceptionPage();
    }
    else
    {
        app.UseExceptionHandler("/Home/Error");
        app.UseHsts();
    }

    app.UseHttpsRedirection();
    app.UseStaticFiles();
    app.UseRouting();
    app.UseAuthentication();
    app.UseAuthorization();

    app.UseEndpoints(endpoints =>
    {
        endpoints.MapControllers();
    });
}
```

4. Utilizing Secrets Management in Development

For sensitive settings, such as connection strings or API keys, ASP.NET Core supports user secrets, which allow you to store sensitive data during development without exposing it in your codebase.

1. Enabling User Secrets

To enable user secrets, right-click on your project in Visual Studio and select "Manage User Secrets," or use the .NET CLI:

```bash
Copy code
dotnet user-secrets init
```

This command will add a UserSecretsId to your project file. You can then add secrets using:

```bash
Copy code
dotnet user-secrets set "ConnectionStrings:DefaultConnection" "YourConnectionString"
```

These secrets can be accessed in your application via the configuration system:

```csharp
Copy code
public void ConfigureServices(IServiceCollection services)
{
    services.AddDbContext<MyDbContext>(options =>
        options.UseSqlServer(Configuration.GetConnectionString("DefaultConnection")));
}
```

Environment-based security settings in ASP.NET Core provide developers with the flexibility to adapt configurations for different stages of the application lifecycle. By utilizing environment-specific configuration files, applying tailored security measures, and leveraging user secrets, you can enhance the security of your applications while maintaining ease of development.

Managing security based on the environment ensures that your application is both secure and functional, adapting to the needs of development and production. This structured approach to configuration will help safeguard sensitive data and maintain the integrity of your web application across all environments.

Performance Optimization Techniques in ASP.NET Core

Asynchronous Programming with async/await in ASP.NET Core

In the realm of modern web applications, performance and responsiveness are paramount. Asynchronous programming in ASP.NET Core using the async and await keywords allows developers to write non-blocking code that can handle numerous requests efficiently without tying up system resources. This chapter delves into the principles and implementation of asynchronous programming in ASP.NET Core, demonstrating how it enhances application performance, improves scalability, and provides a better user experience.

1. Understanding Asynchronous Programming

Asynchronous programming is a programming paradigm that allows a program to perform tasks concurrently. In traditional synchronous programming, each operation must complete before the next one starts, potentially leading to resource contention and slow performance, especially under heavy load.

In contrast, asynchronous programming enables the execution of tasks without blocking the main thread. When a task is initiated, the program can continue executing other code while waiting for the task to complete, thus improving responsiveness and throughput.

Key Benefits of Asynchronous Programming:

- **Increased Scalability**: By freeing up threads to handle other requests, asynchronous programming enables applications to scale more effectively under load.
- **Improved Responsiveness**: Asynchronous operations prevent applications from freezing or becoming unresponsive during long-running tasks.
- **Efficient Resource Utilization**: Reduced blocking leads to better use of system resources, making it possible to handle more simultaneous operations.

2. The async and await Keywords

In C#, the async and await keywords simplify the implementation of asynchronous programming. Here's how they work:

- **async**: This modifier is added to a method declaration to indicate that the method contains asynchronous operations. It allows the method to run asynchronously and return a Task or Task<T>, enabling the caller to await its completion.
- **await**: This keyword is used to pause the execution of the asynchronous method until the awaited task is complete. It allows the program to return control to the caller without blocking the thread.

Example of an Asynchronous Method:

```csharp
Copy code
public async Task<string> GetDataAsync()
{
    // Simulate a long-running operation
    await Task.Delay(1000); // Asynchronously wait for 1 second
    return "Data retrieved successfully!";
}
```

In this example, the GetDataAsync method simulates a long-running operation (like fetching data from a database) without blocking the calling thread.

3. Implementing Asynchronous Programming in ASP.NET Core

When developing web applications with ASP.NET Core, it's crucial to leverage asynchronous programming to enhance performance, especially when dealing with I/O-bound operations like database access, file operations, or network calls.

1. Asynchronous Action Methods in Controllers

ASP.NET Core supports asynchronous action methods in controllers. By defining an action method as asynchronous, the framework can handle requests more efficiently.

Example of an Asynchronous Controller Action:

```csharp
Copy code
public class MyController : Controller
{
    private readonly IMyService _myService;

    public MyController(IMyService myService)
    {
        _myService = myService;
    }

    public async Task<IActionResult> GetItem(int id)
    {
        var item = await _myService.GetItemAsync(id);
        return Ok(item);
    }
}
```

In this example, the GetItem action method retrieves an item asynchronously from a service, allowing ASP.NET Core to handle other requests while waiting for the data retrieval to complete.

2. Asynchronous Database Operations with Entity Framework Core

PERFORMANCE OPTIMIZATION TECHNIQUES IN ASP.NET CORE

Entity Framework Core provides asynchronous methods for database operations, enabling developers to perform CRUD operations without blocking the executing thread.

Example of Asynchronous Database Access:

```csharp
Copy code
public class MyService : IMyService
{
    private readonly MyDbContext _context;

    public MyService(MyDbContext context)
    {
        _context = context;
    }

    public async Task<Item> GetItemAsync(int id)
    {
        return await _context.Items.FindAsync(id);
    }
}
```

In this example, the GetItemAsync method uses FindAsync to retrieve an item from the database asynchronously.

4. Best Practices for Asynchronous Programming

While asynchronous programming is a powerful tool, it is essential to follow best practices to ensure optimal performance and maintainability.

1. Use Asynchronous APIs

When working with asynchronous methods, ensure that the APIs you are using also support asynchronous operations. This applies to database calls, file I/O, network calls, etc. Using synchronous methods in asynchronous workflows can lead to thread pool exhaustion and performance bottlenecks.

2. Avoid Blocking Calls

Avoid blocking calls such as Task.Wait() or Task.Result within asynchronous methods, as they can negate the benefits of asynchronous programming and lead to deadlocks.

```csharp
Copy code
// Bad practice
var result = task.Result; // Blocks the thread
```

3. ConfigureAwait

When awaiting tasks in libraries that will be consumed by ASP.NET Core applications, consider using ConfigureAwait(false). This practice helps avoid deadlocks in certain synchronization contexts by not capturing the current synchronization context.

```csharp
Copy code
public async Task<string> GetDataAsync()
{
    // Use ConfigureAwait(false) to avoid capturing the context
    await Task.Delay(1000).ConfigureAwait(false);
    return "Data retrieved successfully!";
}
```

4. Handle Exceptions Gracefully

Asynchronous methods can throw exceptions just like synchronous methods. Ensure that you handle exceptions appropriately within asynchronous methods to prevent unhandled exceptions from propagating.

```csharp
Copy code
try
{
    var item = await GetItemAsync();
}
catch (Exception ex)
```

PERFORMANCE OPTIMIZATION TECHNIQUES IN ASP.NET CORE

```
{
    // Handle exception
}
```

5. Testing Asynchronous Methods

Testing asynchronous methods is crucial for maintaining code quality. Use frameworks that support asynchronous unit tests, like xUnit or NUnit.

Example of Testing an Asynchronous Method:

```csharp
Copy code
[Fact]
public async Task GetItem_ReturnsCorrectItem()
{
    // Arrange
    var service = new MyService(mockDbContext);

    // Act
    var result = await service.GetItemAsync(1);

    // Assert
    Assert.NotNull(result);
    Assert.Equal(1, result.Id);
}
```

6. Profiling and Monitoring Asynchronous Code

Monitoring the performance of asynchronous code is vital for identifying bottlenecks and improving application responsiveness. Utilize built-in tools like Application Insights or third-party libraries to track the performance of asynchronous operations and identify areas for optimization.

Key Metrics to Monitor:

- **Request Latency**: Measure how long requests take to process asynchronously.
- **Thread Pool Usage**: Monitor thread pool utilization to ensure

efficient resource management.
- **Exception Rates**: Track exceptions occurring within asynchronous methods to detect issues.

Asynchronous programming with async and await is a cornerstone of building high-performance web applications in ASP.NET Core. By adopting asynchronous patterns, developers can create responsive applications that scale efficiently under load, utilize system resources effectively, and provide a better user experience.

Following best practices, testing thoroughly, and monitoring performance are crucial steps in implementing asynchronous programming successfully. By mastering these techniques, you can enhance the performance and reliability of your ASP.NET Core applications, ensuring they meet the demands of modern web development.

Caching Strategies: In-Memory, Distributed, and Response Caching

Caching is a powerful technique for improving application performance by temporarily storing frequently accessed data in a fast-access storage layer. In ASP.NET Core, caching strategies can significantly reduce the time it takes to retrieve data, minimize database load, and enhance the overall user experience. This section will explore three primary caching strategies: In-Memory Caching, Distributed Caching, and Response Caching, providing an in-depth understanding of how to implement and leverage them effectively.

1. In-Memory Caching

In-memory caching is one of the simplest forms of caching, where data is stored directly in the memory of the web server hosting the application. This method allows for quick access to data, making it suitable for scenarios where the same data is frequently requested within the lifespan of the application.

Advantages of In-Memory Caching:

PERFORMANCE OPTIMIZATION TECHNIQUES IN ASP.NET CORE

- **Speed**: Accessing data from memory is significantly faster than retrieving it from a database or external source.
- **Simplicity**: Setting up in-memory caching is straightforward and does not require additional infrastructure.
- **Low Latency**: Since data is stored in the application's memory, there is minimal delay in accessing cached data.

Implementation of In-Memory Caching:
Install Required Package

To use in-memory caching in ASP.NET Core, ensure that the required package is included in your project. If you are using the default project template, this package should already be available:

```bash
Copy code
dotnet add package Microsoft.Extensions.Caching.Memory
```

Configure Services

In the Startup.cs file, configure the in-memory caching service:

```csharp
Copy code
public void ConfigureServices(IServiceCollection services)
{
    services.AddControllers();
    services.AddMemoryCache(); // Add in-memory caching
}
```

Using In-Memory Cache

Inject IMemoryCache into your services or controllers and use it to store and retrieve cached data:

```csharp
Copy code
public class MyService
{
    private readonly IMemoryCache _cache;

    public MyService(IMemoryCache cache)
    {
        _cache = cache;
    }

    public string GetData(string key)
    {
        if (!_cache.TryGetValue(key, out string value))
        {
            // Simulate data retrieval
            value = "Expensive Data Retrieval";

            // Set cache options
            var cacheEntryOptions = new MemoryCacheEntryOptions()
                .SetSlidingExpiration(TimeSpan.FromMinutes(5));
                // Cache for 5 minutes

            // Save data in cache
            _cache.Set(key, value, cacheEntryOptions);
        }
        return value;
    }
}
```

In this example, the service checks if the requested data is available in the cache. If not, it retrieves the data (simulated as an expensive operation), stores it in the cache, and sets an expiration time.

2. Distributed Caching

Distributed caching is used in scenarios where multiple instances of an application run simultaneously, such as in a cloud-based environment or microservices architecture. This caching strategy allows multiple servers

to share a common cache, enabling them to access the same cached data.
Advantages of Distributed Caching:

- **Scalability**: Multiple application instances can access the same cache, providing a scalable solution for larger applications.
- **Persistence**: Distributed caches can often persist data across application restarts, unlike in-memory caches that lose data when the application is shut down.
- **Centralized Storage**: Distributed caches provide a centralized data store that can be accessed by multiple applications.

Popular Distributed Caching Providers:

- **Redis**: An in-memory data structure store, often used as a distributed cache.
- **SQL Server**: Using SQL Server as a distributed cache.
- **NCache**: A distributed cache specifically designed for .NET applications.

Implementation of Distributed Caching with Redis:
Install Required Packages

To use Redis for distributed caching, install the following NuGet packages:

```bash
Copy code
dotnet add package
Microsoft.Extensions.Caching.StackExchangeRedis
```

Configure Services

In the Startup.cs file, configure the distributed cache service:

```csharp
Copy code
public void ConfigureServices(IServiceCollection services)
{
    services.AddControllers();
    services.AddStackExchangeRedisCache(options =>
    {
        options.Configuration = "localhost:6379"; // Redis
        server configuration
        options.InstanceName = "SampleInstance"; // Instance
        name for cache
    });
}
```

Using Distributed Cache

Inject IDistributedCache into your services or controllers and use it for caching data:

```csharp
Copy code
public class MyService
{
    private readonly IDistributedCache _distributedCache;

    public MyService(IDistributedCache distributedCache)
    {
        _distributedCache = distributedCache;
    }

    public async Task<string> GetDataAsync(string key)
    {
        var value = await _distributedCache.GetStringAsync(key);

        if (value == null)
        {
            // Simulate data retrieval
            value = "Expensive Data Retrieval";
```

```
        // Set cache options
        var options = new DistributedCacheEntryOptions()
            .SetSlidingExpiration(TimeSpan.FromMinutes(5));
            // Cache for 5 minutes

        await _distributedCache.SetStringAsync(key, value,
        options);
    }
    return value;
    }
}
```

In this example, the service retrieves data from the distributed cache. If the data is not found, it performs the expensive operation and stores the result in the cache.

3. Response Caching

Response caching is a technique where the output of a request (the HTTP response) is cached, allowing subsequent requests for the same resource to be served directly from the cache. This approach is particularly useful for improving performance in scenarios where the same content is requested multiple times.

Advantages of Response Caching:

- **Reduced Latency**: Serving cached responses is faster than generating responses dynamically.
- **Decreased Server Load**: Reduces the number of times the server has to process requests, saving resources and time.
- **Improved User Experience**: Users experience faster load times for frequently accessed resources.

Implementation of Response Caching:
Install Required Package

Make sure to install the response caching package if it's not included in your project:

```bash
Copy code
dotnet add package Microsoft.AspNetCore.ResponseCaching
```

Configure Services

In the Startup.cs file, enable response caching:

```csharp
Copy code
public void ConfigureServices(IServiceCollection services)
{
    services.AddControllers();
    services.AddResponseCaching(); // Add response caching
}
```

Using Response Caching

To use response caching, you can decorate your controller actions with the [ResponseCache] attribute, specifying the duration and other caching options:

```csharp
Copy code
[ApiController]
[Route("[controller]")]
public class MyController : ControllerBase
{
    [HttpGet]
    [ResponseCache(Duration = 60)] // Cache response for 60 seconds
    public IActionResult GetData()
    {
        var data = "Expensive Data Retrieval";
        return Ok(data);
    }
}
```

In this example, the response from the GetData action will be cached for

60 seconds. Subsequent requests made within that time frame will receive the cached response instead of executing the action again.

4. Best Practices for Caching

Implementing caching effectively requires a thoughtful approach. Here are some best practices to consider:

1. **Identify Cacheable Data**: Determine which data is frequently accessed and can be cached without introducing stale data issues. Look for data that does not change often and is computationally expensive to retrieve.
2. **Set Appropriate Expiration Policies**: Use sliding or absolute expiration policies to manage how long cached data should remain valid. This approach helps ensure that users receive fresh data while still benefiting from the speed of cached responses.
3. **Cache Granularity**: Be cautious about caching too much data. Cache individual items rather than entire datasets to reduce the memory footprint and improve cache hit rates.
4. **Monitor Cache Performance**: Keep an eye on cache hit and miss rates. Monitoring helps identify underperforming caches and optimizes caching strategies.
5. **Implement Cache Invalidation**: When data changes (e.g., in a database), ensure that the cache is invalidated or updated accordingly to prevent serving stale data. This can be accomplished through cache expiration policies or explicit cache removal.
6. **Test Cache Behavior**: Make sure to test the application's behavior with caching enabled to identify any unintended consequences, such as stale data being served or increased memory usage.

Caching is a fundamental strategy for optimizing performance in ASP.NET Core applications. By leveraging In-Memory Caching, Distributed Caching, and Response Caching, developers can significantly enhance the responsiveness and efficiency of their applications. Each caching strategy has its own advantages and use cases, allowing developers to choose the most suitable approach based on the specific requirements of their application.

Adopting best practices for caching implementation will ensure that you maximize the benefits of caching while minimizing potential pitfalls. By understanding and effectively utilizing caching techniques, you can create high-performance web applications that deliver an excellent user experience.

Using the Response Compression Middleware for Faster Load Times

In modern web applications, optimizing load times is critical for delivering a seamless user experience. One effective technique to achieve faster load times is through response compression. This method reduces the size of the HTTP responses sent from the server to the client, significantly decreasing the amount of data transmitted over the network. In ASP.NET Core, implementing response compression is straightforward thanks to built-in middleware that facilitates this process.

1. What is Response Compression?

Response compression involves encoding the HTTP response data using compression algorithms such as Gzip or Brotli before sending it to the client. By compressing the data, you reduce the overall payload size, which leads to faster downloads and improved performance, especially for users on slower connections.

Benefits of Response Compression:

- **Reduced Bandwidth Usage**: Compressed responses consume less bandwidth, leading to cost savings and increased efficiency.
- **Improved Load Times**: Smaller response sizes mean faster transmission times, resulting in quicker page loads for users.
- **Better SEO**: Faster websites often rank better in search engine results, contributing to higher visibility and traffic.

2. Configuring Response Compression in ASP.NET Core

To implement response compression in an ASP.NET Core application, follow these steps:

Install the Required Package

First, ensure that the Microsoft.AspNetCore.ResponseCompression package is included in your project. You can add it via NuGet:

```bash
Copy code
dotnet add package Microsoft.AspNetCore.ResponseCompression
```

Configure Services in Startup.cs

In the ConfigureServices method of your Startup class, add response compression services. You can also configure options such as compression providers and their thresholds:

```csharp
Copy code
public void ConfigureServices(IServiceCollection services)
{
    services.AddControllers();
    services.AddResponseCompression(options =>
    {
        options.EnableForHttps = true; // Enable compression
        for HTTPS requests
        options.Providers.Add<GzipCompressionProvider>(); //
        Add Gzip compression
        options.Providers.Add<BrotliCompressionProvider>(); //
        Optionally add Brotli compression
    });
}
```

Add Middleware in the Pipeline

Next, register the response compression middleware in the Configure method before the middleware that handles responses (typically before UseRouting() or UseEndpoints()):

```csharp
Copy code
public void Configure(IApplicationBuilder app, IWebHostEnvironment env)
{
    if (env.IsDevelopment())
    {
        app.UseDeveloperExceptionPage();
    }
    else
    {
        app.UseExceptionHandler("/Home/Error");
        app.UseHsts();
    }

    app.UseHttpsRedirection();
    app.UseStaticFiles();

    app.UseResponseCompression(); // Add the response compression middleware

    app.UseRouting();
    app.UseAuthorization();

    app.UseEndpoints(endpoints =>
    {
        endpoints.MapControllers();
    });
}
```

By including the UseResponseCompression() line, your application will now compress responses for supported content types automatically.

3. Compression Providers

ASP.NET Core supports several compression providers out of the box. The most common are:

- **GzipCompressionProvider**: A widely used compression algorithm that provides a good balance between speed and compression ratio.
- **BrotliCompressionProvider**: A newer compression algorithm that typically achieves better compression ratios than Gzip, particularly for text-based content. It is especially effective for modern web applications that heavily utilize JSON and HTML.

You can configure which compression providers to use and their respective options when setting up response compression services in the ConfigureServices method.

4. Configuring Compression Options

You can customize various settings for response compression to better fit your application's needs:

- **Minimum Response Size**: Set a minimum response size for compression. For example, compress only responses larger than 256 bytes to avoid overhead for small responses:

```csharp
Copy code
options.MinimumResponseSize = 256; // Minimum size for compression
```

- **Enabled Content Types**: You can specify which content types to compress, which can help avoid compressing non-compressible data:

```csharp
Copy code
options.MimeTypes = new[] { "text/plain", "text/css", "application/javascript", "application/json", "text/html" };
```

By default, ASP.NET Core compresses only the text-based content types.

Adjusting these settings can enhance performance and control over how your application handles compression.

5. Testing Response Compression

To verify that response compression is working correctly in your application, you can use several tools:

- **Browser Developer Tools**: Open your web application in a browser, right-click and select "Inspect" to open the Developer Tools. Navigate to the "Network" tab, reload the page, and check the "Content-Encoding" header in the response details. It should indicate "gzip" or "br" for Brotli if compression is applied.
- **Online Tools**: There are several online tools, such as WebPageTest or GTmetrix, that can analyze your site and confirm whether response compression is being applied.

6. Best Practices for Response Compression

To maximize the benefits of response compression, consider the following best practices:

1. **Use Compression Wisely**: Compress responses only for content that benefits from compression, such as text, HTML, CSS, and JavaScript. Avoid compressing binary files (e.g., images, videos) as they are already compressed and may not benefit from additional compression.
2. **Monitor Performance**: Regularly monitor the performance of your application with and without compression to assess its impact. Tools like Application Insights can help track metrics such as response times and server resource usage.
3. **Test on Different Browsers**: Ensure that your application behaves correctly with response compression on various browsers, as implementation may vary slightly between them.
4. **Consider Security Implications**: Be mindful of the security aspects of response compression, especially when dealing with sensitive data.

Ensure that HTTPS is enforced when using response compression to safeguard data integrity and confidentiality.

Implementing response compression in ASP.NET Core is an effective way to enhance your application's performance by reducing response sizes and improving load times. By carefully configuring the response compression middleware and leveraging Gzip and Brotli, you can deliver a faster, more efficient experience for users.

By following best practices and continuously monitoring the impact of response compression, you can ensure that your application remains optimized for performance while maintaining a high level of user satisfaction.

Integrating a Content Delivery Network (CDN) for Static Content

In an era where user experience is paramount, the performance of web applications plays a critical role in determining user engagement and retention. One of the most effective strategies for enhancing the speed and reliability of static content delivery is through the integration of a Content Delivery Network (CDN). This chapter delves into the concept of CDNs, their advantages, and how to integrate them seamlessly into an ASP.NET Core application.

1. Understanding Content Delivery Networks (CDNs)

A Content Delivery Network is a geographically distributed network of servers that work together to provide fast delivery of internet content. By caching static assets such as images, stylesheets, and scripts on multiple servers around the world, a CDN reduces the physical distance between the user and the server, ensuring quicker load times and improved performance.

Key Features of CDNs:

- **Geographical Distribution**: CDNs have numerous servers placed in strategic locations (points of presence, or PoPs) across the globe. This

allows users to access content from the nearest server, minimizing latency.
- **Load Balancing**: CDNs distribute incoming requests across multiple servers to balance the load, which helps maintain optimal performance even during traffic spikes.
- **Content Caching**: CDNs store cached copies of static content, reducing the need to fetch files from the origin server for every request, thus speeding up load times.
- **Reliability and Redundancy**: If one server fails, the CDN can reroute requests to another available server, enhancing the resilience of content delivery.

2. Benefits of Using a CDN

Integrating a CDN into your ASP.NET Core application can yield several benefits:

- **Enhanced Performance**: By serving static files from a nearby CDN server, you can significantly reduce latency and improve the overall user experience, particularly for geographically dispersed users.
- **Reduced Server Load**: CDNs offload bandwidth and resource consumption from the origin server, allowing it to handle dynamic content more efficiently.
- **Improved Security**: Many CDNs offer security features such as DDoS protection, web application firewalls, and secure token authentication, which can bolster the security of your web application.
- **Increased Availability**: CDNs are designed to provide high availability and redundancy, ensuring that your static assets are accessible even if the origin server experiences downtime.

3. Choosing the Right CDN Provider

Selecting a CDN provider that aligns with your project's needs is crucial. Consider the following factors when evaluating CDN options:

- **Geographical Coverage**: Look for a provider with a strong presence in regions where your users are located. This ensures lower latency and faster content delivery.
- **Performance Features**: Some CDNs offer advanced features like real-time analytics, image optimization, and video streaming capabilities. Choose a provider that offers features relevant to your application.
- **Ease of Integration**: Ensure that the CDN can be easily integrated with your existing infrastructure and workflows. Look for providers with straightforward documentation and support.
- **Cost**: Evaluate the pricing structure of each CDN provider. Some charge based on bandwidth usage, while others may have flat-rate pricing models. Consider your expected traffic patterns to find the most cost-effective solution.

Popular CDN providers include:

- **Cloudflare**
- **Amazon CloudFront**
- **Azure CDN**
- **Fastly**
- **Akamai**

4. Integrating a CDN with an ASP.NET Core Application

Integrating a CDN into your ASP.NET Core application is a multi-step process, which includes selecting a CDN provider, configuring your application to utilize the CDN for static content, and validating the setup.

Step-by-Step Integration:

Choose a CDN Provider: Based on your requirements, sign up for a CDN provider and create a CDN endpoint.

Upload Static Content: Depending on your CDN, you may need to upload your static assets (such as images, CSS files, and JavaScript files) to the CDN's storage or point the CDN to your origin server.

Update Static Content URLs: In your ASP.NET Core application, update the references to static files in your views or layout files to use the CDN URLs. For example:

```html
Copy code
<link rel="stylesheet" href="https://cdn.example.com/css/styles.css" />
<script src="https://cdn.example.com/js/scripts.js"></script>
<img src="https://cdn.example.com/images/logo.png" alt="Logo" />
```

You may also utilize the IHostingEnvironment interface to manage URLs dynamically based on the environment (development, staging, production).

Configure Caching and Expiration Policies: Set up caching rules and expiration headers in your CDN configuration. This ensures that users receive the latest versions of your static content without excessive requests to your origin server.

Test the Integration: After implementing the CDN, test your application to ensure that static content is loading correctly from the CDN. You can do this by checking the Network tab in browser developer tools to verify that requests for static files are routed through the CDN.

Monitor Performance: Utilize the analytics provided by your CDN to monitor traffic, cache hit ratios, and performance metrics. This data can help you make informed decisions about further optimizations.

5. Best Practices for Using CDNs

To maximize the benefits of CDNs, consider the following best practices:

- **Minimize Redirects**: Ensure that your CDN URLs do not include unnecessary redirects, as this can add latency. Pointing directly to CDN resources is ideal.
- **Use Versioning for Static Assets**: Implement a versioning strategy for your static files. This allows for easy cache busting when you update your files, ensuring that users receive the latest versions without stale cache issues.
- **Optimize Assets for the Web**: Compress images and minify CSS and JavaScript files before uploading them to the CDN. This reduces file sizes and speeds up load times.
- **Leverage HTTP/2**: Many CDNs support HTTP/2, which can further enhance performance through multiplexing, header compression, and server push capabilities.

Integrating a Content Delivery Network (CDN) into your ASP.NET Core application is a powerful strategy to enhance the delivery of static content. By reducing latency, offloading traffic from the origin server, and improving overall performance, CDNs play a vital role in modern web application architecture.

By carefully selecting a CDN provider, configuring your application correctly, and following best practices, you can ensure a robust and efficient static content delivery strategy that ultimately leads to a better user experience.

Reducing Server Load with Load Balancing and Serverless Architecture

In the realm of modern web application development, maintaining optimal performance while managing server load is crucial for delivering a seamless user experience. As applications scale and user traffic increases, it becomes necessary to implement strategies that not only distribute workloads but also leverage flexible resource management. Two prominent approaches in achieving this are load balancing and serverless architecture.

This chapter explores both methods in detail, illustrating how they can significantly reduce server load and enhance application performance.

1. Understanding Load Balancing

Load balancing is a technique used to distribute incoming network traffic across multiple servers. By ensuring that no single server bears too much load, it enhances application availability and reliability. Load balancers serve as intermediaries between clients and servers, intelligently routing requests based on various factors.

Key Benefits of Load Balancing:

- **Improved Resource Utilization**: By distributing requests evenly, load balancing maximizes the utilization of available server resources, leading to more efficient operations.
- **High Availability**: In the event that one server becomes unavailable, the load balancer can redirect traffic to other operational servers, ensuring that the application remains accessible.
- **Scalability**: Load balancing allows organizations to scale horizontally by adding more servers to accommodate increased traffic, thus enhancing the application's capacity to handle growing user demands.

Common Load Balancing Algorithms:

- **Round Robin**: This method distributes requests sequentially across the available servers.
- **Least Connections**: Traffic is directed to the server with the fewest active connections, ensuring optimal performance.
- **IP Hash**: This technique assigns clients to specific servers based on their IP address, which can help maintain session persistence.

2. Implementing Load Balancing in ASP.NET Core

To integrate load balancing within an ASP.NET Core application, organizations can utilize various solutions depending on their infrastructure.

Common approaches include:

- **Hardware Load Balancers**: These are dedicated devices that manage traffic distribution. They are robust but can be costly.
- **Software Load Balancers**: Solutions like NGINX or HAProxy can be installed on servers to manage traffic efficiently.
- **Cloud-Based Load Balancers**: Cloud service providers, such as AWS Elastic Load Balancing or Azure Load Balancer, offer integrated load balancing solutions that scale automatically based on traffic.

Step-by-Step Implementation:

1. **Choose a Load Balancing Solution**: Select a load balancer that fits your needs, whether it's hardware, software, or cloud-based.
2. **Deploy Multiple Instances**: Set up multiple instances of your ASP.NET Core application across different servers or containers.
3. **Configure the Load Balancer**: Set up your load balancer to route requests to the various instances based on your chosen algorithm.
4. **Test and Monitor**: Regularly monitor load distribution and server performance to ensure that the load balancer is functioning optimally and adjust configurations as necessary.

3. Understanding Serverless Architecture

Serverless architecture is a cloud computing execution model where the cloud provider dynamically manages the allocation of machine resources. In this model, developers focus solely on writing code without worrying about server management, which allows for more agile development practices.

Key Features of Serverless Architecture:

- **Automatic Scaling**: Serverless platforms automatically scale applications in response to incoming requests. There's no need to provision servers for peak loads or manage idle resources during low traffic

periods.
- **Pay-as-You-Go Pricing**: Users pay only for the resources consumed during execution, which can significantly reduce costs compared to traditional server models.
- **Simplified Development**: Developers can focus on building features rather than managing infrastructure, enhancing productivity and speed of deployment.

Popular Serverless Platforms:

- **AWS Lambda**
- **Azure Functions**
- **Google Cloud Functions**

4. Integrating Serverless Architecture with ASP.NET Core

Integrating serverless architecture into an ASP.NET Core application allows developers to create highly scalable applications without the overhead of traditional server management. Here's how to effectively implement serverless architecture:

Step-by-Step Integration:

1. **Choose a Serverless Platform**: Select a cloud provider that supports serverless functions. For ASP.NET Core, Azure Functions is a strong choice as it provides native support.
2. **Define Your Functions**: Identify parts of your application that can be converted into serverless functions. Common candidates include API endpoints, data processing tasks, and background jobs.
3. **Develop and Deploy Functions**: Write the serverless functions using ASP.NET Core. You can deploy these functions directly through the provider's management console or CLI tools.
4. **Set Up Triggers**: Configure triggers for your functions, such as HTTP requests, timers, or events from other services (like queues or storage).

5. **Monitor and Optimize**: Utilize the monitoring tools provided by the cloud platform to track the performance of your serverless functions and optimize them as necessary.

5. Combining Load Balancing and Serverless Architecture

Combining load balancing with serverless architecture can provide enhanced performance and reliability for your ASP.NET Core applications. This hybrid approach allows for flexible scaling of both server-based and serverless components, ensuring that your application can handle varying levels of traffic without performance degradation.

Best Practices:

- **Identify Critical Paths**: Determine which parts of your application can benefit most from load balancing and which can be implemented serverlessly.
- **Use API Gateway**: Utilize an API Gateway to manage requests to both your traditional and serverless endpoints. This can simplify the architecture and provide centralized management for security, routing, and monitoring.
- **Monitor Performance**: Keep an eye on both load-balanced instances and serverless functions to ensure that the application remains performant and responsive under varying traffic conditions.

Reducing server load is essential for maintaining high performance in modern web applications. By implementing load balancing and serverless architecture, developers can create scalable, efficient, and resilient ASP.NET Core applications. Load balancing distributes incoming traffic intelligently across multiple servers, while serverless architecture allows for flexible resource management without the need for server maintenance.

By understanding these concepts and leveraging them effectively, organizations can improve application performance, reduce costs, and enhance user experience, ultimately leading to a more robust web application ecosystem.

Testing and Debugging Your ASP.NET Core Application

Setting Up Unit Tests with xUnit and Moq
Testing is an integral part of the software development lifecycle, ensuring that applications function correctly and meet user requirements. In the context of ASP.NET Core applications, unit testing plays a crucial role in validating individual components, helping to identify and fix issues early in the development process. This chapter focuses on setting up unit tests using xUnit, a popular testing framework, and Moq, a powerful mocking library, to effectively test your ASP.NET Core applications.

1. Introduction to Unit Testing

Unit testing involves testing individual components or pieces of code, known as units, in isolation from the rest of the application. The goal is to validate that each unit behaves as expected, regardless of the surrounding code.

Benefits of Unit Testing:

- **Early Bug Detection**: Finding bugs early in the development process reduces the cost and effort required to fix them.
- **Improved Code Quality**: Writing tests encourages developers to create modular and maintainable code.
- **Facilitated Refactoring**: With a comprehensive suite of unit tests,

developers can refactor code with confidence, knowing that any regressions will be caught.
- **Documentation**: Unit tests serve as a form of documentation, providing examples of how code is intended to be used.

2. Overview of xUnit

xUnit is a popular open-source testing framework for .NET applications. It is designed to be simple and easy to use, making it an excellent choice for unit testing ASP.NET Core applications.

Key Features of xUnit:

- **Flexible Assertions**: xUnit provides a rich set of assertion methods that allow developers to write expressive tests.
- **Data-Driven Testing**: xUnit supports data-driven tests through the use of theories, enabling tests to be run with various inputs.
- **Parallel Test Execution**: Tests can be run in parallel, reducing the overall execution time and improving efficiency.

3. Overview of Moq

Moq is a mocking library for .NET that allows developers to create mock objects for testing purposes. It is particularly useful for isolating the units under test by simulating dependencies, enabling focused and effective testing.

Key Features of Moq:

- **Easy to Use**: Moq's fluent API makes it straightforward to set up and configure mock objects.
- **Flexible Mocking**: Moq allows for the creation of mocks that can simulate behavior for both interfaces and classes.
- **Verification of Interactions**: Moq provides mechanisms to verify that certain interactions with mocks occurred as expected.

4. Setting Up Your ASP.NET Core Project for Testing

TESTING AND DEBUGGING YOUR ASP.NET CORE APPLICATION

Before diving into writing tests, you need to set up your ASP.NET Core project to support unit testing with xUnit and Moq.

Step-by-Step Setup:

Create a Test Project:

- In your solution, add a new project specifically for testing. Choose the **xUnit Test Project** template.
- Name the project appropriately, e.g., YourApp.Tests.

Install Required Packages:

- Open the NuGet Package Manager Console or use the NuGet Package Manager to install the following packages:

```bash
Copy code
Install-Package xunit
Install-Package xunit.runner.visualstudio
Install-Package Moq
```

- These packages will provide the necessary tools to write and run unit tests using xUnit and Moq.

Configure Project References:

- Add a reference from your test project to the main ASP.NET Core project. This allows the test project to access the classes and methods you want to test.

5. Writing Your First Unit Test with xUnit

Now that your testing environment is set up, it's time to write your first unit test.

Example: Testing a Simple Service

Let's consider a simple service that performs operations on a User object.

```csharp
Copy code
public class UserService
{
    private readonly IUserRepository _userRepository;

    public UserService(IUserRepository userRepository)
    {
        _userRepository = userRepository;
    }

    public User GetUser(int id)
    {
        return _userRepository.GetById(id);
    }
}
```

Unit Test for UserService:

```csharp
Copy code
using Moq;
using Xunit;

public class UserServiceTests
{
    [Fact]
    public void GetUser_ValidId_ReturnsUser()
    {
        // Arrange
        var mockRepo = new Mock<IUserRepository>();
        mockRepo.Setup(repo => repo.GetById(1)).Returns(new User { Id = 1, Name = "John Doe" });

        var userService = new UserService(mockRepo.Object);
```

TESTING AND DEBUGGING YOUR ASP.NET CORE APPLICATION

```csharp
    // Act
    var result = userService.GetUser(1);

    // Assert
    Assert.NotNull(result);
    Assert.Equal(1, result.Id);
    Assert.Equal("John Doe", result.Name);
}
}
```

Explanation:

- **Arrange**: Set up the necessary objects, including the mock of the IUserRepository and configuring it to return a user when GetById is called.
- **Act**: Call the method under test, GetUser, with a valid ID.
- **Assert**: Verify that the result is not null and that it matches the expected user details.

6. Using Moq for More Complex Scenarios

Moq can handle more complex scenarios, such as verifying interactions and setting up multiple behaviors.

Example: Verifying Method Calls:

```
csharp
Copy code
[Fact]
public void GetUser_CallsRepositoryOnce()
{
    // Arrange
    var mockRepo = new Mock<IUserRepository>();
    var userService = new UserService(mockRepo.Object);

    // Act
```

```
    userService.GetUser(1);

    // Assert
    mockRepo.Verify(repo => repo.GetById(1), Times.Once);
}
```

In this example, we verify that the GetById method on the repository is called exactly once during the execution of GetUser.

7. Running Your Tests

After writing your tests, you can run them using Visual Studio's Test Explorer or the command line:

- **Using Visual Studio**: Open the Test Explorer (Test > Windows > Test Explorer), and you will see your tests listed. You can run all tests or select individual tests to run.
- **Using Command Line**: Use the dotnet test command in your terminal from the root of your solution to execute all tests.

8. Best Practices for Unit Testing

To ensure effective unit testing with xUnit and Moq, consider the following best practices:

- **Keep Tests Independent**: Each test should be able to run independently of others. This means avoiding shared state between tests.
- **Name Tests Clearly**: Use descriptive names for your test methods to convey the purpose of the test.
- **Test Behavior, Not Implementation**: Focus on testing the behavior of methods rather than their internal implementation details.
- **Utilize Setup Methods**: Use the IClassFixture or CollectionFixture features in xUnit to manage shared setup code for related tests.

TESTING AND DEBUGGING YOUR ASP.NET CORE APPLICATION

Setting up unit tests with xUnit and Moq provides a robust framework for validating your ASP.NET Core applications. By leveraging these tools, you can ensure that individual components of your application function as expected, enhancing code quality and facilitating easier maintenance and refactoring.

Incorporating unit testing into your development workflow not only improves your application's reliability but also builds confidence in your code, allowing for agile development and quicker iterations. With a solid foundation in testing principles, you can create scalable and maintainable ASP.NET Core applications that meet the demands of modern web development.

Testing Controllers, Services, and Middleware Components

Unit testing is essential for validating the functionality of various components in an ASP.NET Core application. In this section, we will delve into the specific practices for testing controllers, services, and middleware components. By mastering these testing strategies, you can ensure that your application behaves correctly and is resilient to changes in the codebase.

1. Testing Controllers

Controllers in ASP.NET Core are responsible for handling HTTP requests and returning responses. They typically interact with services and model data, making them a key component of the application architecture. Testing controllers involves verifying that they respond correctly to various input scenarios and that they interact properly with the services they depend on.

Example Controller:

```
csharp
Copy code
public class UserController : ControllerBase
{
```

```
    private readonly IUserService _userService;

    public UserController(IUserService userService)
    {
        _userService = userService;
    }

    [HttpGet("{id}")]
    public ActionResult<User> GetUser(int id)
    {
        var user = _userService.GetUser(id);
        if (user == null)
        {
            return NotFound();
        }
        return Ok(user);
    }
}
```

Unit Test for UserController:

```csharp
Copy code
using Microsoft.AspNetCore.Mvc;
using Moq;
using Xunit;

public class UserControllerTests
{
    [Fact]
    public void GetUser_ExistingId_ReturnsOkResult()
    {
        // Arrange
        var mockService = new Mock<IUserService>();
        mockService.Setup(service =>
        service.GetUser(1)).Returns(new User { Id = 1, Name = "John Doe" });

        var controller = new UserController(mockService.Object);
```

TESTING AND DEBUGGING YOUR ASP.NET CORE APPLICATION

```csharp
    // Act
    var result = controller.GetUser(1);

    // Assert
    var okResult = Assert.IsType<OkObjectResult>(result);
    var user = Assert.IsType<User>(okResult.Value);
    Assert.Equal(1, user.Id);
    Assert.Equal("John Doe", user.Name);
}

[Fact]
public void GetUser_NonExistingId_ReturnsNotFound()
{
    // Arrange
    var mockService = new Mock<IUserService>();
    mockService.Setup(service =>
    service.GetUser(2)).Returns((User)null);

    var controller = new UserController(mockService.Object);

    // Act
    var result = controller.GetUser(2);

    // Assert
    Assert.IsType<NotFoundResult>(result);
}
}
```

Explanation:

- **Arrange**: Set up the mock IUserService and configure it to return a user when GetUser is called with an existing ID and null for a non-existing ID.
- **Act**: Call the GetUser method on the controller.
- **Assert**: Verify that the result is an OkObjectResult containing the expected user or a NotFoundResult when the user does not exist.

2. Testing Services

Services encapsulate business logic and are typically the core components of an application. Testing services involves checking that the business logic functions correctly and that the service interacts with the data layer as expected.

Example Service:

```csharp
Copy code
public class UserService : IUserService
{
    private readonly IUserRepository _userRepository;

    public UserService(IUserRepository userRepository)
    {
        _userRepository = userRepository;
    }

    public User GetUser(int id)
    {
        return _userRepository.GetById(id);
    }
}
```

Unit Test for UserService:

```csharp
Copy code
public class UserServiceTests
{
    [Fact]
    public void GetUser_ExistingId_ReturnsUser()
    {
        // Arrange
        var mockRepo = new Mock<IUserRepository>();
        mockRepo.Setup(repo => repo.GetById(1)).Returns(new User { Id = 1, Name = "John Doe" });
```

TESTING AND DEBUGGING YOUR ASP.NET CORE APPLICATION

```csharp
        var userService = new UserService(mockRepo.Object);

        // Act
        var result = userService.GetUser(1);

        // Assert
        Assert.NotNull(result);
        Assert.Equal(1, result.Id);
        Assert.Equal("John Doe", result.Name);
    }
}
```

Explanation:

- The testing strategy for services is similar to that of controllers. In this case, we check whether the service returns the expected user when given a valid ID.

3. Testing Middleware Components

Middleware components are crucial for processing requests and responses in ASP.NET Core applications. They can handle tasks such as logging, authentication, and error handling. Testing middleware involves ensuring that they behave correctly when processing requests.

Example Middleware:

```
csharp
Copy code
public class LoggingMiddleware
{
    private readonly RequestDelegate _next;

    public LoggingMiddleware(RequestDelegate next)
    {
        _next = next;
    }
```

```csharp
public async Task InvokeAsync(HttpContext context)
{
    // Log the request
    Console.WriteLine($"Request: {context.Request.Method} {context.Request.Path}");

    // Call the next middleware in the pipeline
    await _next(context);
}
```

Unit Test for LoggingMiddleware:

```csharp
csharp
Copy code
using Microsoft.AspNetCore.Http;
using Moq;
using System;
using System.IO;
using System.Threading.Tasks;
using Xunit;

public class LoggingMiddlewareTests
{
    [Fact]
    public async Task InvokeAsync_LogsRequest()
    {
        // Arrange
        var mockNext = new Mock<RequestDelegate>();
        var middleware = new LoggingMiddleware(mockNext.Object);
        var context = new DefaultHttpContext();
        context.Request.Method = "GET";
        context.Request.Path = "/api/users";

        using (var sw = new StringWriter())
        {
            Console.SetOut(sw); // Redirect console output to capture logs
```

TESTING AND DEBUGGING YOUR ASP.NET CORE APPLICATION

```
        // Act
        await middleware.InvokeAsync(context);

        // Assert
        var loggedOutput = sw.ToString();
        Assert.Contains("Request: GET /api/users",
        loggedOutput);
    }
  }
}
```

Explanation:

- In this test, we create a mock RequestDelegate and pass it to the LoggingMiddleware. The HttpContext is set up with a sample request, and we redirect console output to verify that the logging behavior works as expected.

4. Mocking Dependencies in Tests

When testing controllers, services, or middleware, it's essential to mock dependencies to isolate the unit under test. Moq provides powerful tools for creating mock objects and verifying interactions.

Common Mocking Patterns:

- **Setup**: Use Setup to define how a mock should respond to method calls.
- **Returns**: Specify the return value for a method when it is called.
- **Verifications**: Use Verify to ensure a method was called with the expected parameters and the expected number of times.

5. Running All Tests

With unit tests for controllers, services, and middleware in place, you can run your entire test suite using Visual Studio's Test Explorer or from the command line using:

```bash
Copy code
dotnet test
```

This command will execute all tests in your solution and provide feedback on their success or failure.

6. Best Practices for Testing Components

To ensure effective testing of controllers, services, and middleware, follow these best practices:

- **Isolate Tests**: Ensure that each test runs independently and does not rely on the state left by other tests.
- **Use Meaningful Names**: Name your test methods descriptively to convey what each test verifies.
- **Maintain Test Coverage**: Aim for high test coverage across your components, including edge cases and error conditions.
- **Keep Tests Fast**: Ensure that tests run quickly to encourage frequent execution during development.

Testing controllers, services, and middleware is critical for maintaining the reliability and performance of your ASP.NET Core applications. By leveraging xUnit and Moq, you can create effective unit tests that verify the functionality of individual components in isolation.

Through diligent testing practices, you can catch bugs early, improve code quality, and facilitate easier refactoring. The ability to confidently modify your codebase while ensuring the correctness of your application empowers you to build scalable, maintainable, and robust ASP.NET Core applications.

Integration Testing for Data Access and Business Logic Layers

TESTING AND DEBUGGING YOUR ASP.NET CORE APPLICATION

Integration testing plays a crucial role in ensuring that various components of your ASP.NET Core application work together as intended. Unlike unit tests, which focus on testing individual components in isolation, integration tests verify the interaction between different layers of the application, including the data access layer and business logic layer. In this section, we will discuss the importance of integration testing, how to set it up, and best practices for writing effective integration tests.

1. Understanding Integration Testing

Integration testing aims to identify issues that arise when components interact with each other. This is especially important in applications that involve multiple services, databases, and external APIs. By performing integration tests, you can ensure that:

- The data access layer correctly retrieves and stores data.
- The business logic layer processes data as expected.
- Components interact seamlessly without errors.

Integration tests typically involve spinning up an actual database or a mock database that mimics the production environment to test the complete flow of data and logic through the application.

2. Setting Up Integration Tests

To get started with integration testing in an ASP.NET Core application, follow these steps:

a. Create an Integration Test Project

Add a New Test Project: Create a new test project in your solution, typically using the xUnit framework. You can do this via the .NET CLI:

```bash
Copy code
dotnet new xunit -n MyApp.IntegrationTests
```

Add Necessary References: Ensure that your integration test project references the main application project and any required NuGet packages:

```bash
Copy code
dotnet add MyApp.IntegrationTests/MyApp.IntegrationTests.csproj reference ../MyApp/MyApp.csproj
dotnet add MyApp.IntegrationTests package Microsoft.AspNetCore.Mvc.Testing
dotnet add MyApp.IntegrationTests package Microsoft.EntityFrameworkCore.InMemory
```

b. Configure the Test Host

Use the WebApplicationFactory<TEntryPoint> class provided by Microsoft.AspNetCore.Mvc.Testing to create a test host. This will allow you to run your integration tests against the full application, including middleware and services.

Example Integration Test Setup:

```csharp
Copy code
using Microsoft.AspNetCore.Mvc.Testing;
using Xunit;

public class IntegrationTests : IClassFixture<WebApplicationFactory<Startup>>
{
    private readonly HttpClient _client;

    public IntegrationTests(WebApplicationFactory<Startup> factory)
    {
        _client = factory.CreateClient();
    }

    // Integration tests will be written here
}
```

In this example, the WebApplicationFactory<Startup> is used to create an instance of your application, allowing you to send HTTP requests to it during the tests.

3. Writing Integration Tests

Integration tests typically involve setting up data in a test database, executing operations through your API, and verifying the results. Below are common scenarios you might test:

a. Testing Data Retrieval and Insertion
Example Integration Test:

```csharp
Copy code
[Fact]
public async Task GetUser_ReturnsUser_WhenUserExists()
{
    // Arrange: Seed the database with a user
    var userId = 1;
    await SeedUserAsync(userId, "John Doe");

    // Act: Send a GET request to the API
    var response = await
    _client.GetAsync($"/api/users/{userId}");

    // Assert: Verify the response is successful and contains
    the expected data
    response.EnsureSuccessStatusCode();
    var userResponse = await
    response.Content.ReadAsAsync<User>();
    Assert.Equal(userId, userResponse.Id);
    Assert.Equal("John Doe", userResponse.Name);
}

private async Task SeedUserAsync(int id, string name)
{
    // Code to insert a user into the test database
    using (var scope = _factory.Services.CreateScope())
    {
        var dbContext =
```

```
            scope.ServiceProvider.GetRequiredService<MyDbContext>();
        dbContext.Users.Add(new User { Id = id, Name = name });
        await dbContext.SaveChangesAsync();
    }
}
```

In this test:

- A user is seeded into the database before the test runs.
- An HTTP GET request is sent to retrieve that user.
- The response is verified to ensure it matches the seeded data.

b. Testing Business Logic Execution

Integration tests should also validate that the business logic behaves as expected when interacting with the data access layer.

Example Integration Test:

```csharp
Copy code
[Fact]
public async Task CreateUser_AddsUserToDatabase()
{
    // Arrange: Prepare a new user
    var newUser = new User { Name = "Jane Doe" };

    // Act: Send a POST request to create a user
    var response = await _client.PostAsJsonAsync("/api/users", newUser);

    // Assert: Verify the response is successful and the user is in the database
    response.EnsureSuccessStatusCode();
    var createdUser = await response.Content.ReadAsAsync<User>();

    using (var scope = _factory.Services.CreateScope())
```

TESTING AND DEBUGGING YOUR ASP.NET CORE APPLICATION

```csharp
    {
        var dbContext =
        scope.ServiceProvider.GetRequiredService<MyDbContext>();
        var userInDb = await
        dbContext.Users.FindAsync(createdUser.Id);
        Assert.NotNull(userInDb);
        Assert.Equal("Jane Doe", userInDb.Name);
    }
}
```

In this test:

- A new user is created via an HTTP POST request.
- The test then checks if the user was successfully added to the database by querying it directly.

4. Cleaning Up After Tests

After running integration tests that modify the database, it's crucial to clean up the data to maintain a consistent test environment. This can be accomplished in several ways:

- **Using In-Memory Database**: If you are using an in-memory database for tests, it will automatically clear the data after each test run.
- **Database Transactions**: Wrap each test in a transaction and roll it back at the end, which is particularly useful when using a real database for integration tests.

Example of Transaction Cleanup:

```csharp
csharp
Copy code
public class IntegrationTests :
IClassFixture<WebApplicationFactory<Startup>>
```

```
{
    private readonly HttpClient _client;
    private readonly MyDbContext _dbContext;

    public IntegrationTests(WebApplicationFactory<Startup>
    factory)
    {
        _client = factory.CreateClient();

        using (var scope = factory.Services.CreateScope())
        {
            _dbContext =
            scope.ServiceProvider.GetRequiredService<MyDbContext>();
            _dbContext.Database.BeginTransaction();
        }
    }

    public void Dispose()
    {
        _dbContext.Database.RollbackTransaction();
    }
}
```

5. Best Practices for Integration Testing

To ensure the effectiveness of your integration tests, consider the following best practices:

- **Use Realistic Data**: Seed the database with realistic data to better simulate real-world scenarios.
- **Keep Tests Independent**: Ensure that tests can run independently of one another, avoiding shared state that might affect outcomes.
- **Run Integration Tests Regularly**: Include integration tests in your CI/CD pipeline to catch integration issues early.
- **Limit the Scope of Tests**: Each test should ideally validate a specific behavior to make it easier to diagnose failures.

Integration testing is a critical aspect of ensuring the reliability of your ASP.NET Core applications. By validating the interactions between the data access layer and business logic, you can identify issues that may not be evident during unit testing. With the right setup and practices, you can create robust integration tests that enhance the quality and maintainability of your codebase. By leveraging tools like xUnit and in-memory databases, you can streamline the testing process and focus on delivering high-quality software.

End-to-End Testing Strategies with Selenium or Playwright

End-to-end (E2E) testing is a crucial aspect of the software development lifecycle, particularly for web applications. It ensures that the entire application flow, from the user interface to the backend, works as intended. In this section, we will explore strategies for implementing E2E testing in ASP.NET Core applications using popular tools like Selenium and Playwright.

1. Understanding End-to-End Testing

End-to-end testing simulates real user scenarios to validate the entire system's functionality. It checks whether all integrated components work together seamlessly. E2E tests help identify issues related to user interactions, data integrity, and the flow of information across the application layers.

Key objectives of E2E testing include:

- **Verifying Functional Requirements**: Ensure that the application behaves as expected when users perform actions.
- **Detecting Integration Issues**: Identify problems that may occur due to interactions between different parts of the application.
- **Validating User Experience**: Confirm that the application is user-friendly and meets design expectations.

2. Choosing Between Selenium and Playwright

Selenium and Playwright are two of the most popular tools for E2E testing, each with its strengths and use cases.

a. Selenium

Selenium has been a long-standing leader in the E2E testing landscape. It supports multiple programming languages and can automate browsers to simulate user interactions. Key features of Selenium include:

- **Cross-Browser Support**: Selenium can test on various browsers, including Chrome, Firefox, Safari, and Edge.
- **Wide Language Support**: It can be used with various programming languages, such as C#, Java, Python, and Ruby.
- **Community and Ecosystem**: A vast ecosystem of tools and libraries has developed around Selenium, providing various extensions and utilities.

b. Playwright

Playwright is a relatively newer tool that offers modern features for E2E testing. It is designed to handle complex scenarios more easily and provides excellent support for modern web applications. Key features of Playwright include:

- **Built-in Support for Multiple Browsers**: Playwright can automate Chromium, Firefox, and WebKit, making it easy to test across different environments.
- **Headless Mode**: Playwright runs tests in headless mode, which can improve performance and speed up testing.
- **Parallel Execution**: Playwright supports running tests in parallel, allowing for faster feedback during the testing process.
- **Rich API for Interaction**: Playwright offers a robust API for interacting with web elements, making it simpler to write tests.

When deciding between Selenium and Playwright, consider your project requirements, team familiarity with the tools, and the specific features

TESTING AND DEBUGGING YOUR ASP.NET CORE APPLICATION

needed for your testing strategy.

3. Setting Up E2E Tests

To set up E2E tests in an ASP.NET Core application, follow these general steps:

a. Install Necessary Packages

For both Selenium and Playwright, you need to install the respective NuGet packages.

- **For Selenium**:

```bash
Copy code
dotnet add package Selenium.WebDriver
dotnet add package Selenium.WebDriver.ChromeDriver
dotnet add package Selenium.Support
```

- **For Playwright**:

```bash
Copy code
dotnet add package Microsoft.Playwright
```

b. Create the Test Project

Create a separate project for your E2E tests to keep them organized. You can use xUnit or NUnit for your testing framework.

```bash
Copy code
dotnet new xunit -n MyApp.E2ETests
```

c. Configure the Testing Environment

For both Selenium and Playwright, you will need to configure the test environment, including the URL of your application and any necessary setup for browser drivers.

Example Setup for Selenium:

```csharp
Copy code
using OpenQA.Selenium;
using OpenQA.Selenium.Chrome;
using Xunit;

public class E2ETests : IClassFixture<WebApplicationFactory<Startup>>
{
    private readonly IWebDriver _driver;

    public E2ETests(WebApplicationFactory<Startup> factory)
    {
        _driver = new ChromeDriver();
        _driver.Navigate().GoToUrl("http://localhost:5000"); // URL of the running app
    }

    // E2E tests will be written here

    public void Dispose()
    {
        _driver.Quit();
    }
}
```

Example Setup for Playwright:

```csharp
Copy code
using Microsoft.Playwright;
using Xunit;
```

TESTING AND DEBUGGING YOUR ASP.NET CORE APPLICATION

```
public class E2ETests : IAsyncLifetime
{
    private IPlaywright _playwright;
    private IBrowser _browser;
    private IBrowserContext _context;
    private IPage _page;

    public async Task InitializeAsync()
    {
        _playwright = await Playwright.CreateAsync();
        _browser = await _playwright.Chromium.LaunchAsync(new
        BrowserTypeLaunchOptions { Headless = true });
        _context = await _browser.NewContextAsync();
        _page = await _context.NewPageAsync();
        await _page.GotoAsync("http://localhost:5000"); // URL
        of the running app
    }

    public async Task DisposeAsync()
    {
        await _browser.CloseAsync();
    }

    // E2E tests will be written here
}
```

4. Writing E2E Tests

Once the setup is complete, you can start writing E2E tests to simulate user interactions with your application.

a. Simulating User Interactions
Selenium Example:

```
csharp
Copy code
[Fact]
public void UserCanLogin()
{
```

```csharp
    // Arrange
    var loginButton = _driver.FindElement(By.Id("loginButton"));

    // Act
    loginButton.Click();
    var emailField = _driver.FindElement(By.Id("email"));
    emailField.SendKeys("test@example.com");
    var passwordField = _driver.FindElement(By.Id("password"));
    passwordField.SendKeys("Password123!");
    var submitButton =
    _driver.FindElement(By.Id("submitButton"));
    submitButton.Click();

    // Assert
    var welcomeMessage =
    _driver.FindElement(By.Id("welcomeMessage"));
    Assert.True(welcomeMessage.Displayed);
}
```

Playwright Example:

```csharp
Copy code
[Fact]
public async Task UserCanLogin()
{
    // Arrange
    var loginButton = await _page.Locator("#loginButton");
    await loginButton.ClickAsync();

    // Act
    await _page.FillAsync("#email", "test@example.com");
    await _page.FillAsync("#password", "Password123!");
    var submitButton = await _page.Locator("#submitButton");
    await submitButton.ClickAsync();

    // Assert
    var welcomeMessage = await
    _page.Locator("#welcomeMessage").IsVisibleAsync();
```

TESTING AND DEBUGGING YOUR ASP.NET CORE APPLICATION

```
    Assert.True(welcomeMessage);
}
```

In these examples, we are simulating a user logging into the application by filling out the login form and verifying that the user is greeted with a welcome message upon successful login.

b. Verifying Application State

In addition to simulating user actions, it's essential to verify the application state after performing actions. This can include checking for elements on the page, validating URLs, or verifying the content displayed.

Example of Verifying URL After Navigation:

```csharp
Copy code
[Fact]
public async Task UserCanNavigateToDashboardAfterLogin()
{
    // Arrange
    await _page.Locator("#loginButton").ClickAsync();
    await _page.FillAsync("#email", "test@example.com");
    await _page.FillAsync("#password", "Password123!");
    await _page.Locator("#submitButton").ClickAsync();

    // Act
    var currentUrl = _page.Url;

    // Assert
    Assert.Equal("http://localhost:5000/dashboard", currentUrl);
}
```

5. Running E2E Tests

Running your E2E tests can be done through the command line or integrated into your CI/CD pipeline. Ensure that your ASP.NET Core application is running before executing the tests to allow the testing tools to interact with it.

Using Command Line:

```bash
Copy code
dotnet test MyApp.E2ETests
```

This command will run all tests in the specified test project, and you should see the results in your terminal.

6. Best Practices for E2E Testing

To maximize the effectiveness of your E2E tests, consider the following best practices:

- **Keep Tests Isolated**: Ensure that tests do not depend on the state left by other tests. This helps maintain test reliability and reduces flakiness.
- **Use Mock Services When Appropriate**: For external APIs or services, consider mocking them to isolate the test environment and focus on the application logic.
- **Optimize Test Performance**: Minimize the time taken to run E2E tests by reducing unnecessary steps, using headless browsers, and running tests in parallel when possible.
- **Implement Continuous Testing**: Integrate E2E tests into your CI/CD pipeline to catch issues early and ensure that your application remains stable with each code change.

End-to-end testing is an essential component of the development process for ASP.NET Core applications. By leveraging tools like Selenium and Playwright, you can effectively simulate user interactions and validate the application's functionality from start to finish. By following best practices and incorporating E2E testing into your development workflow, you can ensure a high-quality user experience and minimize potential issues in production.

Debugging Techniques and Tools for Troubleshooting

Debugging is an integral part of the software development process. In ASP.NET Core applications, effective debugging can help identify and resolve issues quickly, ensuring a smoother user experience and more stable applications. This section discusses various debugging techniques and tools that can assist developers in troubleshooting ASP.NET Core applications.

1. Understanding the Debugging Process

The debugging process involves a systematic approach to identifying, isolating, and fixing bugs or issues within the code. The primary goals of debugging are:

- **Identify the Source of the Problem**: Determine where in the code the issue is occurring.
- **Understand the Context**: Gather information about the application's state when the issue arises.
- **Test Fixes**: Apply changes to the code and test to see if the issue is resolved.

Effective debugging requires a combination of skills, including analytical thinking, familiarity with the application, and knowledge of the tools available.

2. Using Visual Studio Debugger

Visual Studio is one of the most popular IDEs for ASP.NET Core development, and it comes with a powerful built-in debugger that provides a range of features for troubleshooting applications.

a. Setting Breakpoints

Breakpoints are markers placed in your code to pause execution at a specific line. This allows you to inspect variables, evaluate expressions, and observe the flow of control.

To set a breakpoint:

1. Click in the left margin next to the line of code where you want to pause execution.
2. A red dot will appear, indicating a breakpoint has been set.

When you run your application in debug mode (F5), execution will stop at the breakpoint, allowing you to analyze the current state.

b. Step Through Code

Once execution is paused at a breakpoint, you can use various commands to step through the code:

- **Step Over (F10)**: Executes the current line and moves to the next line, skipping any function calls.
- **Step Into (F11)**: If the current line contains a function call, this command steps into the function to debug it line by line.
- **Step Out (Shift + F11)**: If you are inside a function, this command executes the remaining lines of the function and returns to the calling function.

Using these commands helps in understanding how the application behaves at runtime.

c. Inspecting Variables and Watch Expressions

While debugging, you can hover over variables to see their current values. Additionally, you can use the Watch window to monitor specific variables or expressions continuously.

1. **Locals Window**: Automatically displays all local variables in the current scope.
2. **Watch Window**: You can manually add variables or expressions you want to track.
3. **Immediate Window**: Allows you to execute commands or evaluate

TESTING AND DEBUGGING YOUR ASP.NET CORE APPLICATION

expressions while debugging.

These tools provide valuable insights into the application's state, helping identify issues.

d. Exception Handling

The debugger will typically break on unhandled exceptions, allowing you to investigate the issue. You can customize exception settings to break on specific exceptions, whether they are caught or uncaught.

To configure exceptions:

1. Go to the **Debug** menu.
2. Select **Windows > Exception Settings**.
3. Check the exceptions you want to break on.

This feature is particularly useful for identifying issues early in the debugging process.

3. Logging for Debugging

Logging is a crucial technique for troubleshooting ASP.NET Core applications. It provides insights into the application's behavior and helps diagnose issues without needing to rely solely on breakpoints.

a. Built-in Logging Framework

ASP.NET Core includes a built-in logging framework that allows you to log messages at various levels: Trace, Debug, Information, Warning, Error, and Critical. This framework can log to various outputs, including console, files, and third-party services.

To implement logging:

1. Inject the ILogger<T> service into your classes, where T is the class type.
2. Use the logger instance to log messages.

Example:

```csharp
public class HomeController : Controller
{
    private readonly ILogger<HomeController> _logger;

    public HomeController(ILogger<HomeController> logger)
    {
        _logger = logger;
    }

    public IActionResult Index()
    {
        _logger.LogInformation("Index action called.");
        return View();
    }
}
```

b. Configuring Logging Levels

You can configure logging levels in the appsettings.json file. This allows you to control which messages are logged based on the environment (development, production, etc.).

Example Configuration:

```json
{
  "Logging": {
    "LogLevel": {
      "Default": "Information",
      "Microsoft": "Warning",
      "System": "Warning"
    }
  }
}
```

This configuration sets the default logging level to Information, while Microsoft and System namespaces will only log Warning-level messages or higher.

  c. Structured Logging

  Structured logging involves capturing logs in a structured format (e.g., JSON) that allows for easier querying and analysis. This is particularly useful for monitoring applications in production.

  Integrating libraries like Serilog or NLog can facilitate structured logging in your ASP.NET Core applications.

4. Remote Debugging

Remote debugging is useful when you need to debug applications running in different environments, such as a staging server or a container.

a. Remote Debugging with Visual Studio

Visual Studio supports remote debugging for ASP.NET Core applications. You can attach the Visual Studio debugger to a remote process running on another machine or in a container.

1. Install the Visual Studio Remote Tools on the target machine.
2. Start the Remote Debugger application.
3. In Visual Studio, go to **Debug > Attach to Process**.
4. Enter the remote machine's name and connect to the appropriate process.

This allows you to debug applications running in different environments as if they were local.

b. Debugging in Containers

If your ASP.NET Core application runs in Docker containers, you can debug it using Visual Studio or the command line. Visual Studio provides built-in support for Docker, allowing you to run and debug applications within a container.

To enable debugging:

1. Add a Dockerfile to your project.
2. Run the application using Docker Compose or directly with Docker.
3. Attach the debugger to the running container.

This method provides valuable insights into the application's behavior in containerized environments.

5. Debugging ASP.NET Core Middleware

ASP.NET Core middleware is critical in handling requests and responses. Debugging middleware can help identify issues related to request processing and application flow.

a. Writing Middleware for Debugging

You can create custom middleware that logs the details of incoming requests and outgoing responses. This can be particularly useful for diagnosing issues in the request pipeline.

Example Middleware:

```csharp
Copy code
public class RequestLoggingMiddleware
{
    private readonly RequestDelegate _next;

    public RequestLoggingMiddleware(RequestDelegate next)
    {
        _next = next;
    }

    public async Task InvokeAsync(HttpContext context)
    {
        // Log request details
        Console.WriteLine($"Incoming request: {context.Request.Method} {context.Request.Path}");

        await _next(context);
```

```
        // Log response details
        Console.WriteLine($"Outgoing response:
        {context.Response.StatusCode}");
    }
}
```

To use this middleware, register it in the Configure method of Startup.cs:

```csharp
Copy code
public void Configure(IApplicationBuilder app,
IHostingEnvironment env)
{
    app.UseMiddleware<RequestLoggingMiddleware>();
    // other middleware registrations
}
```

b. Monitoring Request and Response Performance

In addition to logging, you can monitor the performance of middleware by measuring the time taken to process requests. This can help identify bottlenecks in the application.

Example of Timing Requests:

```csharp
Copy code
public class PerformanceMonitoringMiddleware
{
    private readonly RequestDelegate _next;

    public PerformanceMonitoringMiddleware(RequestDelegate next)
    {
        _next = next;
    }

    public async Task InvokeAsync(HttpContext context)
    {
```

```
        var watch = Stopwatch.StartNew();

        await _next(context);

        watch.Stop();
        Console.WriteLine($"Request took
        {watch.ElapsedMilliseconds} ms");
    }
}
```

6. Debugging Third-Party Libraries

When using third-party libraries, issues may arise due to integration problems or unexpected behavior. Debugging these issues can be challenging, but several strategies can help.

a. Read Documentation and Check Issues

Before diving into debugging, ensure you thoroughly read the documentation for the third-party library. This can often provide insights into common pitfalls or configuration options that may affect behavior. Additionally, check the library's issue tracker on platforms like GitHub to see if others have encountered similar issues.

b. Enable Detailed Logging

Many libraries provide logging options to help diagnose issues. Enable detailed logging in the library's configuration to gain insights into its internal workings. This can often point out what's going wrong.

c. Use Debug Symbols

If the library offers debug symbols (PDB files), you can attach them in Visual Studio to step into the library's code during debugging. This allows you to observe its behavior and interactions with your application.

Debugging is an essential skill for any ASP.NET Core developer. By leveraging the built-in Visual Studio debugger, effective logging practices, remote debugging, and middleware insights, you can identify and resolve issues more efficiently. Implementing structured logging and monitoring can further enhance your debugging capabilities, making it easier to maintain high-quality, reliable applications. Adopting these techniques and tools will ultimately lead to a smoother development experience and a better end-user experience.

Deployment and Continuous Integration/Continuous Delivery (CI/CD)

Deployment Strategies for ASP.NET Core Applications

Deploying an ASP.NET Core application is a critical step in the software development lifecycle, ensuring that your application is accessible to users in a production environment. This chapter delves into various deployment strategies, offering insights into how to effectively deploy your application while leveraging Continuous Integration and Continuous Delivery (CI/CD) practices.

1. Understanding Deployment Environments

Before deploying an application, it is essential to understand the different environments involved in the deployment process:

- **Development**: The initial phase where the application is developed and tested by developers.
- **Staging**: A pre-production environment that mirrors the production environment as closely as possible. It is used for final testing before deployment.
- **Production**: The live environment where end users interact with the application. This environment must be stable, secure, and perform well.

2. Deployment Models

There are several deployment models available for ASP.NET Core applications, each with its own set of advantages and considerations:

a. On-Premises Deployment

Deploying on on-premises servers involves hosting the application on physical or virtual machines managed by the organization. This model offers full control over the hardware, network, and security configurations.

Considerations:

- **Pros**: Complete control, customization options, and compliance with specific security policies.
- **Cons**: Higher maintenance costs, requires infrastructure management, and limited scalability.

b. Cloud Deployment

Cloud deployment leverages cloud service providers (CSPs) such as Microsoft Azure, AWS, or Google Cloud. These platforms offer various services for hosting ASP.NET Core applications, including infrastructure as a service (IaaS) and platform as a service (PaaS).

Considerations:

- **Pros**: Scalability, cost-effectiveness, reduced management overhead, and access to a range of cloud services.
- **Cons**: Dependency on the service provider, potential vendor lock-in, and concerns about data privacy.

c. Containerized Deployment

Containerization involves packaging the application and its dependencies into containers using technologies like Docker. This approach ensures consistency across environments, making it easier to deploy and manage applications.

Considerations:

- **Pros**: Portability, consistency, isolation, and scalability. Easier to manage dependencies and configurations.
- **Cons**: Requires a learning curve for container management and orchestration.

3. Preparing for Deployment

Before deploying an ASP.NET Core application, certain preparations should be made to ensure a smooth deployment process:

a. Build Configuration

Use the appropriate build configuration for deployment. Typically, the "Release" configuration should be used for production deployments to optimize performance.

```bash
Copy code
dotnet publish -c Release
```

This command compiles the application, applies transformations, and creates a self-contained deployment in the bin/Release/netcoreapp3.1/publish folder.

b. Environment Configuration

Configure environment variables and settings specific to the deployment environment. ASP.NET Core allows you to use different configuration files for different environments (e.g., appsettings.Development.json, appsettings.Production.json).

Use the ASPNETCORE_ENVIRONMENT environment variable to specify the current environment:

```bash
Copy code
set ASPNETCORE_ENVIRONMENT=Production
```

c. Database Migrations

Ensure that your database schema is up to date before deploying the application. Use Entity Framework Core migrations to apply any pending changes:

```bash
Copy code
dotnet ef database update
```

This command applies the latest migrations to the database, ensuring that your application can function correctly with the expected data structure.

4. Deployment Options

There are several common options for deploying ASP.NET Core applications:

a. Using Web Deploy

Web Deploy (MSDeploy) is a Microsoft tool that simplifies the deployment of ASP.NET applications to IIS servers. It allows you to deploy your application, manage settings, and synchronize content easily.

Steps:

1. Publish your application to a package.
2. Use Web Deploy to push the package to the target IIS server.

b. Deploying to Azure App Service

Azure App Service is a fully managed platform for building, deploying, and scaling web apps. It provides features such as auto-scaling, custom domains, and built-in CI/CD integration.

Steps:

1. Create an Azure App Service instance through the Azure portal.
2. Publish your application using Visual Studio, Azure CLI, or GitHub Actions.

c. Deploying via Docker

When using Docker, you can build a Docker image of your application and deploy it to a container orchestration platform like Kubernetes or Azure Kubernetes Service (AKS).

Steps:

1. Create a Dockerfile for your ASP.NET Core application.
2. Build the Docker image:

```bash
Copy code
docker build -t myapp:latest .
```

1. Push the image to a container registry (e.g., Docker Hub, Azure Container Registry).
2. Deploy the image to your chosen orchestration platform.

5. Continuous Integration and Continuous Delivery (CI/CD)

CI/CD practices streamline the deployment process, reducing the time and effort required to release new features and fixes. Implementing CI/CD involves automating the build, test, and deployment processes.

a. Setting Up CI/CD Pipelines

Use tools like Azure DevOps, GitHub Actions, or Jenkins to set up CI/CD pipelines for your ASP.NET Core application.

Example with GitHub Actions: Create a .github/workflows/ci-cd.yml file in your repository:

```yaml
Copy code
name: CI/CD Pipeline
```

```yaml
on:
  push:
    branches:
      - main

jobs:
  build:
    runs-on: ubuntu-latest
    steps:
      - name: Checkout Code
        uses: actions/checkout@v2

      - name: Setup .NET
        uses: actions/setup-dotnet@v1
        with:
          dotnet-version: '3.1.x'

      - name: Restore Dependencies
        run: dotnet restore

      - name: Build Application
        run: dotnet build --configuration Release

      - name: Run Tests
        run: dotnet test

      - name: Publish Application
        run: dotnet publish --configuration Release --output ./publish

      - name: Deploy to Azure
        uses: Azure/webapps-deploy@v2
        with:
          app-name: 'your-app-name'
          publish-profile: ${{ secrets.AZURE_PUBLISH_PROFILE }}
          package: ./publish
```

In this example, the CI/CD pipeline automatically builds, tests, and publishes the application to Azure whenever changes are pushed to the main branch.

b. Monitoring Deployments

After deploying your application, it's essential to monitor its performance and availability. Tools like Azure Application Insights, New Relic, or ELK Stack can provide valuable insights into your application's health.

6. Rollback Strategies

Despite thorough testing, issues may still arise in production. It's vital to have rollback strategies in place to quickly revert to a previous stable version.

- **Versioned Releases**: Keep track of versions in your deployment process. Use semantic versioning to differentiate releases.
- **Backup and Restore**: Maintain backups of the database and application state before each deployment, allowing for quick restoration in case of failures.
- **Feature Flags**: Implement feature flags to enable or disable features without requiring a new deployment. This allows you to mitigate issues with specific features without affecting the entire application.

Deploying ASP.NET Core applications involves a well-planned approach that considers various deployment models, configurations, and CI/CD practices. By understanding the deployment landscape, preparing your application, and implementing continuous integration and delivery, you can ensure a smooth deployment process. Additionally, having robust monitoring and rollback strategies in place will help maintain application stability and performance in production environments. This comprehensive approach to deployment will ultimately lead to a more reliable and efficient application lifecycle management process.

Setting Up CI/CD Pipelines with GitHub Actions, Azure DevOps, and GitLab

Continuous Integration (CI) and Continuous Delivery (CD) are essential practices in modern software development, allowing teams to deliver

DEPLOYMENT AND CONTINUOUS INTEGRATION/CONTINUOUS DELIVERY...

high-quality applications at a faster pace. This section focuses on setting up CI/CD pipelines using three popular tools: GitHub Actions, Azure DevOps, and GitLab CI/CD. Each tool offers unique features, and the choice will depend on your team's workflow, preferences, and existing infrastructure.

1. CI/CD with GitHub Actions

GitHub Actions provides a robust framework for automating software workflows directly within GitHub. It allows developers to define workflows using YAML files, making it easy to set up CI/CD pipelines for their ASP.NET Core applications.

a. Creating a CI/CD Workflow

To create a CI/CD pipeline with GitHub Actions, follow these steps:

1. **Create a Workflow File**: Navigate to your repository and create a new directory called .github/workflows. Inside this directory, create a YAML file (e.g., ci-cd-pipeline.yml).
2. **Define the Workflow**: Below is an example workflow configuration that builds, tests, and deploys an ASP.NET Core application to Azure.

```yaml
Copy code
name: CI/CD Pipeline

on:
  push:
    branches:
      - main

jobs:
  build:
    runs-on: ubuntu-latest

    steps:
```

```yaml
- name: Checkout code
  uses: actions/checkout@v2

- name: Setup .NET Core
  uses: actions/setup-dotnet@v1
  with:
    dotnet-version: '3.1.x'

- name: Restore dependencies
  run: dotnet restore

- name: Build
  run: dotnet build --configuration Release --no-restore

- name: Run tests
  run: dotnet test --configuration Release --no-build
  --verbosity normal

- name: Publish
  run: dotnet publish --configuration Release --output
  ./publish

- name: Deploy to Azure
  uses: Azure/webapps-deploy@v2
  with:
    app-name: 'YourAppName'
    publish-profile: ${{ secrets.AZURE_PUBLISH_PROFILE }}
    package: ./publish
```

b. Managing Secrets

For deployment to Azure, you need to store sensitive information like the Azure publish profile in GitHub Secrets. Navigate to your repository settings, find the "Secrets" section, and add the AZURE_PUBLISH_PROFILE secret. This ensures that your credentials are not exposed in the workflow file.

c. Monitoring Workflow Runs

After committing the workflow file, you can monitor the workflow runs

DEPLOYMENT AND CONTINUOUS INTEGRATION/CONTINUOUS DELIVERY...

from the "Actions" tab in your GitHub repository. Each push to the main branch will trigger the defined actions, providing immediate feedback on the build and deployment process.

2. CI/CD with Azure DevOps

Azure DevOps is a comprehensive platform that includes services for building, testing, and deploying applications. Its CI/CD capabilities are robust and support a variety of programming languages, including C# and .NET.

a. Creating a New Pipeline

1. **Navigate to Azure DevOps**: Go to your Azure DevOps project.
2. **Create a Pipeline**: Click on "Pipelines" in the left sidebar and then click on "New Pipeline."
3. **Select Your Repository**: Choose the source where your code resides (e.g., GitHub, Azure Repos).
4. **Configure the Pipeline**: Select "Starter Pipeline" to begin with a basic YAML configuration. The following example demonstrates a CI/CD pipeline for an ASP.NET Core application:

```yaml
yaml
Copy code
trigger:
  branches:
    include:
      - main

pool:
  vmImage: 'windows-latest'

steps:
- task: UseDotNet@2
  inputs:
    packageType: 'sdk'
```

```yaml
    version: '3.1.x'
    installationPath: $(Agent.ToolsDirectory)/dotnet

- script: dotnet restore
  displayName: 'Restore Dependencies'

- script: dotnet build --configuration Release
  displayName: 'Build Solution'

- script: dotnet test --configuration Release
  displayName: 'Run Tests'

- script: dotnet publish --configuration Release --output $(Build.ArtifactStagingDirectory)
  displayName: 'Publish'

- task: AzureWebApp@1
  inputs:
    azureSubscription: 'YourAzureSubscription'
    appName: 'YourAppName'
    package: '$(Build.ArtifactStagingDirectory)/**'
```

b. Deploying to Azure

In the Azure DevOps pipeline configuration, ensure that you have set up the necessary service connection to your Azure account, which allows Azure DevOps to deploy your application to Azure.

3. CI/CD with GitLab CI/CD

GitLab CI/CD is a powerful tool integrated into GitLab that automates the software development process. It supports multi-stage pipelines, enabling teams to implement complex workflows with ease.

a. Setting Up the .gitlab-ci.yml File

To create a CI/CD pipeline in GitLab, you will need to define a .gitlab-ci.yml file in the root of your repository. Here's a basic example for an ASP.NET Core application:

```yaml
Copy code
stages:
  - build
  - test
  - deploy

variables:
  DOTNET_VERSION: '3.1'

before_script:
  - apt-get update && apt-get install -y apt-transport-https
  - wget https://packages.microsoft.com/config/ubuntu/$(lsb_release -rs)/packages-microsoft-prod.deb
  - dpkg -i packages-microsoft-prod.deb
  - apt-get update
  - apt-get install -y dotnet-sdk-$DOTNET_VERSION

build:
  stage: build
  script:
    - dotnet restore
    - dotnet build --configuration Release

test:
  stage: test
  script:
    - dotnet test --configuration Release

deploy:
  stage: deploy
  script:
    - dotnet publish --configuration Release --output ./publish
    - echo "Deploying to Azure..."
    # Add deployment steps here
```

b. Deployment Steps

The deployment script can vary based on your deployment target. You can use Azure CLI commands, SSH to connect to your server, or integrate with other services.

Setting up CI/CD pipelines is a crucial step toward automating the deployment process of your ASP.NET Core applications. Whether using GitHub Actions, Azure DevOps, or GitLab CI/CD, the right setup can greatly enhance your development workflow, allowing for rapid releases and increased software quality. Each tool offers unique benefits and integration options, enabling teams to choose the best solution based on their specific requirements and existing infrastructure. By adopting CI/CD practices, you not only improve the efficiency of your deployment process but also facilitate collaboration and innovation within your development teams.

Deploying to Cloud Platforms (Azure, AWS, Google Cloud)

Deploying ASP.NET Core applications to cloud platforms is a crucial part of modern web development. This section explores how to deploy applications to three leading cloud services: Microsoft Azure, Amazon Web Services (AWS), and Google Cloud Platform (GCP). Each cloud provider has unique features and deployment methods that can be leveraged to host your applications effectively.

1. Deploying to Microsoft Azure

Azure is a popular choice for hosting ASP.NET Core applications due to its seamless integration with the .NET ecosystem and its extensive services.

a. Deployment Options

- **Azure App Service**: A fully managed platform for building, deploying, and scaling web apps. Ideal for rapid development without managing infrastructure.
- **Azure Virtual Machines**: Provides full control over the server environment but requires more management effort.
- **Azure Kubernetes Service (AKS)**: Perfect for containerized applica-

DEPLOYMENT AND CONTINUOUS INTEGRATION/CONTINUOUS DELIVERY...

tions, allowing you to manage Kubernetes clusters.

b. Deploying to Azure App Service
Create an Azure App Service:

- Go to the Azure portal and create a new App Service.
- Select your subscription and resource group, and choose a unique name for your app.
- Choose the runtime stack (ASP.NET Core 3.1 or later).

Deploying via Visual Studio:

- In Visual Studio, right-click on your project and select **Publish**.
- Choose **Azure** as the target and follow the prompts to select your Azure subscription and App Service.

Using GitHub Actions for CI/CD:

- If you are using GitHub, you can configure a GitHub Action workflow to automate deployment.
- Use the Azure Web Apps Deploy action in your workflow file, specifying the App Service name and your publish profile secret.

c. Monitoring and Scaling

Once deployed, you can monitor application performance and scale the app directly from the Azure portal. Azure provides insights into application health and usage metrics.

2. Deploying to Amazon Web Services (AWS)

AWS offers a variety of services suitable for hosting ASP.NET Core applications, including Elastic Beanstalk, EC2, and ECS.

a. Deployment Options

- **AWS Elastic Beanstalk**: A platform as a service (PaaS) that handles deployment, from capacity provisioning to load balancing and auto-scaling.
- **Amazon EC2**: Offers full control over your server, allowing for custom configurations.
- **Amazon ECS/EKS**: Ideal for containerized applications, using Docker and Kubernetes.

b. Deploying to AWS Elastic Beanstalk
Create an Elastic Beanstalk Application:

- In the AWS Management Console, navigate to Elastic Beanstalk and create a new application.
- Select the appropriate platform (e.g., .NET Core).

Package Your Application:

- Build your project and create a zip package of the output files.

Deploy the Application:

- Upload the zip file through the Elastic Beanstalk console or use the AWS CLI for deployment.
- Example AWS CLI command:

```bash
Copy code
eb init -p "dotnetcore" my-app
eb create my-app-env
eb deploy
```

Monitoring:

DEPLOYMENT AND CONTINUOUS INTEGRATION/CONTINUOUS DELIVERY...

- Elastic Beanstalk provides monitoring tools through the AWS console to track application performance and health.

3. Deploying to Google Cloud Platform (GCP)

GCP provides various services suitable for deploying ASP.NET Core applications, including Google App Engine, Google Kubernetes Engine (GKE), and Compute Engine.

a. Deployment Options

- **Google App Engine**: A fully managed serverless platform that automatically handles traffic and scaling.
- **Google Kubernetes Engine (GKE)**: For containerized applications, managing Kubernetes clusters on GCP.
- **Google Compute Engine**: Provides VMs for custom server setups.

b. Deploying to Google App Engine
Create a New App:

- In the Google Cloud Console, create a new project and enable App Engine for that project.

Prepare Your Application:

- Create an app.yaml file in your project directory to define the runtime and handlers:

```yaml
Copy code
runtime: aspnetcore
handlers:
- url: /.*
  script: auto
```

Deploy the Application:

- Use the Google Cloud SDK to deploy:

```bash
Copy code
gcloud app deploy
```

Monitoring:

- Google Cloud provides monitoring and logging capabilities that allow you to track your application's performance.

Choosing the right cloud platform for deploying your ASP.NET Core application depends on your specific needs, budget, and team expertise. Each provider offers unique benefits and tools to help automate deployment processes, monitor application health, and scale resources according to demand. By understanding the deployment options available across Azure, AWS, and Google Cloud, you can select the best solution for your project, ensuring smooth operations and high availability for your users. Whether you choose a managed service like Azure App Service, a platform like AWS Elastic Beanstalk, or container orchestration with Google Kubernetes Engine, the right deployment strategy will enhance your application's reliability and performance.

Configuring Docker and Kubernetes for Scalable Deployment

In the realm of modern application development, Docker and Kubernetes have emerged as the de facto standards for containerization and orchestration. This section delves into how to configure Docker and Kubernetes to deploy ASP.NET Core applications in a scalable manner. By utilizing these technologies, developers can achieve consistent environments, streamlined deployment processes, and efficient resource management.

1. Understanding Docker

Docker is a platform that enables developers to automate the deployment of applications inside lightweight, portable containers. A Docker container packages an application and its dependencies into a single unit, ensuring that it runs consistently across different environments.

a. Creating a Dockerfile

The first step in containerizing your ASP.NET Core application is creating a Dockerfile. This file defines the environment in which your application will run.

Basic Structure: Here's an example of a simple Dockerfile for an ASP.NET Core application:

```dockerfile
Copy code
# Use the official .NET Core SDK image for building the application
FROM mcr.microsoft.com/dotnet/sdk:3.1 AS build-env
WORKDIR /app

# Copy the csproj file and restore dependencies
COPY *.csproj ./
RUN dotnet restore

# Copy the entire project and build the application
COPY . ./
RUN dotnet publish -c Release -o out

# Use the official ASP.NET Core runtime image for running the application
FROM mcr.microsoft.com/dotnet/aspnet:3.1
WORKDIR /app
COPY --from=build-env /app/out ./
```

```
# Expose the application on port 80
EXPOSE 80

# Start the application
ENTRYPOINT ["dotnet", "YourAppName.dll"]
```

Build the Docker Image: Run the following command in the terminal at the directory containing your Dockerfile:

```bash
Copy code
docker build -t yourappname:latest .
```

Running the Docker Container: After building the image, you can run it with:

```bash
Copy code
docker run -d -p 8080:80 yourappname:latest
```

This command maps port 80 inside the container to port 8080 on your host machine.

2. Configuring Kubernetes

Kubernetes is an open-source orchestration platform that automates deploying, scaling, and managing containerized applications.

a. Setting Up a Kubernetes Cluster

Using Minikube: For local development, you can use Minikube to create a single-node Kubernetes cluster:

```bash
Copy code
```

DEPLOYMENT AND CONTINUOUS INTEGRATION/CONTINUOUS DELIVERY...

```
minikube start
```

Using a Managed Service: For production, consider using managed services like Azure Kubernetes Service (AKS), Amazon EKS, or Google Kubernetes Engine (GKE).

b. Creating Kubernetes Manifests

Kubernetes uses YAML files to define the desired state of your applications. You will need at least a Deployment and a Service manifest to deploy your ASP.NET Core application.

Deployment Manifest: Create a file named deployment.yaml:

```yaml
Copy code
apiVersion: apps/v1
kind: Deployment
metadata:
  name: yourappname
spec:
  replicas: 3
  selector:
    matchLabels:
      app: yourappname
  template:
    metadata:
      labels:
        app: yourappname
    spec:
      containers:
      - name: yourappname
        image: yourappname:latest
        ports:
        - containerPort: 80
```

This configuration defines a deployment with three replicas of your application for load balancing.

Service Manifest: Create a file named service.yaml:

```yaml
Copy code
apiVersion: v1
kind: Service
metadata:
  name: yourappname
spec:
  type: LoadBalancer
  ports:
    - port: 80
      targetPort: 80
  selector:
    app: yourappname
```

This service exposes your application to the outside world, allowing access through a **LoadBalancer.**

c. Deploying to Kubernetes

Apply Manifests: Use the following commands to deploy your application:

```bash
Copy code
kubectl apply -f deployment.yaml
kubectl apply -f service.yaml
```

Accessing Your Application: If you're using Minikube, you can access your application using:

```bash
Copy code
minikube service yourappname
```

For managed services, you'll receive an external IP after deploying, which you can use to access your application.

3. Scaling Your Application

One of the primary benefits of using Kubernetes is its ability to scale applications seamlessly.

Scaling Up: To increase the number of replicas, you can modify the replicas field in your Deployment manifest and reapply it, or use the command:

```bash
Copy code
kubectl scale deployment yourappname --replicas=5
```

Horizontal Pod Autoscaling: For automated scaling based on CPU or memory usage, enable Horizontal Pod Autoscaling:

```bash
Copy code
kubectl autoscale deployment yourappname --cpu-percent=50 --min=1 --max=10
```

4. Best Practices for Docker and Kubernetes

- **Use Multi-Stage Builds**: This optimizes image size and improves build time by separating the build environment from the runtime environment.
- **Manage Secrets Securely**: Use Kubernetes Secrets to manage sensitive information, keeping them out of your Docker images and manifests.
- **Implement Health Checks**: Configure readiness and liveness probes in your Kubernetes manifests to ensure the application is running correctly.
- **Monitor Your Applications**: Use tools like Prometheus, Grafana, or Azure Monitor to keep an eye on your application's performance and resource usage.

Configuring Docker and Kubernetes for deploying ASP.NET Core applications enables developers to leverage containerization and orchestration for efficient, scalable deployments. By utilizing these technologies, you can ensure that your applications run consistently across different environments, scale seamlessly to meet demand, and integrate into modern CI/CD pipelines. As you adopt Docker and Kubernetes, consider best practices for security, monitoring, and resource management to optimize your deployment strategy and improve application reliability.

Monitoring and Logging for Production Applications

Effective monitoring and logging are essential for maintaining the health and performance of production applications. In an ASP.NET Core environment, proper monitoring and logging help developers identify issues, track performance metrics, and ensure the application is running as expected. This section covers the best practices and tools for implementing robust monitoring and logging in ASP.NET Core applications deployed in production.

1. Importance of Monitoring and Logging

Monitoring involves continuously tracking the performance and health of your application, while logging records events that occur during execution. Both practices are critical for:

- **Identifying Performance Bottlenecks**: Monitoring tools can help pinpoint slow operations, allowing you to optimize your code or infrastructure.
- **Error Tracking**: Logs capture exceptions and errors, making it easier to diagnose and fix issues.
- **Understanding User Behavior**: Monitoring user interactions can provide insights into how the application is used, guiding future enhancements.
- **Compliance and Auditing**: Logging can help you meet regulatory requirements by keeping a record of access and changes to sensitive

data.

2. Implementing Logging in ASP.NET Core

ASP.NET Core has built-in support for logging through the Microsoft.Extensions.Logging namespace, allowing you to use various logging providers.

a. Setting Up Logging

Configure Logging in Startup.cs: You can configure logging in the ConfigureServices method of your Startup class:

```csharp
Copy code
public void ConfigureServices(IServiceCollection services)
{
    services.AddLogging(config =>
    {
        config.AddConsole();
        config.AddDebug();
        config.AddEventSourceLogger();
    });

    // Other service configurations
}
```

Using Logging in Your Application: Inject the ILogger<T> interface into your classes to log messages:

```csharp
Copy code
public class MyService
{
    private readonly ILogger<MyService> _logger;

    public MyService(ILogger<MyService> logger)
    {
        _logger = logger;
    }
```

```
    public void DoWork()
    {
        _logger.LogInformation("Work started.");
        try
        {
            // Your logic here
        }
        catch (Exception ex)
        {
            _logger.LogError(ex, "An error occurred while doing
            work.");
        }
        _logger.LogInformation("Work finished.");
    }
}
```

b. Logging Levels

ASP.NET Core supports multiple logging levels, allowing you to categorize messages according to their importance:

- **Trace**: Most detailed logs, used for debugging.
- **Debug**: Information useful for developers during debugging.
- **Information**: General application flow logs.
- **Warning**: An indication that something unexpected happened, but the application is still functioning.
- **Error**: Logs for failures that need to be investigated.
- **Critical**: Logs for fatal errors that require immediate attention.

3. Monitoring Application Performance

Monitoring involves using tools that provide insights into your application's health and performance. Below are some popular monitoring solutions compatible with ASP.NET Core applications.

a. Application Performance Monitoring (APM) Tools

Application Insights: Part of Azure Monitor, Application Insights is a powerful APM tool that automatically collects performance data, exceptions, and custom events.

- **Setup**: To use Application Insights, install the NuGet package:

```bash
Copy code
dotnet add package Microsoft.ApplicationInsights.AspNetCore
```

- **Configure in Startup.cs**:

```csharp
Copy code
public void ConfigureServices(IServiceCollection services)
{
    services.AddApplicationInsightsTelemetry(Configuration["ApplicationInsights:InstrumentationKey"]);
}
```

- **Benefits**: Provides rich telemetry data, including request rates, response times, failure rates, and user insights.

New Relic, Dynatrace, and Datadog: These are additional APM solutions that provide comprehensive monitoring features, including performance metrics, transaction tracing, and infrastructure monitoring.

b. Custom Metrics with Prometheus and Grafana

For more advanced monitoring, consider integrating Prometheus for metrics collection and Grafana for visualization:

Integrating Prometheus:

- Use the prometheus-net library to expose metrics from your ASP.NET Core application:

```bash
dotnet add package prometheus-net
```

- In your Startup.cs:

```csharp
public void Configure(IApplicationBuilder app, IWebHostEnvironment env)
{
    app.UseRouting();
    app.UseEndpoints(endpoints =>
    {
        endpoints.MapMetrics(); // Expose /metrics endpoint for Prometheus
    });
}
```

Visualizing Metrics with Grafana:

- Set up Grafana and configure it to pull metrics from your Prometheus instance. Create dashboards to visualize application performance metrics such as request latency, error rates, and resource usage.

4. Centralized Logging Solutions

While logging locally is useful during development, centralized logging is crucial in production environments. Centralized logging tools aggregate logs from multiple sources for easier analysis and troubleshooting.

a. ELK Stack (Elasticsearch, Logstash, Kibana)

The ELK stack is a popular choice for centralized logging:

- **Elasticsearch**: A search engine that stores logs and allows for powerful querying.
- **Logstash**: A server-side data processing pipeline that ingests logs and sends them to Elasticsearch.
- **Kibana**: A visualization tool that provides a user-friendly interface for querying and analyzing log data.

Setting Up ELK Stack:

1. **Install ELK Stack**: Follow the installation instructions for Elasticsearch, Logstash, and Kibana on their official websites.
2. **Configure Logstash**: Create a Logstash configuration file to define input (where to read logs from), filter (processing logs), and output (where to send logs):

```plaintext
Copy code
input {
  file {
    path => "/var/log/yourapp/*.log"
    start_position => "beginning"
  }
}

filter {
  # Add any filters you need here
}

output {
  elasticsearch {
    hosts => ["http://localhost:9200"]
```

```
    index => "yourapp-%{+YYYY.MM.dd}"
  }
}
```

Visualize Logs in Kibana: Open Kibana in your browser, create an index pattern, and start analyzing your logs.

b. Other Centralized Logging Solutions

- **Serilog**: A popular structured logging library that can easily integrate with sinks for various log storage options, including Elasticsearch, SQL Server, and more.
- **Seq**: A structured log server that works well with Serilog, providing a user interface for querying and analyzing log data.

5. Best Practices for Monitoring and Logging

- **Log Only What's Necessary**: Avoid excessive logging that can clutter your log files and make it harder to find relevant information.
- **Use Structured Logging**: Store logs in a structured format (like JSON) to make it easier to parse and analyze them in centralized logging solutions.
- **Set Up Alerts**: Configure alerts in your monitoring tools to notify you of potential issues, such as high error rates or performance degradation.
- **Regularly Review Logs and Metrics**: Conduct periodic reviews of your logs and metrics to identify trends and potential issues before they escalate.
- **Ensure Compliance**: Follow industry regulations regarding data privacy and log retention, especially when handling sensitive information.

Implementing robust monitoring and logging strategies is essential for maintaining the health and performance of ASP.NET Core applications in production. By leveraging built-in logging capabilities, integrating APM tools, and employing centralized logging solutions, developers can gain valuable insights into application performance and user behavior. With these practices in place, teams can quickly diagnose issues, enhance user experience, and ensure their applications run smoothly and efficiently in a production environment.

Building a Full-Scale Real-World Projec

Project Overview: Building an E-Commerce Web Application
In today's digital marketplace, e-commerce applications are critical for businesses aiming to reach a wider audience and increase sales. Building a robust e-commerce web application involves several components, including product management, user authentication, payment processing, and an intuitive user interface. This chapter provides a comprehensive overview of creating a full-scale e-commerce web application using ASP.NET Core 3, emphasizing best practices, architectural patterns, and essential features.

1. Understanding E-Commerce Applications

E-commerce applications enable online transactions and services, allowing users to browse products, manage their shopping carts, and complete purchases. The primary components of an e-commerce application include:

- **User Management**: Handling user accounts, authentication, and authorization.
- **Product Catalog**: Displaying products, including images, descriptions, and pricing.
- **Shopping Cart**: Allowing users to add products and manage their selections before checkout.
- **Order Management**: Processing orders, managing inventory, and

handling returns.
- **Payment Processing**: Integrating payment gateways for secure transactions.
- **Administration Panel**: Providing an interface for administrators to manage products, orders, and users.

2. Project Scope and Objectives

This project aims to develop a scalable and maintainable e-commerce web application that provides a seamless shopping experience. Key objectives include:

- **User-Friendly Interface**: Designing an intuitive front-end to enhance user experience.
- **Robust Backend Architecture**: Implementing a secure and efficient backend using ASP.NET Core and Entity Framework Core.
- **Extensible Design**: Ensuring the application can easily accommodate future features and integrations.
- **High Performance**: Optimizing the application for fast load times and efficient database operations.
- **Security Best Practices**: Incorporating measures to protect user data and transactions.

3. Technical Stack

For this e-commerce web application, the following technologies will be utilized:

- **Backend**: ASP.NET Core 3, Entity Framework Core for ORM (Object-Relational Mapping).
- **Frontend**: Razor Pages for server-side rendering or a JavaScript framework like React, Angular, or Vue.js for a more dynamic single-page application (SPA) experience.
- **Database**: SQL Server or PostgreSQL for data storage.
- **Authentication**: ASP.NET Core Identity for user management and

security.
- **Payment Processing**: Integration with a payment gateway such as Stripe or PayPal for handling transactions.
- **Hosting**: Azure, AWS, or any other cloud provider for deployment.

4. Application Architecture

A well-structured architecture is essential for maintaining scalability and flexibility. The architecture can be divided into the following layers:

- **Presentation Layer**: This is where user interactions occur. The frontend application communicates with the backend through APIs or server-rendered pages.
- **Business Logic Layer**: This layer contains the application's core logic, managing operations like user authentication, product catalog management, and order processing.
- **Data Access Layer**: Utilizing Entity Framework Core to interact with the database, this layer abstracts database operations, providing a clean interface for the business logic layer.

5. Key Features of the E-Commerce Application

The following features will be implemented to provide a comprehensive e-commerce experience:

a. User Authentication and Authorization

- **Registration and Login**: Users can create accounts, log in, and manage their profiles.
- **Role Management**: Different roles (e.g., Admin, User) will define access levels and permissions throughout the application.

b. Product Management

- **Product Catalog**: Display a list of products with options to filter and sort based on categories, prices, and ratings.

- **Product Details Page**: Each product will have a dedicated page with detailed information, images, and an "Add to Cart" button.

c. Shopping Cart Functionality

- **Add to Cart**: Users can add items to their cart and adjust quantities.
- **View Cart**: A dedicated page to review items, update quantities, or remove items before proceeding to checkout.

d. Checkout Process

- **Order Summary**: Review order details before finalizing the purchase.
- **Payment Integration**: Implement secure payment processing using a payment gateway, including handling transactions and refunds.

e. Order Management

- **Order History**: Users can view their past orders, including status updates (e.g., pending, shipped, completed).
- **Admin Panel**: An administrative interface for managing products, viewing orders, and handling user inquiries.

f. Search Functionality

- **Product Search**: Allow users to search for products using keywords, categories, and filters to enhance discoverability.

g. Responsive Design

- **Mobile-Friendly UI**: Ensure the application is responsive and works seamlessly on various devices, enhancing accessibility.

6. Development Process

The development process will follow a structured approach, typically involving the following stages:

a. Planning and Design

1. **Requirements Gathering**: Define the project's scope and gather requirements through discussions with stakeholders.
2. **Wireframing and Prototyping**: Create wireframes and prototypes to visualize the application's layout and user flow.

b. Setting Up the Development Environment

1. **IDE and Tools**: Use Visual Studio or Visual Studio Code for development, along with necessary extensions and tools for ASP.NET Core.
2. **Version Control**: Implement Git for version control, allowing for collaborative development and easy tracking of changes.

c. Development Phases

1. **Database Design**: Create the database schema using Entity Framework Core, defining models for products, users, orders, etc.
2. **Implementing Features**: Develop features incrementally, starting from user authentication to product management and order processing.
3. **Unit Testing**: Write unit tests to ensure code quality and functionality throughout the development process.

d. Deployment

1. **Continuous Integration/Continuous Deployment (CI/CD)**: Set up CI/CD pipelines using GitHub Actions, Azure DevOps, or GitLab to automate builds and deployments.

2. **Cloud Hosting**: Deploy the application to a cloud platform, ensuring scalability and availability.

Building an e-commerce web application using ASP.NET Core 3 requires careful planning, an understanding of user needs, and attention to detail in both frontend and backend development. By following best practices and leveraging the powerful features of ASP.NET Core, you can create a robust, scalable, and user-friendly e-commerce platform that meets the demands of modern consumers. In the subsequent sections of this chapter, we will delve into the implementation details, focusing on specific features and best practices to ensure the success of your e-commerce application.

Step-by-Step Guide to Application Architecture and Design

In this section, we will outline a detailed, step-by-step guide to designing and architecting your e-commerce web application using ASP.NET Core 3. Proper architecture is fundamental for ensuring scalability, maintainability, and performance of your application. The following guide will cover the essential components of application architecture and design principles tailored for an e-commerce solution.

1. Defining the Architecture Style
Choosing an Architectural Pattern
Start by selecting an architectural pattern that fits the project requirements. Common patterns for web applications include:

- **Layered Architecture**: This separates concerns into distinct layers (Presentation, Business Logic, Data Access), making it easier to manage and scale the application.
- **Microservices**: In this approach, different components of the application (e.g., user management, product catalog, order processing) are built as independent services. This promotes scalability and allows teams to work on different services simultaneously.

- **Domain-Driven Design (DDD)**: This focuses on modeling the application around the business domain, ensuring that the design reflects the real-world processes and rules.

For our e-commerce application, a **Layered Architecture** is suitable due to its simplicity and clear separation of concerns.

2. Identifying Key Components
Defining the Core Components

1. **User Management**: This module handles user registration, authentication, and role management. It leverages ASP.NET Core Identity for user security.
2. **Product Management**: This component manages the product catalog, including product details, inventory, and categories. It will involve CRUD (Create, Read, Update, Delete) operations.
3. **Shopping Cart**: This module allows users to add, update, and remove items from their shopping cart, providing an intuitive user experience.
4. **Order Processing**: This encompasses order placement, status tracking, and history management. This module also interfaces with payment gateways for transaction processing.
5. **Administration Panel**: A secure interface for administrators to manage users, products, and orders, providing analytics and reporting features.
6. **Search Functionality**: This allows users to search products based on various criteria and filters.

3. Designing the Database Schema
Creating the Entity Relationship Diagram (ERD)

The database design is crucial for data integrity and performance. Begin by identifying the key entities and their relationships:

- **User**: Represents customers and administrators, containing fields like UserId, Username, PasswordHash, and Role.
- **Product**: Represents items available for purchase, with fields such as ProductId, Name, Description, Price, and StockQuantity.
- **Order**: Contains order information, linking users and products, with fields like OrderId, UserId, OrderDate, and TotalAmount.
- **Cart**: Temporary storage for user-selected products before checkout, including fields like CartId, UserId, and ProductId.

Using Entity Framework Core, define these models and their relationships:

```csharp
Copy code
public class User
{
    public int UserId { get; set; }
    public string Username { get; set; }
    public string PasswordHash { get; set; }
    public string Role { get; set; }
}

public class Product
{
    public int ProductId { get; set; }
    public string Name { get; set; }
    public string Description { get; set; }
    public decimal Price { get; set; }
    public int StockQuantity { get; set; }
}

public class Order
{
    public int OrderId { get; set; }
    public int UserId { get; set; }
    public DateTime OrderDate { get; set; }
    public decimal TotalAmount { get; set; }
```

```
}

public class Cart
{
    public int CartId { get; set; }
    public int UserId { get; set; }
    public int ProductId { get; set; }
}
```

4. Setting Up the Project Structure
Creating a Scalable Project Structure

Organizing your project files effectively is essential for maintainability. A recommended structure is as follows:

```lua
Copy code
ECommerceApp/
|-- Controllers/
|-- Models/
|-- Views/
|-- Services/
|-- Data/
|-- wwwroot/
|-- Middleware/
|-- wwwroot/
|-- appsettings.json
|-- Startup.cs
|-- Program.cs
```

- **Controllers/**: Contains the application controllers that handle incoming requests.
- **Models/**: Defines the data models and their properties.
- **Views/**: Contains Razor views for server-side rendering.
- **Services/**: Implements business logic and reusable services.
- **Data/**: Includes the database context and migrations.
- **Middleware/**: Contains custom middleware components.

- **wwwroot/**: Hosts static files such as images, CSS, and JavaScript.

5. Implementing the User Interface
Designing the Frontend

The user interface is critical for user engagement. Consider the following best practices for the UI:

- **Responsive Design**: Ensure the application is usable on various devices using frameworks like Bootstrap or CSS Grid.
- **User Experience (UX)**: Design with the user in mind, making navigation intuitive and minimizing the number of steps to complete a purchase.

A sample layout structure for the views could look like this:

```html
html
Copy code
<!DOCTYPE html>
<html>
<head>
    <title>E-Commerce Application</title>
    <link rel="stylesheet" href="~/css/bootstrap.min.css" />
    <link rel="stylesheet" href="~/css/styles.css" />
</head>
<body>
    <header>
        <nav>
            <!-- Navigation links -->
        </nav>
    </header>
    <main>
        @RenderBody()
    </main>
    <footer>
        <p>&copy; 2024 E-Commerce App</p>
    </footer>
```

```
    <script src="~/js/jquery.min.js"></script>
    <script src="~/js/bootstrap.bundle.min.js"></script>
</body>
</html>
```

6. Security Considerations
Implementing Security Best Practices
Given the sensitive nature of e-commerce applications, security should be a top priority:

- **Authentication**: Use ASP.NET Core Identity for managing user authentication and authorization.
- **HTTPS**: Ensure that all communication is secured with HTTPS.
- **Input Validation**: Implement strict input validation to prevent SQL injection and XSS attacks.
- **Error Handling**: Implement custom error handling middleware to manage exceptions gracefully and log error details.

7. Testing Strategy
Creating a Testing Plan
Testing is essential for ensuring that the application is reliable and functions as intended. Include:

- **Unit Tests**: Write tests for individual components (services, controllers) using xUnit and Moq.
- **Integration Tests**: Ensure that different parts of the application work together seamlessly.
- **End-to-End Tests**: Utilize tools like Selenium or Playwright to simulate user interactions and verify the overall user experience.

8. Deployment Considerations
Planning for Deployment
Decide on deployment strategies early in the development process:

- **Continuous Integration/Continuous Deployment (CI/CD)**: Implement pipelines using GitHub Actions or Azure DevOps to automate testing and deployment.
- **Cloud Hosting**: Choose a cloud provider like Azure or AWS for scalable hosting solutions, enabling load balancing and autoscaling features.

By following this step-by-step guide, you will have a well-structured and robust architecture for your e-commerce web application. This foundation will allow you to build a scalable, secure, and user-friendly platform that meets modern e-commerce needs. As you proceed to implementation, each component will contribute to the overall functionality and success of your application, ensuring that it can grow and adapt to changing market demands. In the next section, we will delve deeper into implementing specific features and best practices for the e-commerce application.

Implementing Core Features: Product Catalog, Shopping Cart, and Checkout

In this section, we will focus on the implementation of the core features of the e-commerce application: the Product Catalog, Shopping Cart, and Checkout processes. These components are crucial for providing a seamless shopping experience and will be structured to ensure maintainability, scalability, and performance.

1. Implementing the Product Catalog
1.1 Defining the Product Model

The first step is to establish the data model for products. This model will contain all necessary fields that describe a product. Here's an updated Product model that includes additional attributes relevant to e-commerce:

```
csharp
Copy code
```

```csharp
public class Product
{
    public int ProductId { get; set; }
    public string Name { get; set; }
    public string Description { get; set; }
    public decimal Price { get; set; }
    public int StockQuantity { get; set; }
    public string ImageUrl { get; set; }  // URL to product image
    public string Category { get; set; }   // Category of the product
}
```

1.2 Creating the Product Repository

To manage data access for products, a repository pattern is beneficial. This separates data access logic from business logic. Here's an example of a simple repository for products:

```csharp
Copy code
public interface IProductRepository
{
    IEnumerable<Product> GetAllProducts();
    Product GetProductById(int id);
    void AddProduct(Product product);
    void UpdateProduct(Product product);
    void DeleteProduct(int id);
}

public class ProductRepository : IProductRepository
{
    private readonly AppDbContext _context;

    public ProductRepository(AppDbContext context)
    {
        _context = context;
    }
```

```
public IEnumerable<Product> GetAllProducts() =>
_context.Products.ToList();

public Product GetProductById(int id) =>
_context.Products.Find(id);

public void AddProduct(Product product)
{
    _context.Products.Add(product);
    _context.SaveChanges();
}

public void UpdateProduct(Product product)
{
    _context.Products.Update(product);
    _context.SaveChanges();
}

public void DeleteProduct(int id)
{
    var product = _context.Products.Find(id);
    if (product != null)
    {
        _context.Products.Remove(product);
        _context.SaveChanges();
    }
}
}
```

1.3 Building the Product Catalog View

Next, we will create a Razor view to display the list of products. This view will iterate over the list of products and display their details.

```razor
Copy code
@model IEnumerable<Product>

<h1>Product Catalog</h1>
```

```razor
<div class="row">
    @foreach (var product in Model)
    {
        <div class="col-md-4">
            <div class="card">
                <img src="@product.ImageUrl"
                class="card-img-top" alt="@product.Name" />
                <div class="card-body">
                    <h5 class="card-title">@product.Name</h5>
                    <p
                    class="card-text">@product.Description</p>
                    <p class="card-text">Price:
                    @product.Price.ToString("C")</p>
                    <a href="@Url.Action("Details", "Products",
                    new { id = product.ProductId })" class="btn
                    btn-primary">View Details</a>
                </div>
            </div>
        </div>
    }
</div>
```

1.4 Creating Product Details Page

Implement a product details page that shows more detailed information about a specific product.

```razor
Copy code
@model Product

<h1>@Model.Name</h1>
<img src="@Model.ImageUrl" class=
"img-fluid" alt="@Model.Name" />
<p>@Model.Description</p>
<p>Price: @Model.Price.ToString("C")</p>
<p>In Stock: @Model.StockQuantity</p>
```

```html
<form asp-action="AddToCart" method="post">
    <input type="hidden" name="productId" value="@Model.ProductId" />
    <button type="submit" class="btn btn-success">Add to Cart</button>
</form>
```

2. Implementing the Shopping Cart
2.1 Defining the Shopping Cart Model

The shopping cart can be represented as a model that holds the selected products for a user. This model can also keep track of quantities.

```csharp
Copy code
public class ShoppingCartItem
{
    public int ProductId { get; set; }
    public string ProductName { get; set; }
    public decimal Price { get; set; }
    public int Quantity { get; set; }
}

public class ShoppingCart
{
    public List<ShoppingCartItem> Items { get; set; } = new List<ShoppingCartItem>();

    public void AddItem(Product product, int quantity)
    {
        var existingItem = Items.FirstOrDefault(i => i.ProductId == product.ProductId);
        if (existingItem != null)
        {
            existingItem.Quantity += quantity;
        }
        else
        {
            Items.Add(new ShoppingCartItem
```

```csharp
            {
                ProductId = product.ProductId,
                ProductName = product.Name,
                Price = product.Price,
                Quantity = quantity
            });
        }
    }

    public void RemoveItem(int productId)
    {
        var item = Items.FirstOrDefault(i => i.ProductId == productId);
        if (item != null)
        {
            Items.Remove(item);
        }
    }

    public decimal CalculateTotal() =>
 Items.Sum(i => i.Price * i.Quantity);
}
```

2.2 Creating the Shopping Cart Controller

A controller is needed to manage cart operations like adding and removing items.

```csharp
csharp
Copy code
public class CartController : Controller
{
    private readonly IProductRepository _productRepository;

    public CartController(IProductRepository productRepository)
    {
        _productRepository = productRepository;
    }
```

```csharp
    public IActionResult Index()
    {
        var cart = 
        HttpContext.Session.GetObject<ShoppingCart>("ShoppingCart")
        ?? new ShoppingCart();
        return View(cart);
    }

    [HttpPost]
    public IActionResult AddToCart(int productId)
    {
        var product = _productRepository.
GetProductById(productId);
        if (product != null)
        {
            var cart = HttpContext.Session
.GetObject<ShoppingCart>("ShoppingCart")
?? new ShoppingCart();
            cart.AddItem(product, 1);
            HttpContext.Session.SetObject
("ShoppingCart", cart);
        }
        return RedirectToAction("Index");
    }

    [HttpPost]
    public IActionResult RemoveFromCart(int productId)
    {
        var cart = HttpContext.Session.
GetObject<ShoppingCart>("ShoppingCart");
        if (cart != null)
        {
            cart.RemoveItem(productId);
            HttpContext.Session.SetObject
("ShoppingCart", cart);
        }
        return RedirectToAction("Index");
    }
}
```

2.3 Building the Shopping Cart View

Create a Razor view to display the contents of the shopping cart.

```razor
Copy code
@model ShoppingCart

<h1>Your Shopping Cart</h1>

@if (!Model.Items.Any())
{
    <p>Your cart is empty.</p>
}
else
{
    <table class="table">
        <thead>
            <tr>
                <th>Product</th>
                <th>Price</th>
                <th>Quantity</th>
                <th>Subtotal</th>
                <th>Actions</th>
            </tr>
        </thead>
        <tbody>
            @foreach (var item in Model.Items)
            {
                <tr>
                    <td>@item.ProductName</td>
                    <td>@item.Price.ToString("C")</td>
                    <td>@item.Quantity</td>
                    <td>@(item.Price * item.Quantity).ToString("C")</td>
                    <td>
                        <form asp-action="RemoveFromCart" method="post">
<input type="hidden" name="productId" value="@item.ProductId" />
<button type="submit" class="btn btn-danger">Remove</button>
```

```
                </form>
            </td>
        </tr>
        }
        <tr>
            <td colspan="3" class="text-right">Total:</td>
            <td colspan="2">@Model.
CalculateTotal().ToString("C")</td>
        </tr>
    </tbody>
</table>
<a href="@Url.Action("Checkout", "Order")" class="btn
btn-primary">Proceed to Checkout</a>
}
```

3. Implementing the Checkout Process
3.1 Defining the Order Model

The order model represents a completed order in the system.

```csharp
Copy code
public class Order
{
    public int OrderId { get; set; }
    public int UserId { get; set; }
    public DateTime OrderDate { get; set; }
    public decimal TotalAmount { get; set; }
    public List<OrderItem> OrderItems { get; set; }
}

public class OrderItem
{
    public int OrderItemId { get; set; }
    public int OrderId { get; set; }
    public int ProductId { get; set; }
    public decimal Price { get; set; }
    public int Quantity { get; set; }
}
```

3.2 Creating the Checkout Controller

Implement a controller to handle the checkout process.

```csharp
Copy code
public class OrderController : Controller
{
    private readonly IProductRepository _productRepository;
    private readonly AppDbContext _context;

    public OrderController
(IProductRepository productRepository, AppDbContext context)
    {
        _productRepository = productRepository;
        _context = context;
    }

    public IActionResult Checkout()
    {
        var cart = HttpContext.Session.GetObject<ShoppingCart>("ShoppingCart");
        return View(cart);
    }

    [HttpPost]
    public IActionResult PlaceOrder()
    {
        var cart =
        HttpContext.Session.GetObject<ShoppingCart>("ShoppingCart");
        if (cart == null || !cart.Items.Any())
        {
            return RedirectToAction("Index", "Cart");
        }

        var order = new Order
        {
            UserId = /* get the current user's ID */,
            OrderDate = DateTime.Now,
            TotalAmount = cart.CalculateTotal(),
            OrderItems = cart.Items.Select
```

BUILDING A FULL-SCALE REAL-WORLD PROJEC

```
(i => new OrderItem
            {
                ProductId = i.ProductId,
                Price = i.Price,
                Quantity = i.Quantity
            }).ToList()
    };

    _context.Orders.Add(order);
    _context.SaveChanges();

    HttpContext.Session.Remove
("ShoppingCart");  // Clear the cart after successful order placement
    return RedirectToAction
("OrderConfirmation", new { orderId = order.OrderId });
    }
}
```

3.3 Creating the Checkout View

The checkout view allows users to review their cart and place an order.

```razor
Copy code
@model ShoppingCart

<h1>Checkout</h1>

@if (!Model.Items.Any())
{
    <p>Your cart is empty.</p>
}
else
{
    <table class="table">
        <thead>
            <tr>
                <th>Product</th>
```

```html
                <th>Price</th>
                <th>Quantity</th>
                <th>Subtotal</th>
            </tr>
        </thead>
        <tbody>
            @foreach (var item in Model.Items)
            {
                <tr>
                    <td>@item.ProductName</td>
                    <td>@item.Price.ToString("C")</td>
                    <td>@item.Quantity</td>
                    <td>@(item.Price * item.Quantity).ToString("C")</td>
                </tr>
            }
            <tr>
<td colspan="3" class="text-right">Total:</td>
                <td>@Model.CalculateTotal().ToString("C")</td>
            </tr>
        </tbody>
    </table>
    <form asp-action="PlaceOrder" method="post">
        <button type="submit" class="btn btn-success">Place Order</button>
    </form>
}
```

In this section, we have covered the implementation of essential features for the e-commerce application: the Product Catalog, Shopping Cart, and Checkout process. These components are designed with best practices in mind, ensuring that they are both user-friendly and maintainable. The next steps involve enhancing these features with additional functionality, such as payment processing, user authentication, and order management, to create a comprehensive e-commerce platform.

Securing Payments and Customer Data

In an e-commerce application, security is paramount, especially regarding payment processing and the protection of sensitive customer data. As online transactions involve the exchange of personal and financial information, it's essential to implement robust security measures to safeguard this data against threats such as data breaches, fraud, and identity theft. This section will explore various strategies for securing payments and customer data in your ASP.NET Core e-commerce application.

1. Understanding Payment Security Fundamentals
1.1 PCI Compliance

The Payment Card Industry Data Security Standard (PCI DSS) provides guidelines for securely handling credit card transactions. Achieving PCI compliance is not only a legal requirement for processing credit card payments but also crucial for building trust with customers. Key requirements include:

- **Secure Network:** Implement firewalls and encryption to protect cardholder data.
- **Data Protection:** Store cardholder information securely and only keep what is necessary.
- **Access Control:** Limit access to payment information to authorized personnel only.
- **Regular Testing:** Conduct security testing and vulnerability assessments regularly.

1.2 Tokenization

Tokenization is a process that replaces sensitive data with a unique identifier, or token, that cannot be reversed without access to the tokenization system. This ensures that even if attackers gain access to your system, they cannot retrieve actual credit card details. Implementing tokenization can significantly reduce your PCI compliance burden.

2. Implementing Secure Payment Gateways

2.1 Choosing a Payment Processor

When selecting a payment processor, consider the following factors:

- **Reputation:** Choose a reputable processor known for strong security measures.
- **Compliance:** Ensure the processor is PCI compliant.
- **Integration:** Look for a processor that offers easy integration with ASP.NET Core applications.

Popular payment gateways include:

- **Stripe:** Provides comprehensive API support and excellent documentation.
- **PayPal:** Offers secure transactions and a well-known brand.
- **Authorize.Net:** Known for its robust fraud detection tools.

2.2 Integrating Payment Processors

Integrating a payment processor involves using their API to handle transactions securely. Below is an example of integrating Stripe into an ASP.NET Core application.

Step 1: Install Stripe NuGet Package

You can install the Stripe library via NuGet:

```bash
Copy code
dotnet add package Stripe.net
```

Step 2: Configure Stripe in Startup.cs

```csharp
Copy code
public void ConfigureServices(IServiceCollection services)
{
```

```
    services.AddControllersWithViews();
    // Configure Stripe API Key
    StripeConfiguration.ApiKey =
Configuration["Stripe:SecretKey"];
}
```

Step 3: Create Payment Controller

Create a controller to handle payment requests:

```csharp
Copy code
public class PaymentController : Controller
{
    [HttpPost]
    public IActionResult Charge(string stripeEmail, string
    stripeToken)
    {
        var options = new ChargeCreateOptions
        {
            Amount = 5000, // Amount in cents
            Currency = "usd",
            Description = "Sample Charge",
            Source = stripeToken,
        };
        var service = new ChargeService();
        Charge charge = service.Create(options);
        // Process the charge response
        return View();
    }
}
```

Step 4: Payment View

Create a Razor view to capture payment information:

```razor
Copy code
```

```html
<form action="/Payment/Charge" method="post">
    <script src="https://js.stripe.com/v3/"></script>
    <input type="email" name="stripeEmail"
 placeholder="Email" required />
    <div id="card-element"></div>
    <button type="submit">Submit Payment</button>
</form>

<script>
    var stripe = Stripe('your-publishable-key');
    var elements = stripe.elements();
    var cardElement = elements.create('card');
    cardElement.mount('#card-element');
</script>
```

This code captures user payment information securely without storing sensitive data on your server.

3. Protecting Customer Data
3.1 Encryption

Always encrypt sensitive data, both in transit and at rest. Use HTTPS to encrypt data in transit. For data at rest, you can use techniques such as:

- **Database Encryption:** Encrypt sensitive fields in your database.
- **File Encryption:** If you store files (like invoices), encrypt them using strong algorithms (e.g., AES).

3.2 Data Minimization

Collect only the necessary information needed for processing transactions. This not only reduces risk but also enhances customer trust. For instance, avoid collecting unnecessary details like phone numbers or secondary addresses unless required.

4. Implementing Strong Authentication and Access Control
4.1 Multi-Factor Authentication (MFA)

Implementing MFA adds an additional layer of security by requiring users to provide two or more verification factors to gain access to their accounts. This could include:

- Something they know (password).
- Something they have (a mobile device for SMS codes or an authenticator app).
- Something they are (biometric verification).

4.2 Role-Based Access Control (RBAC)

Implement RBAC to ensure that only authorized users can access sensitive data. Assign roles to users (e.g., admin, customer) and restrict actions based on these roles. This can prevent unauthorized access to customer data and payment information.

5. Regular Security Audits and Monitoring

5.1 Conduct Regular Security Audits

Regular security audits help identify vulnerabilities in your application. You should:

- Review access logs for suspicious activity.
- Perform penetration testing to identify weaknesses.
- Assess third-party libraries and services for vulnerabilities.

5.2 Monitoring for Fraudulent Activity

Integrate tools that can help monitor transactions for signs of fraud. Look for:

- Unusual transaction patterns (e.g., multiple charges from the same IP address).
- High-value transactions from new accounts.
- Transactions that exceed a certain threshold without prior activity.

Securing payments and customer data in your ASP.NET Core e-commerce application is critical to maintaining customer trust and complying with legal requirements. By following best practices such as PCI compliance, implementing tokenization, using secure payment gateways, and employing strong authentication mechanisms, you can significantly enhance the security of your application. Regular audits and monitoring will help you stay ahead of potential threats and ensure a safe shopping experience for your customers.

Adding User Accounts, Roles, and Order History

To create a robust e-commerce application, implementing user accounts, role management, and an order history feature is essential. These components not only enhance user experience but also facilitate better data management and security. This section outlines how to implement these features in your ASP.NET Core application effectively.

1. Implementing User Accounts

1.1 Setting Up ASP.NET Core Identity

ASP.NET Core Identity is a membership system that adds login functionality to your application. It provides features such as user registration, authentication, and user management out of the box.

Step 1: Install ASP.NET Core Identity

You can add Identity support to your project using the following command:

```bash
Copy code
dotnet add package Microsoft.AspNetCore.Identity.EntityFrameworkCore
```

Step 2: Configure Identity Services

In your Startup.cs, add the Identity services to the ConfigureServices method:

BUILDING A FULL-SCALE REAL-WORLD PROJEC

```csharp
Copy code
public void ConfigureServices
(IServiceCollection services)
{
    services.AddDbContext<ApplicationDbContext>(options =>
        options.UseSqlServer(Configuration.
GetConnectionString("DefaultConnection")));

    services.AddIdentity<IdentityUser, IdentityRole>()
        .AddEntityFrameworkStores<ApplicationDbContext>()
        .AddDefaultTokenProviders();

    services.AddControllersWithViews();
}
```

Step 3: Configure Authentication Middleware

In the Configure method of Startup.cs, enable authentication:

```csharp
Copy code
public void Configure(IApplicationBuilder app,
IWebHostEnvironment env)
{
    app.UseRouting();
    app.UseAuthentication(); // Enable authentication
    app.UseAuthorization(); // Enable authorization
    app.UseEndpoints(endpoints =>
    {
        endpoints.MapControllerRoute(
            name: "default",
            pattern: "{controller=Home}/{action=Index}/{id?}");
    });
}
```

1.2 User Registration and Login

Create views and controllers to handle user registration and login.

Registration Controller:

```csharp
Copy code
public class AccountController : Controller
{
    private readonly UserManager<IdentityUser> _userManager;
    private readonly SignInManager<IdentityUser> _signInManager;

    public AccountController(UserManager<IdentityUser> userManager, SignInManager<IdentityUser> signInManager)
    {
        _userManager = userManager;
        _signInManager = signInManager;
    }

    [HttpGet]
    public IActionResult Register() => View();

    [HttpPost]
    public async Task<IActionResult> Register(RegisterViewModel model)
    {
        if (ModelState.IsValid)
        {
            var user = new IdentityUser { UserName = model.Email, Email = model.Email };
            var result = await _userManager.CreateAsync(user, model.Password);
            if (result.Succeeded)
            {
                await _signInManager.SignInAsync(user, isPersistent: false);
                return RedirectToAction("Index", "Home");
            }
            foreach (var error in result.Errors)
            {
```

BUILDING A FULL-SCALE REAL-WORLD PROJEC

```
                ModelState.AddModelError(string.Empty,
                error.Description);
            }
        }
        return View(model);
    }
}
```

Login Controller:

```csharp
Copy code
[HttpGet]
public IActionResult Login() => View();

[HttpPost]
public async Task<IActionResult> Login(LoginViewModel model)
{
    if (ModelState.IsValid)
    {
        var result = await _signInManager.PasswordSignInAsync
(model.Email, model.Password, model.RememberMe, lockoutOnFailure: false);
        if (result.Succeeded)
        {
            return RedirectToAction("Index", "Home");
        }
        ModelState.AddModelError
(string.Empty, "Invalid login attempt.");
    }
    return View(model);
}
```

1.3 Creating User Views

Create Razor views for the registration and login forms:

Register.cshtml:

```razor
Copy code
@model RegisterViewModel

<form asp-action="Register" method="post">
    <input asp-for="Email" placeholder="Email" required />
    <input asp-for="Password" type="password" placeholder="Password" required />
    <input asp-for="ConfirmPassword" type="password" placeholder="Confirm Password" required />
    <button type="submit">Register</button>
</form>
```

Login.cshtml:

```razor
Copy code
@model LoginViewModel

<form asp-action="Login" method="post">
    <input asp-for="Email" placeholder="Email" required />
    <input asp-for="Password" type="password" placeholder="Password" required />
    <input asp-for="RememberMe" type="checkbox" /> Remember Me
    <button type="submit">Login</button>
</form>
```

2. Implementing Roles
2.1 Creating Roles
Role management allows you to assign specific permissions to users. You can use ASP.NET Core Identity to manage roles easily.
Step 1: Seed Roles in the Database
You can create roles when your application starts by modifying your Startup.cs or creating a dedicated seed method:

```csharp
Copy code
public void Configure(IApplicationBuilder app, 
IWebHostEnvironment env)
{
    CreateRoles(app).Wait();
    // Other configurations...
}

private async Task CreateRoles(IApplicationBuilder app)
{
    var roleManager = app.
ApplicationServices.GetRequiredService
<RoleManager<IdentityRole>>();
    var userManager = app.
ApplicationServices.GetRequiredService
<UserManager<IdentityUser>>();

    string[] roleNames = { "Admin", "Customer" };
    IdentityResult roleResult;

    foreach (var roleName in roleNames)
    {
        var roleExist = await roleManager.
RoleExistsAsync(roleName);
        if (!roleExist)
        {
            roleResult = await roleManager.CreateAsync(new 
            IdentityRole(roleName));
        }
    }

    // Create a default admin user if necessary
    var poweruser = new IdentityUser
    {
        UserName = "admin@yourdomain.com",
        Email = "admin@yourdomain.com",
    };
    string userPassword = "Admin@123";
    var user = await userManager.
```

```
FindByEmailAsync(poweruser.Email);

    if (user == null)
    {
        var createPowerUser = await
        userManager.CreateAsync(poweruser, userPassword);
        if (createPowerUser.Succeeded)
        {
            await userManager.
AddToRoleAsync(poweruser, "Admin");
        }
    }
}
```

2.2 Assigning Roles to Users

You can assign roles to users in your account controller:

```
csharp
Copy code
public async Task<IActionResult>
AssignRole(string userId, string role)
{
    var user = await _userManager.FindByIdAsync(userId);
    if (user != null)
    {
        await _userManager.AddToRoleAsync(user, role);
    }
    return RedirectToAction("Index");
}
```

3. Implementing Order History
3.1 Modifying the Order Model

Extend your existing Order model to include user information. This will help link orders to users effectively.

```csharp
Copy code
public class Order
{
    public int OrderId { get; set; }
    public string UserId { get; set; } // Foreign key
    public DateTime OrderDate { get; set; }
    public decimal TotalAmount { get; set; }
    public List<OrderItem> OrderItems { get; set; }
}
```

3.2 Saving User Order Information

When a user places an order, save the associated user ID:

```csharp
Copy code
public IActionResult PlaceOrder()
{
    var cart = HttpContext.Session.GetObject<ShoppingCart>("ShoppingCart");
    if (cart == null || !cart.Items.Any())
    {
        return RedirectToAction("Index", "Cart");
    }

    var order = new Order
    {
        UserId = User.FindFirstValue(ClaimTypes.NameIdentifier), // Get current user's ID
        OrderDate = DateTime.Now,
        TotalAmount = cart.CalculateTotal(),
        OrderItems = cart.Items.Select(i => new OrderItem
        {
            ProductId = i.ProductId,
            Price = i.Price,
            Quantity = i.Quantity
        }).ToList()
    };
```

```
    _context.Orders.Add(order);
    _context.SaveChanges();

    HttpContext.Session.Remove
("ShoppingCart"); // Clear the cart after successful order
placement
    return RedirectToAction
("OrderConfirmation", new { orderId = order.OrderId });
}
```

3.3 Creating an Order History View

To display a user's order history, create a new action in your controller and a corresponding view.

Order History Controller Action:

```csharp
Copy code
public IActionResult OrderHistory()
{
    var userId = User.FindFirstValue(ClaimTypes.NameIdentifier);
    var orders = _context.Orders
        .Include(o => o.OrderItems)
        .Where(o => o.UserId == userId)
        .ToList();

    return View(orders);
}
```

Order History View (OrderHistory.cshtml):

```razor
Copy code
@model List<Order>

<h1>Your Order History</h1>
```

```html
<table class="table">
    <thead>
        <tr>
            <th>Order ID</th>
            <th>Order Date</th>
            <th>Total Amount</th>
            <th>Items</th>
        </tr>
    </thead>
    <tbody>
        @foreach (var order in Model)
        {
            <tr>
                <td>@order.OrderId</td>
                <td>@order.OrderDate.ToShortDateString()</td>
                <td>@order.TotalAmount.ToString("C")</td>
                <td>
                    <ul>
@foreach (var item in order.OrderItems)
                        {
<li>@item.ProductId - @item.Quantity</li>
                        }
                    </ul>
                </td>
            </tr>
        }
    </tbody>
</table>
```

In this section, we explored how to implement user accounts, roles, and order history in your ASP.NET Core e-commerce application. By leveraging ASP.NET Core Identity for user management and creating robust role-based access control, you can enhance the security and functionality of your application. Additionally, providing users with an order history feature fosters trust and transparency, contributing to a better overall user experience. With these components in place, your e-commerce application is better equipped to handle real-world scenarios effectively.

Final Deployment and Production Testing

Once your e-commerce application is developed, it is crucial to ensure that it is deployed correctly and tested thoroughly before going live. This section will cover the steps involved in final deployment, including environment setup, deployment strategies, and production testing methods to ensure your application is reliable, secure, and performs well under real-world conditions.

1. Preparing for Deployment
1.1 Environment Configuration

Before deploying your application, it's essential to configure the different environments (development, staging, production) properly. Each environment may have different settings, including connection strings, logging levels, and third-party service configurations.

Configuration Files:

Utilize the appsettings.json file for managing your application settings. For production, consider creating an appsettings.Production.json file that overrides specific settings, such as the connection string:

```json
Copy code
// appsettings.Production.json
{
  "ConnectionStrings": {
    "DefaultConnection":
    "Server=prod_server;Database=ECommerceDb;User Id=prod_user;Password=prod_password;"
  },
  "Logging": {
    "LogLevel": {
      "Default": "Warning"
    }
```

    }
}

Environment Variables:

You can also manage sensitive information through environment variables, ensuring that sensitive data is not hardcoded in your source files.

1.2 Build Configuration

Prepare your application for deployment by creating a production build. In ASP.NET Core, you can use the command line to publish your application:

```bash
Copy code
dotnet publish -c Release -o ./publish
```

This command compiles your application and copies the necessary files to the ./publish directory.

2. Deployment Strategies

2.1 Choosing a Deployment Method

There are various deployment methods available for ASP.NET Core applications, including:

- **Web Hosting Services:** Such as Azure App Service, AWS Elastic Beanstalk, or Google Cloud App Engine.
- **Virtual Machines:** Deploying on a virtual machine using IIS, Nginx, or Apache.
- **Containerization:** Using Docker containers for deploying your application.
- **Serverless:** Using Azure Functions or AWS Lambda for specific functions within your application.

2.2 Deploying to Azure App Service

Azure App Service is a popular choice for hosting ASP.NET Core applications. Here's a step-by-step guide to deploying your application:

Step 1: Create an Azure App Service

1. Log into the Azure portal.
2. Click on "Create a resource."
3. Choose "Web App" and fill in the required information, such as subscription, resource group, and app name.
4. Select the runtime stack as ".NET Core."

Step 2: Configure Deployment

1. In your web app settings, navigate to "Deployment Center."
2. Choose a deployment source (e.g., GitHub, Azure Repos, or local Git).
3. Follow the prompts to connect your repository and configure deployment options.

Step 3: Monitor and Scale

Once deployed, monitor your application's performance through Azure Monitor. You can set up alerts for performance metrics and scale your application based on demand.

3. Production Testing

3.1 Importance of Production Testing

Before going live, conduct thorough testing to ensure your application behaves as expected in a production environment. This helps identify any issues that were not caught during development and can lead to significant improvements in reliability and user satisfaction.

3.2 Types of Testing

1. **Smoke Testing:** Conduct smoke tests to verify that critical func-

tionalities work after deployment. This includes checking the home page, user registration, login, and shopping cart features.
2. **Load Testing:** Perform load testing to simulate multiple users interacting with your application simultaneously. Tools such as Apache JMeter or k6 can help identify performance bottlenecks under heavy traffic.
3. **User Acceptance Testing (UAT):** Engage real users to test the application's usability and functionality. Gather feedback and make necessary adjustments before going live.
4. **Security Testing:** Conduct security assessments to identify vulnerabilities. Utilize tools such as OWASP ZAP or Burp Suite to test for common vulnerabilities like SQL injection and cross-site scripting (XSS).

3.3 Automated Testing in Production

In addition to manual testing, consider implementing automated tests as part of your deployment pipeline. Automated tests can include unit tests, integration tests, and end-to-end tests. Tools like xUnit, NUnit, and Selenium can be integrated into your CI/CD pipeline to ensure ongoing reliability.

Example of Automated Testing:

```csharp
Copy code
[Fact]
public async Task Login_ValidUser_RedirectsToHome()
{
    // Arrange
    var controller = new AccountController(userManager,
    signInManager);
    var model = new LoginViewModel
{ Email = "test@example.com", Password = "Password123" };

    // Act
    var result = await controller.Login(model);
```

```
    // Assert
    var redirectToActionResult =
    Assert.IsType<RedirectToActionResult>(result);
    Assert.Equal("Index",
redirectToActionResult.ActionName);
    Assert.Equal("Home",
redirectToActionResult.ControllerName);
}
```

4. Post-Deployment Monitoring

Once your application is live, it is crucial to monitor its performance continuously. Implement logging and monitoring strategies to track errors, performance metrics, and user behavior.

4.1 Logging

ASP.NET Core provides built-in logging capabilities. Configure logging in your Startup.cs:

```csharp
Copy code
public void Configure(IApplicationBuilder app, IWebHostEnvironment env, ILogger<Startup> logger)
{
    if (env.IsDevelopment())
    {
        app.UseDeveloperExceptionPage();
    }
    else
    {
        app.UseExceptionHandler("/Home/Error");
        app.UseHsts();
    }

    app.UseHttpsRedirection();
    app.UseStaticFiles();
    app.UseRouting();
    app.UseAuthentication();
```

```
    app.UseAuthorization();

    app.UseEndpoints(endpoints =>
    {
        endpoints.MapControllerRoute(
            name: "default",
            pattern: "{controller=Home}/
{action=Index}/{id?}");
    });

    logger.LogInformation
("Application has started successfully.");
}
```

4.2 Application Insights
Consider using Azure Application Insights for advanced monitoring and telemetry. This tool provides real-time performance monitoring, crash reporting, and usage analytics.

4.3 Regular Updates and Maintenance
After deployment, regularly update your application to address any security vulnerabilities, add new features, or improve performance. Plan for maintenance windows to minimize disruption to your users.

In summary, deploying your ASP.NET Core e-commerce application requires careful preparation, the selection of an appropriate deployment strategy, and thorough testing before going live. By following best practices for deployment and implementing rigorous production testing, you can ensure that your application is robust, secure, and ready to handle user demands. Continuous monitoring and maintenance will further enhance your application's reliability and user experience in the long run. With these strategies in place, your application will be well-equipped to serve its users effectively.

ASP.NET Core 3 Beyond the Basics

Clean Architecture and Domain-Driven Design (DDD) in ASP.NET Core

Implementing a well-organized architecture is essential for building scalable, maintainable, and flexible applications. In ASP.NET Core, adopting Clean Architecture principles alongside Domain-Driven Design (DDD) can help achieve this structure, especially in complex systems with evolving business logic. This section will explore the fundamentals of Clean Architecture and Domain-Driven Design and how to implement these methodologies within an ASP.NET Core application.

1. Overview of Clean Architecture

Clean Architecture, introduced by Robert C. Martin (Uncle Bob), is an architectural pattern that emphasizes separation of concerns and independence between different layers of an application. The primary goal is to create a system that is flexible to change, easy to test, and organized for long-term maintenance.

Clean Architecture organizes an application into distinct layers, typically in a concentric circle pattern, with the core business logic at the center. This central positioning reinforces the independence of business logic from other application concerns, such as user interface (UI) and database management.

Layers in Clean Architecture:

1. **Entities (Core)** - Represent the fundamental business models and

rules, encapsulating high-level policies.
2. **Use Cases (Application)** - Define specific business operations and application logic.
3. **Interface Adapters** - Serve as bridges between external interfaces (like UI, APIs) and the core application.
4. **Frameworks & Drivers** - Represent infrastructure-level details, including databases, UI frameworks, external APIs, and tools.

In this setup, dependencies point inward toward the core, meaning the business logic is independent of technical details like database choices, frameworks, and UI libraries.

2. Introduction to Domain-Driven Design (DDD)

Domain-Driven Design (DDD), developed by Eric Evans, is a methodology that focuses on modeling the software's domain accurately and efficiently to address business complexities. DDD emphasizes collaboration with domain experts, often resulting in a Ubiquitous Language—a common language shared by developers and business stakeholders for consistent communication.

Core Concepts in DDD:

- **Entities** - Objects with a unique identity that persists across states, such as Customer or Order.
- **Value Objects** - Immutable objects without identity, defined solely by their properties (e.g., Money or Address).
- **Aggregates** - Collections of related entities and value objects treated as a single unit, ensuring business rules are consistently enforced.
- **Repositories** - Responsible for retrieving and persisting aggregates to the database.
- **Services** - Contain business logic that does not naturally belong to entities or value objects.
- **Domain Events** - Represent significant occurrences within the domain, often triggering actions in response.

In DDD, the focus is on understanding the core domain deeply, aligning technical components to reflect business rules and interactions closely.

3. Implementing Clean Architecture with DDD in ASP.NET Core

Combining Clean Architecture with DDD principles provides a robust framework for developing complex ASP.NET Core applications. Here's a breakdown of how to implement Clean Architecture with DDD.

3.1 Defining the Project Structure

A common Clean Architecture folder structure in an ASP.NET Core solution might look like this:

```scss
Copy code
- src/
    - Domain/              // Core domain logic (Entities, Value Objects, Interfaces)
    - Application/         // Use Cases, DTOs, Application Services
    - Infrastructure/      // Database, Repositories, external services
    - WebUI/               // ASP.NET Core Web Application (UI, API)
```

Project Layers:

- **Domain:** This layer contains entities, value objects, domain services, and domain events.
- **Application:** Houses use cases, application services, DTOs, and interfaces that define business operations.
- **Infrastructure:** Implements the interfaces defined in the core layers, managing data access and external dependencies.
- **WebUI:** The UI layer that includes the ASP.NET Core web application, MVC controllers, Razor Pages, or APIs.

3.2 Creating Domain Entities and Value Objects

The Domain layer represents the core business models and logic. Start by defining entities and value objects that reflect your domain.

Example of an Entity in ASP.NET Core:

```csharp
Copy code
public class Product
{
    public Guid Id { get; private set; }
    public string Name { get; private set; }
    public decimal Price { get; private set; }

    public Product(string name, decimal price)
    {
        Id = Guid.NewGuid();
        Name = name;
        Price = price;
    }

    public void UpdatePrice(decimal newPrice)
    {
        if (newPrice <= 0)
            throw new ArgumentException("Price must be
            positive.");
        Price = newPrice;
    }
}
```

Example of a Value Object in ASP.NET Core:

```csharp
Copy code
public class Money
{
    public decimal Amount { get; }
    public string Currency { get; }
```

```csharp
    public Money(decimal amount, string currency)
    {
        Amount = amount;
        Currency = currency;
    }

    public override bool Equals(object obj)
    {
        if (obj is Money money)
        {
            return Amount == money.Amount && Currency ==
            money.Currency;
        }
        return false;
    }

    public override int GetHashCode() =>
    HashCode.Combine(Amount, Currency);
}
```

3.3 Implementing Use Cases and Application Services

Use cases (also called application services) represent operations that the application performs. Each use case encapsulates a specific piece of application logic.

Example of an Application Service:

```csharp
Copy code
public class ProductService
{
    private readonly IProductRepository _productRepository;

    public ProductService(IProductRepository productRepository)
    {
        _productRepository = productRepository;
    }
```

```
    public async Task CreateProductAsync
(string name, decimal price)
    {
        var product = new Product(name, price);
        await _productRepository.AddAsync(product);
    }

    public async Task UpdateProduct
PriceAsync(Guid productId, decimal newPrice)
    {
        var product = await
        _productRepository.GetByIdAsync(productId);
        product.UpdatePrice(newPrice);
        await _productRepository.SaveChangesAsync();
    }
}
```

3.4 Working with Repositories and Infrastructure

Repositories abstract away data persistence details and offer a way to interact with aggregates in the domain. Implementing repositories within the Infrastructure layer allows you to keep your domain logic isolated from data access specifics.

Defining the Repository Interface in the Domain Layer:

```
csharp
Copy code
public interface IProductRepository
{
    Task<Product> GetByIdAsync(Guid id);
    Task AddAsync(Product product);
    Task SaveChangesAsync();
}
```

Implementing the Repository in the Infrastructure Layer:

```csharp
Copy code
public class ProductRepository : IProductRepository
{
    private readonly ApplicationDbContext _context;

    public ProductRepository(ApplicationDbContext context)
    {
        _context = context;
    }

    public async Task<Product> GetByIdAsync(Guid id)
    {
        return await _context.Products.FindAsync(id);
    }

    public async Task AddAsync(Product product)
    {
        await _context.Products.AddAsync(product);
    }

    public async Task SaveChangesAsync()
    {
        await _context.SaveChangesAsync();
    }
}
```

3.5 Adding Domain Events

Domain events capture changes in the system and can trigger other operations. ASP.NET Core supports a built-in event-handling model for managing domain events, enabling you to decouple business operations.

Example of a Domain Event:

```csharp
Copy code
public class ProductCreatedEvent : INotification
{
    public Product Product { get; }
```

```csharp
    public ProductCreatedEvent(Product product)
    {
        Product = product;
    }
}
```

Event Handler:

```csharp
Copy code
public class ProductCreatedEventHandler :
INotificationHandler<ProductCreatedEvent>
{
    public Task Handle(ProductCreatedEvent notification,
    CancellationToken cancellationToken)
    {
        Console.WriteLine($"Product created:
        {notification.Product.Name}");
        return Task.CompletedTask;
    }
}
```

3.6 Benefits of Clean Architecture with DDD in ASP.NET Core

1. **Scalability and Maintainability:** Clean Architecture separates concerns, allowing you to extend or modify components without affecting others.
2. **Business Logic Isolation:** With DDD, the domain logic is isolated and remains consistent, providing flexibility to make technical changes without altering core business logic.
3. **Testability:** The separation of responsibilities makes it easy to test individual layers independently, increasing reliability and reducing time to production.

Clean Architecture and Domain-Driven Design offer powerful tools for managing complex applications. Implementing these methodologies in ASP.NET Core 3 ensures that the software aligns closely with business requirements and can adapt to changing needs. This approach supports scalability, improves testability, and allows the application to evolve alongside the domain it serves.

Advanced Topics: SignalR for Real-Time Applications

Real-time communication has become a critical feature in modern web applications, enabling instant updates and interaction across various clients. ASP.NET Core's SignalR library provides a simple yet powerful solution for building real-time applications by establishing persistent, two-way communication channels between servers and clients. This section explores the architecture, key features, and implementation strategies for using SignalR in ASP.NET Core applications.

1. Introduction to SignalR

SignalR is an open-source library in ASP.NET Core that simplifies the process of adding real-time web functionality to applications. It enables the server to push updates to clients as soon as they occur, rather than relying on clients to continuously poll the server for changes. This is especially useful for applications requiring real-time features, such as:
- **Chat applications** (e.g., messaging platforms, customer support)
- **Live notifications** (e.g., stock price updates, sports scores)
- **Collaboration tools** (e.g., collaborative document editing, whiteboards)
- **Interactive dashboards** (e.g., monitoring systems, analytics)

SignalR manages the complexities of WebSocket connections and provides fallback options (such as Server-Sent Events and Long Polling) when WebSocket isn't supported by clients or the network.

2. How SignalR Works

SignalR allows server-to-client communication through a mechanism known as a "Hub." The Hub serves as a high-level pipeline that clients can connect to and call methods on. Similarly, the server can call methods on connected clients via the Hub.

Key Concepts in SignalR:

- **Hubs:** A central class that clients connect to, which enables methods to be invoked on both clients and servers.
- **Persistent Connections:** Enables long-lived communication, allowing for continuous data exchange.
- **Protocols:** SignalR supports multiple protocols, including JSON and MessagePack, for efficient data transfer.
- **Transport Fallback:** If WebSockets aren't available, SignalR automatically falls back to other protocols like Server-Sent Events or Long Polling.

This versatility and adaptability make SignalR an excellent tool for applications that require reliable real-time data synchronization.

3. Setting Up SignalR in ASP.NET Core

To get started with SignalR in an ASP.NET Core 3 project, you'll first need to install the required SignalR packages and configure the server to handle real-time communication.

3.1 Adding SignalR to Your Project
Install the SignalR Package:

In your ASP.NET Core project, install the SignalR NuGet package:

```bash
Copy code
dotnet add package Microsoft.AspNetCore.SignalR
```

Configure SignalR in Startup.cs:

In the ConfigureServices method, add SignalR services to the dependency injection container:

```csharp
Copy code
public void ConfigureServices(IServiceCollection services)
{
    services.AddControllersWithViews();
    services.AddSignalR();
}
```

Then, configure the SignalR endpoint in the Configure method:

```csharp
Copy code
public void Configure(IApplicationBuilder app, IWebHostEnvironment env)
{
    app.UseRouting();

    app.UseEndpoints(endpoints =>
    {
        endpoints.MapControllers();
        endpoints.MapHub<ChatHub>("/chathub");
    });
}
```

Creating a Hub:

Create a class that inherits from Hub, which defines the methods that clients can call and the methods for the server to invoke on clients.

```csharp
Copy code
public class ChatHub : Hub
{
    public async Task SendMessage(string user, string message)
```

```
    {
        await Clients.All.SendAsync
("ReceiveMessage", user, message);
    }
}
```

In this example, SendMessage is a method that receives a user and a message, then broadcasts it to all connected clients by invoking the ReceiveMessage method.

4. Building a Real-Time Client with SignalR

With the SignalR server set up, you'll need to configure the client-side code to connect to the Hub and respond to server calls.

4.1 Connecting the Client to SignalR

To connect to the SignalR Hub from a JavaScript client, you'll need to include the SignalR JavaScript library.

Include the SignalR JavaScript Library:

Add the SignalR JavaScript library to your HTML file. If using a CDN, you can add this directly:

```html
Copy code
<script src="https://cdnjs.
cloudflare.com/ajax/libs
/microsoft-signalr/3.1.0/
signalr.min.js"></script>
```

Establish a Connection:

Initialize a connection to the SignalR Hub and set up methods to handle messages from the server.

```javascript
const connection = new signalR.HubConnectionBuilder()
    .withUrl("/chathub")
    .build();

connection.on("ReceiveMessage", function (user, message) {
    const msg = `${user}: ${message}`;
    const li = document.createElement("li");
    li.textContent = msg;
    document.getElementById("messagesList").appendChild(li);
});

connection.start().catch(function (err) {
    return console.error(err.toString());
});
```

Calling Server Methods:

Use JavaScript to call methods on the server's Hub. For example, to call SendMessage, you might add the following code to handle a form submission:

```javascript
document.getElementById("sendButton").addEventListener("click",
function (event) {
    const user = document.getElementById("userInput").value;
    const message =
    document.getElementById("messageInput").value;
    connection.invoke("SendMessage", user,
    message).catch(function (err) {
        return console.error(err.toString());
    });
    event.preventDefault();
});
```

This JavaScript client listens for the ReceiveMessage event from the server and appends the messages to a list.

5. Advanced SignalR Features

SignalR offers additional features for advanced real-time scenarios, including:

5.1 Group Management

SignalR supports grouping clients, which is useful for broadcasting messages to specific sets of users rather than all connected clients. For example, in a multi-room chat application, each room can be represented as a group.

Adding Clients to Groups:

```csharp
Copy code
public async Task JoinGroup(string groupName)
{
    await Groups.AddToGroupAsync(Context.ConnectionId,
    groupName);
}

public async Task LeaveGroup(string groupName)
{
    await Groups.RemoveFromGroupAsync(Context.ConnectionId,
    groupName);
}
```

5.2 Connection Management

SignalR allows monitoring and managing client connections, which is helpful for handling user status changes or maintaining a list of active users.

Handling Connection Events:

Override the OnConnectedAsync and OnDisconnectedAsync methods in your Hub to manage connection events.

```csharp
Copy code
public override async Task OnConnectedAsync()
{
```

```
    await base.OnConnectedAsync();
    Console.WriteLine("A client connected.");
}

public override async Task OnDisconnectedAsync(Exception exception)
{
    await base.OnDisconnectedAsync(exception);
    Console.WriteLine("A client disconnected.");
}
```

5.3 Scaling SignalR with Redis

In applications with multiple servers, SignalR can use Redis as a backplane to coordinate messages across instances. This allows real-time updates to be broadcast across a distributed environment.

Configuring Redis as a Backplane:

Install the Redis backplane package:

```bash
Copy code
dotnet add package Microsoft.AspNetCore.SignalR.StackExchangeRedis
```

Then configure SignalR to use Redis in Startup.cs:

```csharp
Copy code
public void ConfigureServices(IServiceCollection services)
{
    services.AddSignalR().AddStackExchangeRedis("localhost:6379");
}
```

6. Benefits and Use Cases of SignalR

Benefits:

- **Low Latency:** Enables real-time updates with minimal delay.

- **Scalability:** Redis and other backplanes can handle high volumes of simultaneous users.
- **Simplified API:** SignalR abstracts WebSocket handling, offering fallback options for compatibility.

Use Cases:

- **Live Chat:** Interactive chat applications, customer service platforms.
- **Collaborative Tools:** Real-time document editing, whiteboards.
- **Notifications:** Real-time alerts and notifications in e-commerce, finance, and monitoring apps.
- **Interactive Dashboards:** Dynamic data updates for dashboards, IoT systems, and analytics.

SignalR provides ASP.NET Core applications with a robust framework for real-time functionality, essential for interactive, data-driven applications. By leveraging its capabilities—like group management, connection events, and Redis backplanes—developers can create responsive and scalable real-time systems that elevate the user experience. As real-time applications continue to grow in importance, SignalR offers a powerful toolset within the ASP.NET Core ecosystem for implementing these features seamlessly.

Introduction to gRPC for High-Performance Communication

In modern distributed systems, achieving efficient, scalable, and high-performance communication between services is crucial. gRPC (gRPC Remote Procedure Call) offers an advanced framework for such communication, designed to connect multiple services with minimal latency. Built on HTTP/2 and Protocol Buffers, gRPC provides a high-performance alternative to REST for inter-service communication. ASP.NET Core 3 integrates gRPC, enabling developers to create fast, efficient, and robust APIs for microservices, internal applications, and complex service-to-service scenarios.

1. What is gRPC?

gRPC, originally developed by Google, is a language-agnostic, open-source RPC (Remote Procedure Call) framework that enables remote procedures across distributed services as if they were local calls. Unlike REST, which relies on HTTP methods (GET, POST, etc.) and typically uses JSON, gRPC leverages HTTP/2 and Protocol Buffers, resulting in faster communication, smaller payloads, and a better fit for real-time data transfer requirements.

Key features of gRPC include:
- **HTTP/2 Transport**: Provides multiplexing, full-duplex communication, and efficient resource utilization.
- **Protocol Buffers (Protobuf)**: A language-neutral, efficient serialization format, creating smaller message sizes.
- **Bi-directional Streaming**: Allows data to flow continuously between client and server.
- **Cross-Language Support**: Offers compatibility with various languages like C#, Java, Python, Go, and more, making it ideal for polyglot environments.

These features make gRPC particularly suitable for high-throughput scenarios, microservices architectures, and low-latency applications.

2. Benefits of Using gRPC

gRPC's performance-focused design provides several advantages, especially in complex applications with extensive inter-service communication requirements.

Main Benefits of gRPC in ASP.NET Core:

1. **High Performance**: With HTTP/2 and Protocol Buffers, gRPC enables faster communication than JSON-based REST APIs.
2. **Strongly Typed Contracts**: Protocol Buffers enforce strict typing

and schema validation, which reduces runtime errors.
3. **Full-Duplex Streaming**: Supports client-server streaming, server-side streaming, and bi-directional streaming, enabling continuous data flow.
4. **Scalability**: Well-suited for cloud-native applications, particularly in Kubernetes environments, where high scalability and low latency are essential.
5. **Cross-Platform Interoperability**: Allows services written in different languages to communicate smoothly, making it ideal for polyglot microservices.

These benefits make gRPC a compelling choice for applications where speed, efficiency, and interoperability are priorities.

3. Setting Up gRPC in ASP.NET Core 3

Implementing gRPC in ASP.NET Core 3 involves creating a service, defining service contracts using Protocol Buffers, and configuring both server and client components.

3.1 Installing Required Packages

First, install the necessary NuGet packages for gRPC. The Grpc.AspNetCore package provides gRPC server support in ASP.NET Core.

```bash
Copy code
dotnet add package Grpc.AspNetCore
```

3.2 Defining a gRPC Service with Protocol Buffers

gRPC relies on Protocol Buffers (or Protobuf) to define services and message types. Protobuf files, typically ending in .proto, define the service contract in a language-neutral syntax.

Create a .proto file (e.g., greet.proto) in your project's Protos folder:

```proto
syntax = "proto3";

option csharp_namespace = "MyApp.GRPC";

service Greeter {
    rpc SayHello (HelloRequest) returns (HelloReply);
}

message HelloRequest {
    string name = 1;
}

message HelloReply {
    string message = 1;
}
```

This example defines a Greeter service with a SayHello RPC method that accepts a HelloRequest message and returns a HelloReply message.

Configure gRPC in Startup.cs:

In the ConfigureServices method, register gRPC services:

```csharp
public void ConfigureServices(IServiceCollection services)
{
    services.AddGrpc();
}
```

In the Configure method, define the endpoint for the gRPC service:

```csharp
public void Configure(IApplicationBuilder app, IWebHostEnvironment env)
```

```
{
    app.UseRouting();

    app.UseEndpoints(endpoints =>
    {
        endpoints.MapGrpcService<GreeterService>();
    });
}
```

Implement the gRPC Service:

Implement the GreeterService by creating a class that inherits from Greeter.GreeterBase (generated automatically based on the .proto file).

```csharp
Copy code
public class GreeterService : Greeter.GreeterBase
{
    public override Task<HelloReply> SayHello(HelloRequest request, ServerCallContext context)
    {
        return Task.FromResult(new HelloReply
        {
            Message = "Hello, " + request.Name
        });
    }
}
```

4. Creating a gRPC Client

To consume a gRPC service, create a client that connects to the server and invokes methods defined in the .proto file.

1. **Install the Client Package:**
2. In a separate client application, add the gRPC client library:

```bash
Copy code
dotnet add package Grpc.Net.Client
```

Set Up the Client Connection:

Use GrpcChannel to connect to the gRPC server. The client then uses the generated GreeterClient class to call the SayHello method.

```csharp
Copy code
var channel = GrpcChannel.ForAddress("https://localhost:5001");
var client = new Greeter.GreeterClient(channel);
var reply = await client.SayHelloAsync(new HelloRequest { Name = "John" });

Console.WriteLine("Greeting: " + reply.Message);
```

This setup enables a client application to interact with the gRPC server, calling methods defined in the service.

5. Advanced gRPC Features in ASP.NET Core

gRPC provides powerful features for sophisticated real-time and streaming applications. These advanced capabilities make gRPC ideal for complex, high-demand applications.

5.1 Streaming with gRPC

gRPC supports four types of RPC (Remote Procedure Call) methods, each with unique streaming capabilities:

- **Unary RPC**: Basic request-response (one client request, one server response).
- **Server-Side Streaming**: Client sends one request, but server sends multiple responses.
- **Client-Side Streaming**: Client sends multiple requests, and server sends one response.

- **Bi-directional Streaming**: Both client and server can read and write streams independently.

Example of Server-Side Streaming:
In the .proto file:

```proto
Copy code
service Weather {
  rpc GetForecast (ForecastRequest) returns (stream ForecastReply);
}

message ForecastRequest {
   string location = 1;
}

message ForecastReply {
   string forecast = 1;
}
```

In the server implementation:

```csharp
Copy code
public class WeatherService : Weather.WeatherBase
{
    public override async Task GetForecast(ForecastRequest request, IServerStreamWriter<ForecastReply> responseStream, ServerCallContext context)
    {
        foreach (var forecast in GetForecastsForLocation(request.Location))
        {
            await responseStream.WriteAsync(new ForecastReply { Forecast = forecast });
            await Task.Delay(1000); // Simulate delay
        }
```

    }
}

5.2 gRPC Interceptors

Interceptors allow developers to intercept and manipulate incoming or outgoing gRPC calls. They are commonly used for logging, validation, authentication, and error handling.

Creating an Interceptor for Logging:

Create a custom interceptor class that inherits from Interceptor.

```csharp
Copy code
public class LoggingInterceptor : Interceptor
{
    public override async Task<TResponse>
    UnaryServerHandler<TRequest, TResponse>(
        TRequest request, ServerCallContext context,
        UnaryServerMethod<TRequest, TResponse> continuation)
    {
        Console.WriteLine($"Request: {typeof(TRequest).Name}");
        var response = await continuation(request, context);
        Console.WriteLine($"Response:
        {typeof(TResponse).Name}");
        return response;
    }
}
```

1. Register the interceptor in Startup.cs:

```csharp
Copy code
services.AddGrpc(options =>
{
```

```
    options.Interceptors.Add<LoggingInterceptor>();
});
```

This interceptor logs each request and response, providing insight into gRPC calls in real-time.

6. Best Practices for Using gRPC in ASP.NET Core

To ensure reliable and efficient communication with gRPC, consider the following best practices:

- **Optimize Protobuf Definitions**: Use Protocol Buffers effectively by defining concise message types and using enums and repeated fields as necessary.
- **Implement Authentication and Authorization**: Use SSL/TLS for secure communication, and consider using metadata for authentication tokens.
- **Monitor and Log**: Leverage interceptors for request logging and error handling, providing observability across gRPC services.
- **Leverage Load Balancing**: In distributed environments, use load balancing to distribute requests evenly across servers.

gRPC offers ASP.NET Core applications an efficient, high-performance alternative to REST APIs, especially in service-oriented and microservices architectures. By harnessing HTTP/2, Protocol Buffers, and real-time streaming capabilities, gRPC enables the development of robust, scalable applications optimized for performance and network efficiency. With ASP.NET Core 3's seamless gRPC integration, developers have a powerful tool for building next-generation, distributed applications that prioritize speed, reliability, and interoperability.

Microservices Architecture with ASP.NET Core and Docker

The microservices architecture pattern has become increasingly popular for building scalable, modular applications. Unlike monolithic applications, which combine all functionality into a single, large codebase, microservices break down an application into smaller, independently deployable services. Each microservice can be developed, deployed, and scaled independently, allowing teams to develop features and deploy updates more efficiently. ASP.NET Core is an ideal framework for microservices due to its lightweight, modular structure and support for containerization. Docker, a leading containerization platform, complements microservices by allowing each service to run in isolated, reproducible environments.

1. Key Concepts of Microservices Architecture

The microservices architecture involves breaking down applications into several autonomous services, each responsible for specific business functionality. Here are some of the core principles:

- **Independence**: Each microservice is a self-contained unit with its own code, database, and dependencies, allowing independent updates and scaling.
- **Loose Coupling**: Services communicate with each other over standard protocols (often HTTP/HTTPS for RESTful APIs or gRPC), reducing direct dependencies and enabling flexibility.
- **Scalability**: Services can scale horizontally, meaning individual services can scale up or down based on demand without impacting other services.
- **Resilience**: Since services operate independently, failure in one service doesn't necessarily bring down the entire system.
- **Technology Diversity**: Different services can be built with different tech stacks or languages, depending on specific needs.

This design approach enhances the flexibility and resilience of applications, making it a popular choice for cloud-based applications where scale and uptime are critical.

2. Benefits of Using Docker for Microservices

Docker provides a lightweight, consistent environment for running applications in isolated containers, making it ideal for microservices deployments. Docker containers encapsulate the application code, runtime, dependencies, and configuration, ensuring that each service behaves consistently across different environments.

Key benefits of using Docker with microservices:

- **Environment Consistency**: Docker containers ensure that code runs the same way in development, testing, and production environments.
- **Scalability**: Containers are lightweight and can be spun up or down quickly, making it easy to scale individual services as needed.
- **Efficient Resource Utilization**: Containers share the host system's kernel, making them more lightweight than virtual machines and allowing efficient use of resources.
- **Portability**: Docker containers are platform-agnostic, meaning they can run anywhere Docker is supported.
- **Isolation**: Each microservice runs in its container, isolating it from other services and making it easier to manage dependencies and avoid conflicts.

3. Building Microservices with ASP.NET Core

With ASP.NET Core's lightweight runtime and dependency injection, it is particularly well-suited for building scalable microservices. Here's a breakdown of how to structure microservices in ASP.NET Core.

3.1 Service Segmentation

To start with microservices, identify core components that can operate independently. For instance, in an e-commerce application, you could separate services into:

- **Product Catalog Service**: Handles product information.

- **Order Service**: Manages customer orders.
- **Payment Service**: Processes payments.
- **Inventory Service**: Tracks stock levels.
- **User Service**: Manages user accounts and profiles.

Each of these services can be built as a separate ASP.NET Core project, each with its own API endpoint, database, and business logic.

3.2 API Gateway Pattern

An **API Gateway** acts as an intermediary between clients and microservices. Rather than having clients communicate directly with multiple services, they interact with a single API gateway. This simplifies client interaction, reduces cross-service communication complexity, and centralizes cross-cutting concerns like authentication and logging.

Popular tools for creating API gateways include **Ocelot** (specifically designed for .NET Core) and **NGINX**. For ASP.NET Core, **Ocelot** is widely used as it is a lightweight, scalable gateway specifically for microservices in .NET.

4. Dockerizing an ASP.NET Core Microservice

The process of Dockerizing an ASP.NET Core microservice involves creating a Docker image that includes the application, its dependencies, and runtime environment.

Add a Dockerfile: Create a Dockerfile in your ASP.NET Core project directory. A basic Dockerfile for an ASP.NET Core microservice might look like this:

```
dockerfile
Copy code
# Use the official .NET Core SDK image to build the app
FROM mcr.microsoft.com/dotnet/core/sdk:3.1 AS build
WORKDIR /app
```

```
# Copy csproj and restore as distinct layers
COPY *.csproj ./
RUN dotnet restore

# Copy everything else and build the application
COPY . ./
RUN dotnet publish -c Release -o out

# Build runtime image
FROM mcr.microsoft.com/dotnet/core/aspnet:3.1 AS runtime
WORKDIR /app
COPY --from=build /app/out ./
ENTRYPOINT ["dotnet", "MyMicroservice.dll"]
```

Build the Docker Image:
  Use Docker CLI to build the image from the Dockerfile:

```
bash
Copy code
docker build -t mymicroservice:latest .
```

Run the Docker Container:
  After building the Docker image, you can run it as a container using:

```
bash
Copy code
docker run -d -p 5000:80 --name mymicroservice mymicroservice:latest
```

This command maps port 80 in the container to port 5000 on your machine, allowing you to access the service at http://localhost:5000.

5. Orchestrating Microservices with Docker Compose

For multi-service applications, managing individual Docker containers for each microservice can become cumbersome. **Docker Compose** simplifies this by allowing you to define multiple services in a single

YAML file.

Example docker-compose.yml for a microservices application:

```yaml
Copy code
version: '3.8'

services:
  product-catalog:
    image: productcatalogservice:latest
    build:
      context: ./ProductCatalog
    ports:
      - "5001:80"

  order:
    image: orderservice:latest
    build:
      context: ./OrderService
    ports:
      - "5002:80"

  payment:
    image: paymentservice:latest
    build:
      context: ./PaymentService
    ports:
      - "5003:80"

  gateway:
    image: api-gateway:latest
    build:
      context: ./ApiGateway
    ports:
      - "5000:80"
    depends_on:
      - product-catalog
      - order
      - payment
```

With Docker Compose, all microservices can be started with a single command:

```bash
Copy code
docker-compose up -d
```

This command initializes and runs all services as defined in docker-compose.yml, making it easy to manage the entire application.

6. Scaling Microservices with Docker Swarm or Kubernetes

For production-grade deployments, orchestrators like **Docker Swarm** or **Kubernetes** are essential for managing and scaling microservices across clusters of servers.

- **Docker Swarm**: A native clustering and orchestration tool for Docker that simplifies deploying and scaling services.
- **Kubernetes**: A more advanced orchestration platform that provides load balancing, auto-scaling, and rolling updates. It's widely adopted for microservices deployments due to its powerful features and extensibility.

Both tools allow you to manage containerized applications across multiple nodes, provide scaling capabilities, and ensure high availability.

7. Service Communication in a Microservices Architecture

Effective inter-service communication is vital in a microservices architecture, and there are several options available:

- **RESTful HTTP/HTTPS**: Suitable for external-facing APIs but may incur overhead in high-performance scenarios.
- **gRPC**: Offers efficient, low-latency communication for internal microservices, leveraging HTTP/2 and Protocol Buffers.

- **Message Brokers**: Tools like **RabbitMQ**, **Kafka**, and **Azure Service Bus** are suitable for event-driven architectures, enabling asynchronous communication and decoupling between services.

Selecting the appropriate communication strategy depends on the specific requirements of each service and the overall system design.

8. Monitoring and Logging in a Microservices Environment

Monitoring and logging are crucial for maintaining the health of a microservices application. With services distributed across multiple containers and nodes, observability becomes complex.

- **Centralized Logging**: Use tools like **ELK Stack** (Elasticsearch, Logstash, Kibana), **Graylog**, or **Azure Monitor** for aggregating logs from multiple services.
- **Distributed Tracing**: Tools like **Jaeger** or **Zipkin** trace requests across microservices, helping to identify latency bottlenecks.
- **Health Checks and Metrics**: Prometheus, Grafana, and custom ASP.NET Core health checks provide real-time insights into service health and performance metrics.

Implementing these tools can provide visibility into the behavior and performance of each service, helping to diagnose issues and optimize the system.

Microservices architecture with ASP.NET Core and Docker offers a powerful approach for building scalable, resilient, and efficient applications. By combining ASP.NET Core's modular design with Docker's containerization capabilities, developers can create, deploy, and manage services independently. The microservices model also enables targeted scaling and rapid deployment, aligning well with agile development practices and cloud-native principles. Through effective orchestration, monitoring, and service communication, ASP.NET Core and Docker create a foundation for modern, enterprise-grade applications that can evolve and scale in response to changing business needs.

Integrating ASP.NET Core 3 with Legacy .NET Framework Applications

The transition from legacy .NET Framework applications to ASP.NET Core 3 can present both challenges and opportunities. Many organizations have existing applications built on the .NET Framework, which may contain critical business logic, extensive features, and a wealth of accumulated knowledge. The need for modernization, improved performance, cross-platform capabilities, and enhanced security often drives the desire to adopt ASP.NET Core. This section will discuss strategies for integrating ASP.NET Core 3 with legacy .NET Framework applications, ensuring a smooth transition while leveraging existing investments.

1. Understanding the Integration Scenarios

Integration between ASP.NET Core and legacy .NET Framework applications can take several forms, depending on the specific requirements of the organization. Here are some common scenarios:
- **Coexistence**: Running ASP.NET Core applications alongside existing .NET Framework applications, allowing both to operate independently but communicate where necessary.
- **Gradual Migration**: Incrementally transitioning components or services from the legacy application to ASP.NET Core, often beginning with less complex or less critical features.
- **Microservices Architecture**: Breaking down monolithic .NET Framework applications into microservices, where new services are built in ASP.NET Core and communicate with the legacy application via APIs.
- **Shared Libraries**: Developing shared libraries that can be used

by both ASP.NET Core and legacy .NET Framework applications, enabling reuse of common functionality.

Each integration scenario has its own considerations and approaches, and the choice will depend on factors such as application complexity, team expertise, and organizational goals.

2. Coexistence of ASP.NET Core and .NET Framework

When running ASP.NET Core alongside legacy applications, it's important to establish clear communication channels and protocols. Here are some approaches for enabling coexistence:

2.1 HTTP APIs

One common method for integration is to expose RESTful APIs in the legacy .NET Framework application. The ASP.NET Core application can consume these APIs to interact with legacy business logic or data.

- **Expose Legacy APIs**: Identify key functionalities in the legacy application that can be exposed as HTTP APIs. Use ASP.NET Web API in the .NET Framework to create endpoints.
- **Consume APIs in ASP.NET Core**: Utilize HttpClient in ASP.NET Core to call the legacy APIs. This allows for interaction without tightly coupling the two applications.

Example: Suppose the legacy application contains a user management system. You can create API endpoints to handle user registration, login, and profile retrieval, which the ASP.NET Core application can then consume.

2.2 Messaging Systems

Using a messaging system can decouple the communication between ASP.NET Core and the legacy application. Systems such as RabbitMQ or Azure Service Bus allow for asynchronous communication.

- **Publish-Subscribe Model**: Implement a publish-subscribe pattern where the legacy application publishes messages to a queue. The ASP.NET Core application subscribes to these messages and processes them accordingly.
- **Event-Driven Architecture**: Adopt an event-driven architecture, allowing services to react to events published by the legacy application. This approach enhances responsiveness and scalability.

2.3 Shared Database

In some scenarios, both the legacy application and ASP.NET Core may need to access the same database. This requires careful consideration of data access patterns.

- **Database Schema Compatibility**: Ensure that changes made in either application do not break functionality in the other. Maintain strict versioning of database schemas.
- **Data Access Layer**: Use a common data access layer that both applications can utilize to interact with the database. This can help enforce business rules and maintain data integrity.

3. Gradual Migration Strategies

Migrating components from a legacy application to ASP.NET Core can be a complex process, but a gradual approach can ease the transition.

3.1 Identify Candidate Components

Start by identifying components of the legacy application that are good candidates for migration. Consider the following criteria:

- **Low Complexity**: Begin with simpler features that have fewer dependencies.
- **High Usage**: Focus on features that are frequently used and would benefit from improved performance.
- **Modular Design**: Components designed with separation of concerns in mind are easier to extract and migrate.

3.2 Create a Modular Architecture

Refactor the legacy application into a more modular architecture if possible. This allows for easier extraction of components into ASP.NET Core.

- **Service Layer**: Implement a service layer in the legacy application that encapsulates business logic, making it easier to expose functionalities as APIs.
- **Plugin Architecture**: Consider designing a plugin architecture where new features can be developed in ASP.NET Core and integrated with the legacy system.

3.3 Migrate Incrementally

Once candidate components are identified, plan for a phased migration:

- **Migrate One Component at a Time**: Focus on migrating individual components or services, testing thoroughly before proceeding to the next.
- **Test and Validate**: Ensure each migrated component works as expected in the ASP.NET Core application, integrating with the legacy application where necessary.

4. Leveraging Microservices

Microservices can provide a structured approach to integrating ASP.NET Core with legacy applications. By breaking down the legacy application into smaller, independent services, it becomes easier to adopt ASP.NET Core for new functionalities.

4.1 Identify Microservice Opportunities

Analyze the legacy application to identify functionalities that can be transformed into microservices.

- **Business Capabilities**: Look for functionalities that represent distinct business capabilities and can operate independently.

- **Complexity**: Favor features that have low complexity and high independence from other parts of the application.

4.2 Build New Features as Microservices

Develop new features in ASP.NET Core as independent microservices. These services can interact with the legacy application using APIs or messaging systems.

- **Communication Protocols**: Ensure robust communication protocols are established for data exchange between the legacy and microservice architectures.
- **Monitoring and Logging**: Implement centralized logging and monitoring for both the legacy and new microservices to maintain visibility across the system.

5. Shared Libraries for Code Reuse

To reduce redundancy and maintain consistency across both ASP.NET Core and legacy applications, consider developing shared libraries.

5.1 Create .NET Standard Libraries

Develop libraries targeting .NET Standard, which can be consumed by both ASP.NET Core and .NET Framework applications. This ensures compatibility and enables code reuse.

- **Business Logic**: Move shared business logic into a .NET Standard library to avoid duplicating code in both applications.
- **Common Utilities**: Create utility libraries for common functionalities such as logging, validation, or data access.

5.2 Versioning and Dependency Management

Manage library versions carefully to avoid conflicts between different applications. Use semantic versioning to indicate breaking changes and maintain backward compatibility.

6. Challenges and Considerations

While integrating ASP.NET Core with legacy .NET Framework applications can yield significant benefits, several challenges need to be addressed:

- **Compatibility Issues**: There may be incompatibilities between the two frameworks, particularly around APIs, libraries, and data access technologies.
- **Performance Overheads**: Inter-service communication may introduce latency, especially if not designed properly. Monitor performance metrics and optimize communication strategies.
- **Testing and Validation**: Ensure thorough testing is conducted after integration to validate that both applications work seamlessly together. Automated tests can be particularly useful in identifying issues.

Integrating ASP.NET Core 3 with legacy .NET Framework applications presents a unique set of challenges and opportunities. By understanding the various integration scenarios and leveraging strategies like coexistence, gradual migration, and shared libraries, organizations can modernize their applications while maximizing existing investments. Whether transitioning to a microservices architecture or simply enhancing the capabilities of legacy systems, careful planning and execution will enable successful integration that meets the evolving needs of businesses.

Looking Forward - Preparing for Future ASP.NET Core Versions

Evolution of ASP.NET Core and Expected Changes in ASP.NET Core 5+

ASP.NET Core has significantly transformed the landscape of web application development since its initial release. As a cross-platform, high-performance framework designed for building modern, cloud-based applications, ASP.NET Core has continually evolved to meet the changing needs of developers and businesses. This section explores the evolution of ASP.NET Core, highlighting key developments, features, and the anticipated changes and improvements in ASP.NET Core 5 and beyond.

1. A Brief History of ASP.NET Core

The ASP.NET Core framework was first introduced in 2016 as a complete re-architecture of the original ASP.NET framework. This transition marked a fundamental shift in how web applications were developed and deployed. Below are some of the pivotal milestones in its evolution:

1.1 ASP.NET Core 1.0

Released in June 2016, ASP.NET Core 1.0 brought with it several foundational features:

- **Unified Framework**: Combining MVC and Web API into a single

framework.
- **Cross-Platform**: Support for Windows, macOS, and Linux environments, allowing developers to build and run applications on any platform.
- **Lightweight and Modular**: Introduction of a modular design, enabling developers to include only the necessary components, resulting in improved performance and reduced application size.

1.2 ASP.NET Core 2.0

Released in August 2017, this version introduced enhancements that improved the developer experience:

- **Simplified Project Structure**: Introduction of the new project template with simplified configuration and a streamlined development experience.
- **Razor Pages**: New programming model for building page-focused web applications, simplifying the structure and organization of code.

1.3 ASP.NET Core 3.0

Launched in September 2019, ASP.NET Core 3.0 was a significant release with multiple features and improvements:

- **Support for Windows Desktop Applications**: Introduction of the Windows Desktop framework (WPF and Windows Forms) for building rich desktop applications using .NET Core.
- **Improvements to Razor and Blazor**: Enhancements in the Razor view engine and the introduction of Blazor for building interactive web UIs using C# instead of JavaScript.
- **Endpoint Routing**: A new routing system that allows for cleaner and more efficient routing configuration.

2. ASP.NET Core 5: Key Features and Improvements

ASP.NET Core 5, released in November 2020, continued the evolution of the framework with numerous enhancements that aimed to improve performance, security, and the overall development experience. Key features and improvements included:

2.1 Unified Platform

One of the most notable changes in ASP.NET Core 5 was the unification of the .NET platform under the .NET 5 umbrella. This allowed developers to use a single framework across different application types, including web, desktop, mobile, cloud, and microservices.

2.2 Performance Improvements

ASP.NET Core 5 introduced various performance optimizations, including:

- **Faster Startup**: Improved application startup time by optimizing the middleware pipeline.
- **Reduced Memory Footprint**: Enhancements in memory allocation and garbage collection, contributing to lower resource usage.

2.3 Enhanced Support for Blazor

Blazor received significant updates in ASP.NET Core 5, including:

- **Blazor WebAssembly**: Improved performance and capabilities for building client-side applications running directly in the browser using WebAssembly.
- **Full-Stack Development**: Streamlined development experience for full-stack applications, enabling developers to use C# across both client and server sides.

2.4 Improved API Support

ASP.NET Core 5 focused on enhancing API development with features such as:

- **API Explorer Enhancements**: Better support for documenting APIs,

making it easier to generate documentation and support tools like Swagger.
- **OpenAPI Specification**: Integration with OpenAPI to facilitate API documentation and client generation.

3. Expected Changes and Features in Future Versions (ASP.NET Core 6 and Beyond)

As the ASP.NET Core framework continues to evolve, several expected changes and features for ASP.NET Core 6 and future releases can significantly impact development practices.

3.1 Simplified Hosting Model

Future versions of ASP.NET Core are likely to streamline the hosting model even further, making it easier for developers to host applications in various environments:

- **Minimal Hosting Model**: Introduction of minimal hosting APIs that allow developers to get started with web applications without needing to define a full Startup class.
- **Improved Web Server Integration**: Continued enhancements in how ASP.NET Core integrates with web servers like Kestrel and Nginx.

3.2 Enhanced Blazor Capabilities

Blazor is expected to undergo further enhancements, including:

- **Improved Performance**: Ongoing optimizations to Blazor's runtime to enhance performance and reduce load times.
- **Full-Stack Capabilities**: Continued support for full-stack development with Blazor, making it easier to build complete applications using C#.

3.3 Advanced API Features

Future releases may introduce advanced features for API development, including:

- **Improved Rate Limiting and Throttling**: Native support for rate limiting and throttling APIs to enhance security and manage resource usage.
- **Versioning Strategies**: More robust built-in support for API versioning to help manage changes over time without breaking existing clients.

3.4 Integration with Cloud Services

As cloud adoption continues to grow, future versions of ASP.NET Core are likely to enhance integration with cloud services:

- **Serverless Architecture**: Better support for building serverless applications and microservices that can be deployed to cloud platforms like Azure Functions and AWS Lambda.
- **Automatic Scaling**: Enhancements that allow ASP.NET Core applications to automatically scale based on load and demand.

3.5 Enhanced Security Features

Security will remain a priority in future versions, with expected enhancements such as:

- **Built-in Security Features**: More comprehensive built-in security features, including support for Zero Trust architectures and enhanced authentication protocols.
- **Simplified Authentication and Authorization**: Streamlined models for handling authentication and authorization to improve developer experience and reduce common pitfalls.

4. The Community and Ecosystem

The ASP.NET Core ecosystem benefits from an active community of developers, contributors, and organizations that help shape its future.

Continued collaboration and feedback from the community play a vital role in prioritizing features and improvements. This collaborative spirit fosters innovation, enabling the framework to adapt and grow according to user needs.

The evolution of ASP.NET Core has been marked by a commitment to modern web application development, offering flexibility, performance, and cross-platform capabilities. With each version, ASP.NET Core has introduced enhancements that simplify the development experience while providing robust tools for building secure, scalable applications.

As we look forward to the future of ASP.NET Core 5 and beyond, it is clear that the framework will continue to evolve, embracing new technologies, patterns, and practices that empower developers to create high-quality applications. The anticipated changes promise to enhance productivity, improve performance, and further establish ASP.NET Core as a leading choice for modern web development.

Migration Tips and Strategies to Keep Code Future-Proof

As the ASP.NET Core framework continues to evolve, migrating to newer versions becomes essential for developers seeking to leverage the latest features, improvements, and security enhancements. However, migration can be a daunting task, especially for larger applications with complex architectures. This section outlines effective migration strategies and tips to ensure your codebase remains future-proof while transitioning to new versions of ASP.NET Core.

1. Assessing the Current Codebase

Before initiating any migration, it's crucial to conduct a thorough assessment of your current codebase. This assessment will help identify potential issues, dependencies, and areas that may require significant changes.

1.1 Analyze Dependencies
- **Identify Third-Party Libraries**: Review all the third-party libraries and packages used in your application. Check for their compatibility with the target version of ASP.NET Core.
- **Evaluate Custom Middleware**: If you have custom middleware, ensure that it aligns with the new pipeline and configuration changes introduced in the latest version.

1.2 Code Analysis Tools
Utilize code analysis tools to evaluate your code quality and identify areas that may pose challenges during migration. Tools like Roslyn analyzers can provide insights into deprecated APIs and usage patterns that may need to be addressed.

2. Create a Migration Plan
A well-structured migration plan is vital for ensuring a smooth transition. This plan should include clear timelines, milestones, and strategies for minimizing disruptions.

2.1 Define Objectives

- **Set Clear Goals**: Define the objectives of the migration, such as performance improvements, new feature implementations, or security enhancements.
- **Prioritize Features**: Identify the key features that are essential for the application's functionality and prioritize them in the migration process.

2.2 Incremental Migration Approach

- **Break Down the Migration**: Instead of migrating the entire application at once, consider an incremental approach. This strategy involves migrating individual components or features, allowing for easier testing and rollback if issues arise.

- **Use Feature Flags**: Implement feature flags to control the activation of new features gradually. This allows you to deploy changes without exposing them to all users immediately.

3. Upgrade Path

Understanding the upgrade path is crucial for a successful migration. Each version of ASP.NET Core may introduce breaking changes that require careful attention.

3.1 Review Release Notes

- **Consult Official Documentation**: Always refer to the official ASP.NET Core documentation and release notes for guidance on breaking changes, deprecated features, and new functionalities introduced in each version.
- **Utilize Upgrade Guides**: Microsoft often provides detailed upgrade guides that outline specific changes to be aware of when migrating from one version to another.

3.2 Compatibility Mode

When migrating, consider using compatibility modes available in newer versions of ASP.NET Core. These modes can help maintain legacy behavior while gradually adopting new features.

4. Testing and Validation

Comprehensive testing is crucial during migration to ensure that existing functionality is preserved and that the application behaves as expected in the new environment.

4.1 Automated Testing

- **Maintain Unit and Integration Tests**: Ensure that your unit tests and integration tests are up-to-date before migration. These tests will serve as a safety net, catching regressions caused by the migration.
- **Expand Test Coverage**: If possible, increase the test coverage of your application to identify potential issues that may arise after the

migration.

4.2 Manual Testing

In addition to automated tests, conduct thorough manual testing to verify that all application features work correctly post-migration. This process should include functional, performance, and security testing.

5. Addressing Breaking Changes

When migrating between versions, you may encounter breaking changes that require code modifications. Being proactive in addressing these changes will help maintain a healthy codebase.

5.1 Refactoring Code

- **Identify Deprecated APIs**: Replace any deprecated APIs with their recommended alternatives. This practice will not only ensure compatibility but also keep your codebase clean and modern.
- **Refactor Middleware and Services**: Review and refactor any custom middleware or services to align with new patterns and practices in the latest version.

5.2 Utilize Analyzer Tools

Leverage tools like the .NET Portability Analyzer and the .NET Upgrade Assistant to assess the compatibility of your codebase with the target framework version. These tools can provide detailed reports on what needs to be changed for a successful migration.

6. Future-Proofing Your Code

Once the migration is complete, adopting best practices will help ensure that your code remains maintainable and adaptable for future changes.

6.1 Follow SOLID Principles

Applying SOLID principles in your design will lead to cleaner, more maintainable code. This will make future migrations easier and more efficient.

6.2 Implement Continuous Integration

Set up a continuous integration (CI) pipeline to automate testing and deployment. This ensures that any changes to the codebase are validated against a suite of tests, helping to catch issues early.

6.3 Stay Updated with Best Practices

Continuously stay informed about best practices and new features in ASP.NET Core. Engage with the developer community, attend workshops, and participate in forums to keep your knowledge current.

Migrating to newer versions of ASP.NET Core is an essential part of maintaining a modern web application. By following a structured approach that includes assessing your current codebase, planning the migration, thoroughly testing, and adhering to best practices, you can ensure a smooth transition that keeps your code future-proof.

As ASP.NET Core continues to evolve, developers must remain vigilant in adapting to changes, embracing new features, and maintaining high-quality code. By implementing the strategies outlined in this section, you can navigate the complexities of migration and position your applications for long-term success in a dynamic development landscape.

Leveraging ASP.NET Core 3 Skills for Other .NET Frameworks

As developers grow more proficient in ASP.NET Core 3, they often find that the skills and knowledge acquired during their experience can be applied to other .NET frameworks and technologies. This ability to transfer skills not only enhances a developer's versatility but also prepares them for a broader range of projects and challenges in the .NET ecosystem. This section explores how the core competencies developed while working with ASP.NET Core 3 can be leveraged across various .NET frameworks, such as the traditional .NET Framework, Xamarin, and Blazor.

1. Understanding Core Principles

The foundational principles of software development that you learn in ASP.NET Core 3—such as modularity, dependency injection, and asynchronous programming—are universally applicable across all .NET frameworks.

1.1 Modularity

- **Separation of Concerns**: ASP.NET Core emphasizes the separation of concerns through its architecture. This principle is not exclusive to ASP.NET Core and can be effectively applied to any .NET application, whether it's a traditional ASP.NET application or a Windows Forms app.
- **Reusable Components**: Understanding how to build and use modular components in ASP.NET Core allows developers to create reusable libraries and packages in other .NET applications, improving maintainability and reducing redundancy.

1.2 Dependency Injection

- **Inversion of Control**: ASP.NET Core's built-in support for dependency injection (DI) teaches developers to implement inversion of control in their applications. This approach can be applied when developing services in the .NET Framework, allowing for better testing and flexibility.
- **Service Lifetimes**: Familiarity with the different service lifetimes in ASP.NET Core (transient, scoped, and singleton) helps developers apply similar patterns in other frameworks, leading to better resource management and performance.

1.3 Asynchronous Programming

- **Task-based Asynchronous Model**: The use of async/await in

ASP.NET Core promotes writing non-blocking code. This concept is also applicable in other .NET technologies, such as Windows Presentation Foundation (WPF) and Universal Windows Platform (UWP), allowing for responsive user interfaces.

2. Cross-Framework Patterns

Certain design patterns that are prevalent in ASP.NET Core can be effectively adapted to other .NET frameworks, enhancing your development practices across the board.

2.1 MVC and MVVM Patterns

- **MVC Framework**: ASP.NET Core follows the Model-View-Controller (MVC) design pattern. Understanding MVC can ease the transition to frameworks like ASP.NET MVC or even client-side frameworks that use similar patterns.
- **MVVM for Desktop Applications**: In WPF or Xamarin applications, the Model-View-ViewModel (MVVM) pattern is commonly used. The principles of separation of concerns and binding learned in ASP.NET Core can be applied to build more organized and maintainable MVVM applications.

2.2 Event-Driven Architecture

- **Microservices and Event-Driven Design**: Knowledge of building microservices in ASP.NET Core can be extended to other frameworks. Understanding how to implement an event-driven architecture allows developers to create loosely coupled systems, regardless of the technology stack.
- **Utilizing Pub/Sub Patterns**: Skills in using ASP.NET Core with message brokers can be leveraged in desktop or mobile applications that require asynchronous processing or event notification systems.

3. Web Development Skills

Web development skills gained in ASP.NET Core can be directly applied to other web-related technologies within the .NET ecosystem.

3.1 Web API Development

- **Building APIs**: The skills for building RESTful APIs in ASP.NET Core can transition to creating APIs in older frameworks such as ASP.NET Web API. Knowledge of HTTP, routing, and content negotiation is invaluable.
- **Consuming APIs**: Understanding how to consume APIs using HttpClient in ASP.NET Core can be applied to any .NET application that needs to integrate with external services, enhancing the ability to work with distributed systems.

3.2 Front-End Integration

- **Client-Side Frameworks**: Skills developed in integrating client-side frameworks (like React or Angular) with ASP.NET Core can be applied to traditional ASP.NET applications, enhancing the interactivity of server-rendered pages.
- **SignalR for Real-Time Communication**: The experience with SignalR in ASP.NET Core can be utilized in other contexts where real-time functionality is needed, such as in WPF or Xamarin applications.

4. Cloud and DevOps Practices

The DevOps practices and cloud deployment strategies learned while working with ASP.NET Core can also be beneficial in other .NET frameworks.

4.1 Continuous Integration and Delivery (CI/CD)

- **Automated Pipelines**: Experience setting up CI/CD pipelines in ASP.NET Core using tools like GitHub Actions and Azure DevOps can be applied to any .NET application, facilitating efficient and reliable software delivery.

- **Testing Strategies**: Knowledge of testing frameworks such as xUnit and NUnit in ASP.NET Core can extend to unit and integration testing in other .NET applications, promoting quality across all projects.

4.2 Cloud Services Integration

- **Utilizing Cloud Platforms**: Understanding how to deploy ASP.NET Core applications to Azure or AWS can enhance skills in deploying any .NET application, making it easier to leverage cloud resources effectively.
- **Serverless Architectures**: Experience with serverless architecture in ASP.NET Core, such as Azure Functions, can be applied to other .NET projects, allowing developers to create scalable, event-driven applications.

The skills and knowledge developed while working with ASP.NET Core 3 provide a solid foundation for working with other .NET frameworks. By understanding core principles, design patterns, web development practices, and cloud technologies, developers can seamlessly transition their expertise across the .NET ecosystem.

As technology continues to evolve, leveraging these skills will not only enhance individual productivity but also improve the overall quality and maintainability of applications developed in any .NET framework. Embracing this cross-functional knowledge prepares developers for a versatile and adaptable career in software development, enabling them to tackle a wide range of projects and challenges with confidence.

www.ingramcontent.com/pod-product-compliance
Lightning Source LLC
Chambersburg PA
CBHW082243220526
45469CB00009B/2857